CONVENIENT SUSPECT

A DOUBLE MURDER,
A FLAWED INVESTIGATION,
AND THE RAILROADING
OF AN INNOCENT WOMAN

TAMMY MAL

CHICAGO
REVIEW
PRESS

Copyright © 2018 by Tammy Mal
All rights reserved
Published by Chicago Review Press Incorporated
814 North Franklin Street
Chicago, Illinois 60610
978-1-61373-979-2

Library of Congress Cataloging-in-Publication Data
Is available from the Library of Congress.

Cover design: Rebecca Lown
Cover images: Photo of woods courtesy of Sherry Sparks, photographer;
    stock photos via Shutterstock
Typesetting: Nord Compo

Printed in the United States of America
5 4 3 2 1

For my sister
Who also knows the pain of loss

ACKNOWLEDGMENTS

This book could not have been written without the help of countless people who sat for interviews, spent hours on the phone, provided me with information, and supported my efforts. I'd especially like to thank my family, and all those who were never too busy to take my calls and answer my questions: Sandy and John Mizgerd, Joan and Paul Weiser, Pat E., Craig Neely, Joe York, Telly and Maria Fiouris, Cindy Mills, Sandy Ireland, and Kim and Liz.

A special thank-you to my friend Sherry Sparks, who chauffeured me around, helped with research, and provided many of the photographs for the book, and also to Regge Episale, who went above and beyond with her help on the manuscript.

To my brother Joe, who helped me in countless ways all through this journey, thank you.

My deepest gratitude to the late Margaret Sneary, whose work on the case enabled me to write this book, and Cindy Wiard, who has more courage than most people I know.

A special thank-you as well to my agent, Mike Hoogland, for his encouragement and sound advice, as well as Chicago Review Press editors Yuval Taylor and Devon Freeny and copyeditor Cathy Bernardy Jones, who worked tirelessly on the manuscript.

Last, but not least, I want to thank Patricia Rorrer, who took a tremendous risk by opening up her heart and her files to me.

For those of you I'm forgetting, I apologize. Please know it is not done intentionally, and that I thank you from the bottom of my heart.

AUTHOR'S NOTE

This is a work of investigative reporting about the Patricia Rorrer case. The book is based on approximately ten thousand pages of trial records and investigative and forensic reports obtained from Patricia Rorrer's defense discovery and the FBI, the interviews that I conducted in the course of my research, and the extensive media coverage of the case, which remains a matter of enduring public interest, concern, and debate.

The facts reported in the book are based on these sources, but all of the opinions are my own. Like others who have studied and reported on the Rorrer case, I have weighed the available evidence, analyzed the various arguments for and against Patty Rorrer's innocence, and shared my conclusions with my readers.

Some names of individuals mentioned in this book have been fictionalized. All fictional names are indicated by the use of SMALL CAPS on first appearance. Any similarity between fictionalized names and the names of real people is strictly coincidental.

PROLOGUE

Sudden and violent death is always tragic, but the kidnapping and murder of a young mother, Joann Katrinak, and her infant son, Alex, only ten days before Christmas 1994, shook the small town of Catasauqua, Pennsylvania, to its core. Three years later, the arrest and conviction of Patricia Rorrer, a young mother herself and the ex-girlfriend of Joann's husband, Andy, was no less shocking. Although Rorrer would forever maintain her innocence, the evidence against her appeared overwhelming.

At the time of the murders, I too was a young mother, raising four children and struggling to make ends meet. Living in Pennsylvania, it was impossible not to have heard of the case, but I knew none of the players so didn't follow it that closely. I never forgot it, however, and sometimes, for no apparent reason, I'd think about Patricia Rorrer and wonder why she had done it.

My interest in criminals and their crimes dated back many years and had led me to seriously consider a career in law enforcement. In the mid-1980s I had applied for and been accepted into the Pennsylvania State Police (PSP) as a trooper cadet, but after arriving at the academy in Hershey, I decided not to pursue that vocation. My real passion was writing, and by 2012, with my children now grown, I finally had the time needed to devote to a writing career. One of the first stories I thought about was the Katrinak murders.

I found the case intriguing, and just strange enough to set it apart from most true crime tales. It all seemed so bizarre: the three-year investigation; Pennsylvania's first use of mitochondrial DNA; the obsessed, psychotic ex-girlfriend who drove five hundred miles to murder her ex-lover's new wife and baby. Believing that the case had all the ingredients needed for a page-turning book, I began researching it, starting with the Internet and old newspaper archives. The media had painted a strong and compelling portrait of Rorrer's guilt, and the more I read, the angrier I became. What kind of person could kill a young mother and then leave her three-month-old baby to die of exposure? *Monster* was too kind a word for this killer.

I found nothing good written about Patricia Rorrer until I came across an article by Bridget DiCosmo of the Innocence Institute of Point Park University in Pittsburgh. The article attempted to cast doubt on the hair evidence used to convict her, which I found surprising. The hair had been DNA tested and matched to Patricia—what stronger evidence could there be? I wondered why the Innocence Institute had accepted her case, and I worried that if Rorrer could garner enough support, our justice system might just let her go. It wouldn't be the first time a cold-blooded killer was set free.

I thought that the world needed to know what Patricia Rorrer had done, and that the best way to do that was by writing a book. By late 2012, I had composed letters to all the main players in the case: Patricia herself; Andy Katrinak; his father, Andrew (Andy's mother, Veronica, had passed away in 2011); and Joann's mother and sister, Sally and Peggy O'Connor. Although Patricia wrote me back very quickly, I received no replies to my other letters. What I did receive was a phone call from former state trooper Joseph Vasquez, one of the original investigators on the case.

Vasquez, now a detective with the Lehigh County District Attorney's Office, told me he was calling on behalf of Joann's mother, Sally, who had no intention of cooperating with me on a book. "What do you want to go digging into this case for anyway?" Vasquez asked. "Nobody wants this case brought back up."

The phone call caught me off guard. Why was a detective with the Lehigh County District Attorney's Office calling me, and why did he sound so unhappy with my plans to write a book?

Recalling the Innocence Institute's article, I tried to convey my concern. "She's always maintained her innocence," I said, "and it looks like she's gaining support."

Vasquez laughed sarcastically. "Yeah, she's innocent. That's why we found her DNA at the scene."

"I know that," I said, "which is why I want to write a book about the case. The public needs to know what this woman did and that she should never be released."

"Oh, you don't have to worry about that," the detective said, dismissing the idea. "She is never getting out of jail. *Never.*"

Vasquez then went on to question my motives for writing a book and my knowledge of the case before finally bringing the call to an abrupt end. "Look," he said firmly, "nobody wants you looking into this case, and nobody is going to cooperate with you. No one wants this case brought back up. The family just wants to be left alone."

I felt terrible when I hung up the phone. I certainly didn't want to do anything that would cause more pain for Joann's family, but the call bothered me. It was the first indication—other than the interest of the Innocence Institute—that perhaps the case against Patricia Rorrer was not as compelling as the public was led to believe. When Detective Vasquez told me that no one wanted me "digging into this case," my first thought was *Why? What's in there that you don't want me to find?*

I wrestled with my decision. I desperately wanted to write this story, but I also understood why Joann's family would be reluctant to have it brought back up. They had endured years of publicity, and I couldn't blame them if they were not anxious for more.

Shortly after my phone call with Detective Vasquez, however, I happened to watch a new documentary on the case in which Joann's family and many of the original investigators—including Detective Vasquez—participated. In it, each of them spoke openly and candidly about the crimes, their feelings, and Sally O'Connor's desire to see Patricia Rorrer "rot" in prison.

So much for no one wanting the case brought back up.

The show confused me. Why was everyone involved so eager to air their views on television but reluctant to speak with a writer? It troubled me as well. The documentary was littered with inaccuracies, omissions, and half-truths—intended, so it seemed, solely to make the case against Patricia Rorrer appear more damning. Over and over again, those involved appeared on screen and related things I knew to be untrue. Why was it necessary to lie about the evidence if the case against Patricia was so strong?

The show only raised more questions for me, but I feared those questions would go unanswered. Detective Vasquez had apparently been right. No one seemed willing to cooperate with me. No one, that is, except Patricia Rorrer, who was not only willing to talk but eager to do so.

I knew that Patricia's story would be crucial for the book. She had never spoken publicly about the crimes despite many offers to do so, but I had no desire to write just one person's side. The book needed to be objective and contain all information relevant to the case. At the time, however, I didn't have much choice. Patricia Rorrer was all I had.

From her very first letter, Patricia fervently protested her innocence and urged me to keep an open mind. I promised her I would and assured her I'd investigate the case to the best of my ability, but I gave her a warning as well.

"I'll follow the evidence wherever it leads," I told her, "but if it leads me to conclude you're guilty, I'll write the book that way." Patricia immediately wrote back and agreed.

Thus began a correspondence between me, a struggling writer trying to start my career, and Patricia Lynne Rorrer, the woman convicted of savagely killing a young mother and her infant son.

––––––––––––

It didn't take long for me to feel relatively comfortable with "Patty," and I think she felt the same way about me. Our letter writing quickly evolved into weekly phone calls in which we'd discuss the case, but I remained skeptical of everything she said. I believed this woman was guilty, and I didn't think she could convince me otherwise.

It took a long time, but eventually, I started gaining Patty's trust, and she began to open up to me. Often during normal conversation, she would mention aspects of the case that I had never heard about—everything from compromised crime scenes to suspects who had never been cleared, polygraphs showing deception, and contaminated evidence used to convict her. Patty spoke as if these things were well-known facts in her case, but they weren't. I had a hard time believing any of them.

Apparently sensing my skepticism, whenever I doubted something Patty told me, she'd follow up her claim with an official report to verify what she said. I was astonished by what I was discovering and grateful that the Pennsylvania State Police and the FBI were the sources of the information. How much more credible sources could one get?

After several months, I decided it was time to meet Patty in person. On a cold February day in 2013, I drove the one hundred miles to the State Correctional Institution at Muncy (SCI Muncy) and sat down with Patricia Rorrer in the prisoner visiting room. I had no idea what to expect. I hadn't seen a picture of her since her face was plastered all over the newspapers more than fifteen years earlier. Patty had been pretty then, but I assumed prison would have taken its toll. I'd already formed a mental picture of what she'd probably look like: a hard woman with a craggy face, washed-out gray hair, and a body thickened by middle age and starchy prison food.

What I saw when she walked into the visiting room was none of that. Instead, I found myself staring at a very tall, slim, attractive woman who looked ten years younger than her current age of forty-nine. Patty had long, dark hair that hung nearly to the middle of her back and a smooth, unlined face with pleasant, almost delicate features. She wore just a hint of makeup—a touch of cobalt enhancing her clear brown eyes—and her voice was soft as she greeted me warmly.

For months Patty had been surprising me, and she did so again when she sat down and looked me squarely in the eye.

"Ask me anything you want," she said in her soft southern drawl. "Anything, and I'll answer it. Because I did not commit these crimes."

I knew that the prosecution's case had been almost entirely circumstantial, but circumstantial evidence could be pretty compelling, and there were still some things I thought Patty needed to explain. In many ways, I hoped she wouldn't be able to. I didn't want to think about the possibility of her being innocent, because not only would that mean that the police had allowed the brutal killer of Joann and Alex to go free, but it would also mean an innocent person had her life destroyed in the process.

I tried not to worry about it. *Patty had to be guilty*, I told myself. *The police would never have brought her all the way from North Carolina and asked a jury to sentence her to death if she weren't. They had to have strong and convincing evidence to do that, didn't they?*

I was anxious to start probing—to see her eyes radiate fear at my questions, to listen as she hemmed and hawed in search of a way to answer. I expected there'd come a time when her face would flush scarlet and she'd turn her head away, unable to look me in the eye, but that time never came. Instead, I found Patty to be sincere in her story. She never looked uncomfortable with what I asked, never attempted to make herself appear in a better light, and never contradicted herself. My questions were probing, personal, and to the point, and she answered each of them with logical and plausible explanations.

Slowly, I began to realize that there *was* more to this case than anyone ever knew. A lot more. But it would take me years to discover just how much.

1

Thursday, December 15, 1994, had been a quiet day at the Lehigh County Communications Center, and the mood inside the small, gray building was one of festive anxiety. With Christmas only ten days away, the coming week would be a hectic one, and those manning the phone lines were anxious for their shift to end.

At 10:40 PM, amid the lighthearted banter, one of the dispatchers answered a call from Andrew (Andy) Katrinak of 740 Front Street in Catasauqua, a suburb of Allentown, Pennsylvania. Katrinak sounded more perplexed than worried as he reported that his twenty-six-year-old wife, Joann, and their three-month-old son, Alex, "have been missing since like two o'clock this afternoon." His wife had planned to go Christmas shopping that day, Andy continued, and "was supposed to pick up my mom first, but I called my mom and she never showed up there." Even more concerning was the fact that he had "just discovered that the downstairs basement door has been jimmied open."

Two Catasauqua police officers, Joseph Kicska and Harold Kleiner, were immediately dispatched to the scene, arriving at the house at 10:42—only two minutes after the 911 call. There, they met with Andy Katrinak, who handed them a picture of his wife and son before giving them a description of Joann's tan 1992 Toyota Corolla, which was also missing.

It was evident from the photo that Joann was a beautiful woman. Standing five feet four inches tall, she had dark eyes, delicate features, and long, luxuriant hair that cascaded past her shoulders. Andy was good looking as well but in a more rugged sort of way. Standing six feet two inches tall, with blond hair, blue eyes, and chiseled features, he had the physique of a weightlifter and might have modeled as one of the Marlboro Men from the old-time cigarette commercials. He was a big guy, with broad shoulders, massive arms, and a bulging chest.

Beyond their difference in size, there was also a significant gap in their ages. Joann, at twenty-six, was a full fourteen years younger than her husband.

A contractor by trade, Andy told the officers that he had left for work early that morning and had not heard from Joann for the rest of the day. He noticed that her car wasn't parked in its normal space when he arrived back home, nor was the porch light left on. This was unusual but not worrisome. He knew his wife had plans to go Christmas shopping that afternoon, and he figured she was just tied up in holiday traffic.

Andy told the police that when he went inside the house he found everything exactly as it had been when he left for work that morning. Noticing nothing amiss, he had turned on the television, glanced through the newspaper, and waited for his family to come home. But as the hours ticked by, with no sign of Joann, Andy began to worry. After making a few phone calls in an attempt to find her, he decided to go downstairs to check the oil level in the tank, and it was there that he discovered the basement door standing ajar and realized that someone had broken into his house.

———————

For the next two decades, Andy would maintain that someone had pried the hasp of an outside padlock away from the basement doorjamb, and that both Officers Kicska and Kleiner had examined the broken cellar door. Neither man had seemed concerned, however, nor had they elected to declare the house a crime scene, a decision for which the Catasauqua Police Department would come under heavy criticism.

Andy's version of events has never been challenged, in part because Officer Joseph Kicska later testified that he had observed the hasp of the padlock on the basement door pried away from the doorjamb. However, Kicska made no mention of this—or of observing any signs of foul play at the Katrinak house—in the report he generated of the incident, and he and Kleiner had stayed at the house for only 18 minutes.

Why didn't the police treat the incident as a crime if they saw clear evidence of foul play at the home of a missing mother and child? Why didn't either officer report seeing signs of a break-in? It would take more than twenty years before a witness would come forward and provide a possible answer to those questions, as well as cast doubt on Officer Kicska's trial testimony.*

In November 2015, Joseph York, a retired Northampton police officer, contacted defense attorney Craig Neely with an unusual story. He and Joe Kicska had worked together in the past, and one night, while the two men were on patrol, the conversation had turned to the Katrinak investigation and Kicska's belief that an innocent person had been convicted of the crime. According to York, Kicska went on to explain that he was the first officer to respond to Andy's 911 call, and that while at the house he had conducted a thorough search, finding everything secure. There was no break-in at 740 Front Street that night, Kicska allegedly said, which is why he had not declared the house a crime scene.

Surprised by this revelation, York asked Kicska if he was sure the basement door was not damaged, and Kicska replied that he was positive, as he specifically remembered checking that door.

York urged Kicska to report what he knew, but Kicska told him he already had. He had contacted someone at the Lehigh County District Attorney's Office, and was ordered to keep his mouth shut if he ever wanted to work in law enforcement again.† Fearful of the repercussions,

---

* Officer Kleiner did not write his own report of the incident, nor did he later testify to seeing signs of a break-in that night.
† A footnote contained in an appeal filed in 2016 by defense attorney Craig Neely states, "Defense counsel offers that he spoke to Officer Kleiner on December 18, 2015 to investigate the veracity of Mr. York's claims. Officer Kleiner advised Defense Counsel that 'the prosecutor threatened me too.' Kleiner, however, declined to sign an affidavit attesting to his claim, so the statement was not included in the defendant's PCRA petition."

Kicska said, he never mentioned the incident to anyone and asked York
to do the same. York was troubled by the story, however, and eventually contacted both a member of the defense team and the media, but
neither seemed interested in the story.*

From all appearances, York was a credible witness: a man who had
worked in law enforcement his entire life and one who had absolutely
nothing to gain by coming forward. More important, his story better
fits the facts than Andy's recollection and Officer Kicska's testimony at
trial. Finding no evidence of a break-in at the Katrinak house provides
a logical explanation for why the Catasauqua police failed to take the
disappearances seriously. If there were no signs of foul play, there would
have been no reason to declare the house a crime scene and no cause
for alarm over Joann's tardiness of only a few hours.

————

At 2:45 AM on the morning of December 16, 1994—only four hours after
Kicska and Kleiner left the Katrinak house—a second call came into the
Lehigh County Communications Center from 740 Front Street. This time,
Joann's sister, Peggy, reported that Joann's tan Toyota Corolla had been
found abandoned in a parking lot right next door to her house.

Officer Kicska had gone off duty at midnight, but Harold Kleiner
responded again, arriving to find fellow officer Gary DeAngelo already
there. Incredibly, Joann's vehicle was located barely fifty yards from her
house, sitting in the parking lot of McCarty's bar.

It seemed odd that no one had spotted the vehicle earlier. Backed
into the second space on the south side of the lot, it was sitting close
to the road and easily visible from Front Street. When the authorities arrived, Joann's sister was waiting near the vehicle, along with her
parents, Sally and David O'Connor, and Andy. As soon as the officers
approached, the family converged on them, insisting that Joann would

————

* In 2016, Officer Kicska signed an affidavit for the Lehigh County District Attorney's
Office denying York's claims. However, Kicska did admit in the affidavit that he recalled
a reporter calling him years earlier to ask if it was true that he believed an innocent
person had been convicted of the Katrinak murders, an indication that Joseph York had
been telling this same story for many years.

never have left her car in the lot and certainly would not have backed it into the space if she had.

"Joann can't back up a car," Andy said anxiously. "She'll drive around the block twenty times just to avoid backing up." Her sister and parents agreed, describing Joann's fear of backing up as a "phobia" and a running joke in the family. For them, finding the Toyota backed into that space indicated that something dreadful had happened.

"I think someone abducted my wife and son," Andy said.

The officers appeared skeptical. The car looked as if it had been sitting there for quite some time; all the doors were locked, and it glistened under a heavy coat of frost. As DeAngelo and Kleiner wandered around it, they noticed no signs of damage: no broken glass, no dents or scratches, not even any dirt or debris. Using flashlights, they peered through the frosted windows and noticed the baby's car seat up front but little else. DeAngelo asked if anyone had opened the vehicle, and Andy shook his head "no," then handed him a set of keys and watched as the officer unlocked the driver's side door.

The interior of the car was as pristine as the outside and showed nothing that would indicate foul play: no signs of a struggle, no blood, and no apparent disarray. According to police reports, Andy noticed that Joann's canister of Mace, which was usually kept in the middle console, was lying on the front passenger floor, and that the driver's seat was in the same position his wife always kept it in to drive. Joann's sister also took note of the driver's seat and agreed with her brother-in-law. It was exactly where Joann always kept it.

Closing the door, the two officers then opened the trunk, which also offered no clue to the missing mother and child. Other than a folded-up baby stroller, the trunk, like the rest of the car, was neat, tidy, and empty.

The parking lot where the car had apparently sat for hours was normally a busy one. Many people used it, including area workers and customers of nearby businesses. Locals also regularly cut through the lot to gain access to the alley behind the Katrinak house, and even Andy was known to pass through it when entering and exiting Front Street.

Other than the car being there—rather than at Joann's house—there was nothing suspicious about it and nothing to suggest foul play. It looked as if the owner had simply backed the car into the space and then just walked away.

Despite the family's obvious fear, neither officer seemed overly concerned. Feeling no need to impound the vehicle, DeAngelo and Kleiner released it to Andy and told him he was free to take it home. Andy would later testify that he was stunned by the suggestion and immediately declined. He believed that someone had kidnapped his wife and son and he had no intention of moving the car and possibly destroying evidence.

Again, the officer's blasé demeanor seems odd, unless you consider Officer York's statement that there hadn't actually been evidence of a break-in when Kleiner and Kicska responded to Andy's first 911 call. If, at that time, Kleiner had found Joann's house broken into and her husband frantic with worry, and now found her car abandoned in an unusual place, would he have just discounted foul play? Would he have let Officer DeAngelo just dismiss it? Chances are he would not. However, if there had been no evidence of a break-in at the house and nothing suspicious about the car, then the officer's lack of concern might be explainable.

In any event, after DeAngelo and Kleiner departed McCarty's parking lot—without taking the tan Toyota into custody—Joann's family returned to the Front Street house to wait and worry. Around 5:00 AM Andy retreated to the master bedroom and picked up the cordless telephone, only to discover there was no dial tone. He checked the battery and jiggled a few wires, but still there was only silence. The cordless phone was dead.

Those gathered in the house watched as Andy came out of the bedroom and went directly down to the basement. In the eerie gloom of the cold, damp space he followed the phone line across the cobwebby ceiling, through two partitioned rooms, to the very front of the house. There, tucked up near the floor joists and almost hidden in the insulation, two wires dangled in the empty air. The phone line had been cut.

There were two phones in the Katrinak house, one located in the living room and the other—a portable phone serviced by a separate feed running off the main phone line—in the master bedroom. The family had apparently used the living room phone to make all the calls up to that point, and Andy did so again to notify the police for the third time that night.

Again, Andy's voice sounded calm as he reminded the 911 dispatcher that his wife was missing, before saying, "The telephone she normally uses in the one bedroom was out when I came home. I just thought maybe the battery was dead and I just went downstairs—just out of curiosity—and the line is cut."

The dispatcher told Andy that he would send someone over, and once again Officers DeAngelo and Kleiner responded to the call. Later, however, DeAngelo would testify that they had actually been dispatched to the Katrinak house for two reasons: "Because Mr. Katrinak thought a phone line had been tampered with, *along with a door.*" Why, if Andy had reported the break-in earlier and the police had already investigated it, would he need to report it again? DeAngelo's recollections of that early-morning call were curious for another reason: when he later testified about examining the basement door at 5:30 AM, he would claim that he observed the hasp "loose in nature."

Not broken. Not pried away from the doorjamb. Only "loose in nature."*

―――――――――――

By the morning of December 16, 1994, everyone at the Catasauqua Police Department was aware of the Katrinak investigation that had unfolded the night before. It was rare to respond to the same address three times in less than seven hours and even more unusual to have a young mother and her baby disappear.

―――――――

* Interestingly, Officer Kleiner responded to all three 911 calls that evening, yet later, at trial, he would be the only officer not questioned about the condition of Andy's house that night.

Andy was already on police radar, but he was not the only suspect; Joann was a suspect as well. Future police reports would reveal that initially, the authorities worked the case under parallel investigations: either Joann was the victim of an abduction, or the scenes at the Katrinak house had been "staged," perhaps by Joann herself.

The latter attitude was deeply upsetting to the family, and so was the fact that many police officers didn't mind sharing their opinion. Joann's mother, Sally O'Connor, would later reveal to the media how angry she was with the authorities, not only because they suspected Andy but for what they said about her daughter. One officer had callously remarked that Joann had probably "just run away with someone," a suggestion that made Sally bristle.

"Never in a million years would Joann have run away," she said adamantly.

The O'Connors had arrived in Catasauqua the previous night fearful and apprehensive, but they left at dawn the next morning terrified and appalled. It was obvious that they were upset by the authorities' lack of concern and found it difficult to understand how anyone could just assume that Joann had left on her own after discovering her house broken into, the phone line cut, and her car abandoned in McCarty's parking lot. To them, the notion was ludicrous.

At 9:25 AM on the morning of December 16, Sally placed a call to the Catasauqua police from her home in New Jersey. Speaking with Detective Sergeant Barry Grube she emphatically insisted that Joann had not run away and that foul play was involved in her disappearance. Andy had had nothing to do with it, she said. He and Joann loved each other and had a happy marriage. Her daughter had no reason to leave, and she was certain she had not walked out on her husband.

Sally thought the police should forget about Andy and focus on Joann's first husband, JHARED STARR. Starr was a violent man, Sally said, and his marriage to her daughter had not been a good one.

Grube listened quietly as the distraught mother struggled to get her point across. It was evident that she feared for the safety of Joann and Alex, but there was little the detective could do. He had no new leads in the case and no information to pass along and bring her hope. He tried to assure her that the police were doing everything they could, but he doubted it assuaged her fears. After promising to keep in touch, the two hung up.

For Joann's sister, Peggy, who watched apprehensively as her mother made the call, Grube's assurances were not good enough. Convinced that the Catasauqua police were wasting precious time, Peggy placed a call to the FBI field office in Philadelphia and reported Joann and Alex's disappearance as a kidnapping. She also gave them Jhared Starr's name.

Less than an hour after Grube's conversation with Sally O'Connor, Andy Katrinak appeared at the station and spoke to the detective as well. Joann's husband denied having anything to do with his wife's disappearance and gave Grube a brief rundown of what had transpired the day before.*

Andy said he left for work at 6:30 AM and returned home twelve hours later to find Joann and her car not there. Although he wasn't worried then, when Joann still wasn't home by 8:00 PM he grew concerned and called his parents to see if they had heard from her. Andy's mother, Veronica Katrinak, told her son that she'd spoken with Joann around 1:15 that afternoon when the two made plans to go Christmas shopping. Joann said she'd pick Veronica up between 1:30 and 1:45, but she never arrived. When Veronica tried to call her, no one had answered, and the answering machine did not pick up.

Grube suggested they return to the Front Street house, and Andy agreed. Noting the immediate surroundings, Grube saw that the basement was accessed by a short flight of stairs leading down from a slab of concrete that served as the Katrinaks' back porch. Just off the porch was a small plot of grass that gradually turned into a gravel area where Joann normally parked her car. Beyond the gravel stood a detached two-car garage, which Andy used to store his work tools and van.

---

* As the reader will soon see, in almost every interview Andy gave the police, his recollections of the times and details of certain events were varied and contradictory. The fact that the police never questioned these discrepancies would make recreating the night of December 15 and the early morning of December 16 almost impossible.

Although this part of the Katrinak house was not visible from Front Street, it was not an isolated area. The house sat sandwiched between a residential home on the left and Colonial Landscape Inc. on the right, a narrow alley separating it from the landscaping business and ending at another alley running north to south at the rear of the property. Both alleys were frequently used, not only by Colonial Landscape and other businesses but also by local residents who, like the Katrinaks, parked their vehicles behind their homes.

On the porch, Andy pointed to the short flight of stairs leading down to the wooden basement door. The door had once contained a large window, now removed and boarded up with two pieces of plywood, one screwed into place from the outside and another similarly attached on the inside.

As Grube descended the steps to examine the door, he could easily see visible signs of a break-in: the padlock pried away from the doorjamb. No officer from the previous night had noted this type of damage to the door; Officer Kicska had not mentioned seeing any signs of a break-in in his initial report from the first 911 call, and Officer DeAngelo would later testify that the hasp was simply "loose in nature" when he responded to the house at 5:30 AM. But now Grube could see not only a popped hasp but also something else even more bizarre: nineteen of the twenty screws used to hold the plywood over the missing window were backed out but not removed. Only one screw remained firmly tightened in place to secure the plywood to the door. None of the officers who had responded to the Katrinak residence the previous night had mentioned anything about loosened screws on the basement door, nor would any of them later testify to seeing this. The indication seemed to be that the scene at the Katrinak house had drastically changed since the night before.

Andy shared a theory about the loosened screws: he thought the intruder must have first tried to gain entry to the house by removing the plywood before simply popping the hasp from the jamb and entering that way. Such a theory might have made sense if the plywood had been completely removed to reveal the second piece of plywood inside, but it hadn't been; the outer piece was still being held in place by the final screw. Why would anyone go through all the trouble of backing out nineteen screws, only to give up one screw short of success? Why bother to do it at all, when it was so much easier just to pop the hasp from the jamb as the intruder eventually did?

As Grube looked more carefully at the loosened screws, Andy made another suggestion: the intruder, he said, might have used a cordless screwdriver to loosen them. Why would Andy hazard a guess as to what tool might have been used?

After inspecting the door, the two men proceeded into the Katrinak basement. It was an old house, built in 1885, and like many homes dating to that period, the cellar was a confined space with a dirt floor and low ceiling. Damp and musty, it was unsuitable to use for storage and thus devoid of the typical basement clutter. The main phone line was intact and visible upon entering the house, but Andy barely glanced at it. Instead, he led the detective through two small partitioned rooms, to the very front of the house, and then pointed toward the ceiling to indicate where he had discovered that the feed to the portable phone had been cut.

The location of this feed line was troubling. Hidden in a lonely recess of the basement where no natural or artificial light penetrated, the area was so dark that Andy had been forced to set up drop lights just to see. Why would an intruder seek out this obscure, hidden phone line when the main line was clearly visible upon entering the basement? How would anyone even know this line existed?

The most alarming thing, however, was not the location of the line but the fact that it was no longer severed. Grube knew that his officers had responded to the cut phone line only hours earlier, yet, in that short amount of time, Andy had already spliced the two wires back together. And that wasn't the only oddity.

The floor beneath the cut line consisted of loose, sandy soil, and clearly visible within were a number of fresh footprints. As Grube bent to inspect them, Andy indicated that he need not bother. The footprints, he said, had been left by the responding officers the night before. There had been no footprints when he initially discovered the cut wire, because whoever had kidnapped Joann and Alex must have wiped away his or her own prints before leaving.

Apparently, the "intruder" had spent a considerable amount of time in the Katrinak basement. Enough time to loosen nineteen screws, pop a padlock, search out and cut a hidden phone line, and then wipe away the footprints.

From the house, both Grube and Andy proceeded to McCarty's parking lot, where Joann's tan Toyota Corolla still sat in the second space from Front Street. Grube chose not to enter the vehicle, but he did open the driver's side door and take a look inside. He noted the car seat secured up front and Joann's canister of Mace resting in the middle console.* Lying next to the Mace was a small piece of black plastic, approximately one and a half inches long. The detective pointed it out to Andy, who peered at it for a moment before saying he thought it looked like a piece of Joann's purse.

When asked what he thought might have happened, Andy mentioned several people who recalled seeing an unfamiliar black truck driving around the neighborhood the day Joann disappeared. He thought that might be important, since Joann's ex-husband, Jhared Starr, drove a black truck.

This was the second time Grube had heard the name Jhared Starr in connection with Joann's disappearance. Like Sally, Andy thought Starr might be involved, but he also mentioned a girl named Patricia Rorrer with whom Joann had recently argued. Rorrer, Andy explained, was an ex-girlfriend of his who had called the Katrinaks' house on Monday, December 12. Joann had answered the phone and, upset by the call, had told Rorrer not to call their house again before hanging up on her.

To Grube, the phone call sounded trivial; Jhared Starr did not. Despite any suspicions Joann's current husband might have raised, the police knew they would have to check out her ex-husband as well.

After returning to the station, Grube sat thinking about the Katrinaks and the events surrounding their disappearance. After a while, he picked up the phone and dialed the number for the Pennsylvania State Police at Troop M Bethlehem Headquarters. Speaking to Trooper Robert Egan,

---

* The Mace had somehow moved from the front passenger floor, where it was seen the previous night, to the middle console.

Grube explained the circumstances of the case and asked if the PSP would be willing to assist.

Egan, his curiosity already piqued, quickly agreed, and the two men made plans to meet on the following day, December 17, 1994, to conduct a search of the Katrinak residence.

2

Local police agencies are often small and ill equipped to handle complex cases, so it's not unusual for state police to become involved early in an investigation. State police have more resources, additional manpower, better equipment, and access to the finest forensic labs in the country.

Impeccably dressed in their slate gray uniforms and black leather boots, the Pennsylvania State Police were considered *the* premier law enforcement agency in the state. Intimidating to many and feared by most, they were known for their tenacious investigating and solving of crimes, but rarely would they encounter a case as complex as that of the missing Katrinaks.

Attention from the media had already begun, and the reporting on local law enforcement was less than friendly. While the press portrayed Andy as a sad and sympathetic figure, its criticism of the authorities' handling of the case was harsh and undeserved. The media was not privy to all the details of the investigation, but early FBI reports give a glimpse into the mind-set of those working the case. They viewed the crime scenes at the Katrinak house as suspicious and Andy's demeanor unsettling. Years later, detective Barry Grube would recall his first impression of Joann's husband: "The thing that stood out with Andrew was his calmness, his demeanor," Grube said. "He was not a distraught husband. He wasn't saying 'You have to find my wife! What are you going to do?' There was none of that."

Although Grube knew that people responded differently in stressful situations, it wasn't just Andy's demeanor that troubled him. "Probably one of the main things was that he spliced that phone line back together before we came down." There was another working phone in the house, so "there was no reason to do that." Nor did Andy's theorizing about the crime go unnoticed. "I guess my first impression," Grube said with a laugh, "was that he sort of had everything figured out."

———————

On the afternoon of December 17, 1994, state troopers Robert Egan and Kenneth Coia met with Detective Grube, and together the three men proceeded to 740 Front Street to present Andy with a consent-to-search form. Andy was under no obligation to sign it, but he readily did, granting the officers permission to search his home and garage.

Trooper Coia, of the records and identification (R&I) unit, first took pictures and cast impressions of the pry marks left on the basement door, then began photographing the exterior of the house. Meanwhile, Trooper Egan and Detective Grube began a meticulous search inside.

The Katrinak house was well maintained, with hardwood floors, original woodwork, and high ceilings. Although not yet decorated for the holidays, Christmas cards stood among numerous pictures of baby Alex. Neither Egan nor Grube saw anything unusual in the house—no visible signs of a struggle nor anything out of place.

One of the first things they did notice, however, was a hammer bearing rust-colored stains at the claw end, lying on the kitchen table. Taking the hammer into evidence, they proceeded to the bathroom where they collected several pieces of bloody tissue and a number of used tampons from the bathroom wastebasket. In the hallway, they noticed a suspicious-looking stain on the hardwood floor and took scrapings of that as well.*

———————

* Of the evidence collected from the Katrinak's house that was processed by the crime lab—and not all of the evidence taken was tested—none would yield any incriminating results.

From the outside, the Katrinak house appeared to be a single-family dwelling, but in reality, it was a two-family house. Andy and Joann lived on the ground floor and used the upstairs as a rental, though it was not currently rented out. The police found nothing of significance on either level, and dusting for prints revealed no foreign ones.

The break-in was puzzling and the motive for it elusive. The authorities quickly discounted robbery when they determined that nothing was missing, and with no signs of a struggle, an abduction seemed unlikely too. Lack of motive was not the only problem; by securing the basement door and repairing the cut phone line, Andy most likely would have obliterated any fingerprints or fibers an intruder might have left.

When the three investigators finished at the house, they walked the short distance to McCarty's parking lot, where Joann's car still sat in the second space. Trooper Egan took custody of the Toyota and summoned a flatbed truck to transport it to the state police crime lab. Afterward, he and Detective Grube returned to 740 Front Street to conduct a formal interview with Joann's husband.

Andy began by telling the lawmen that he had met Joann in April 1992 at the Maingate Club in Allentown. He was thirty-seven and she just twenty-three. For him, at least, it was love at first sight. "As soon as I saw her," Andy said, "I knew I was going to marry her." Despite the age difference, the two began dating, and in February 1993, Joann moved in with him at the Front Street house. Two months later, on May 29, the couple married in a posh ceremony in Allentown. Before that, Andy admitted, he had been a "confirmed bachelor" who never thought he'd marry.

Describing his marriage as "perfect" and "still in the honeymoon phase," Andy denied he and Joann had any marital problems. He insisted they had never had a fight, "not even an argument," and Joann was "extremely happy." He claimed Alex was a planned baby, whose birth on August 29, 1994, had only brought the couple closer together.

Recalling the days leading up to the disappearances, Andy described everything as "normal." On Wednesday, December 14, the day before his family disappeared, he had left for work at approximately 6:15 AM and arrived back home around 6:00 PM. Both Joann and Alex were there, and Andy fed the baby while Joann made dinner. Afterward, the couple watched some television and Joann had mentioned her plans to go Christmas shopping the following day. By 10:00 PM both of them were in bed.

The next day, Thursday, December 15, Andy said, he awoke around 6:00 AM and left for work "within fifteen minutes," leaving Joann in bed with the baby. He drove to the home of his best friends, LAUREN and JIM BRENNER, where he was contracted to put an addition on their house. His father, Andrew Sr.,* who was working with him, showed up a little later, and neither of them left the job site all day, "not even for lunch," Andy told detectives.

When Andy arrived home around 6:00 PM, Joann was not there, but this had not concerned him. He remembered her plans to go shopping and said he assumed she had gotten tied up in holiday traffic. Around 7:30, he called her sister, Peggy, to see if she had heard from her, but Peggy hadn't. At 8:00 he went downstairs to check the oil in the tank, and discovered the basement door pried open and standing ajar. He'd gone out to the garage, gathered the necessary tools, and secured the door from the inside.

One of the officers interrupted to ask if the break-in had concerned him, but Andy shook his head. "No, not then," he replied, but later, when he called his mother and learned that Joann had not shown up for their shopping trip, he suddenly realized something was wrong. He didn't call the police, however. Instead, he called Peggy back. By this time, Joann's sister was extremely worried and told Andy that she and the family were leaving for Catasauqua "directly."

Despite the obvious concern of his in-laws, Andy still didn't call the police. Instead, he said, he began calling local hospitals to see if Joann had been in an accident. When those calls proved fruitless, he called the Allentown Police and the Pennsylvania State Police, but again, only to inquire about any accidents. It was not until the PSP told him that if his wife and son were missing, he should report it to the Catasauqua authorities that Andy finally did.

---

* Because Andy and his father share the same name, to avoid confusion, Andrew Sr. will be referred to as Andrew at all times.

Andy said the O'Connors arrived from New Jersey around 1:00 AM, and everyone went out to search for Joann and Alex. They walked around the neighborhood, questioned anyone they encountered, and stopped vehicles along Front Street. Around 2:40 AM, Joann's father, David, went outside to have a cigarette but returned shortly to say he thought he had found Joann's car parked next door in McCarty's parking lot. He'd written down the license plate number and asked Andy to verify it, which Andy did. However, he said that when the police arrived they didn't seem too concerned and told him to take the car home. Andy refused, telling them that he didn't want to destroy any evidence "the kidnapper" might have left inside.

After returning home, Andy said he tried to use the cordless phone but discovered that it was dead. "Later," he found that someone had cut the phone line.

Andy's story did little but raise more questions. Why was he unconcerned when he found his house broken into? Why had he waited so long to call the police—*more than two hours* after discovering the break-in? How could the family have searched the entire neighborhood and no one notice Joann's car sitting right next door?

––––––––––

Grube and Egan also interviewed several other people that afternoon. Andy's mother, Veronica, confirmed her son's story and told the officers that she had spoken to Joann around 1:15 Thursday afternoon when she agreed to go Christmas shopping with her. Joann had told her she would pick her up in ten minutes, but Veronica had waited until 3:15 and Joann never arrived.

DAVE WILSON, one of the Katrinaks' neighbors, reported that during the early morning hours of December 15, he had heard two gunshots in close succession, followed by two more spaced about thirty seconds apart. Wilson thought the shots had come from the direction of Front Street and sounded like they were fired from a small-caliber weapon, possibly a .22.

A man named JOSH BLOOM called Grube to say that he and Joann had become friends when they both worked at Six Flags amusement park in Parsippany, New Jersey. Bloom said he had just seen Joann on Tuesday, December 13, when she and Alex traveled to New Jersey to have lunch with him and three other former coworkers. Joann had been in good spirits at the time and had given no indication that anything was troubling her.

Though the authorities remained reluctant to call the disappearances an abduction, Joann's family was not. They had already printed up hundreds of fliers bearing pictures of the missing pair and sporting the bold head-line "ABDUCTED 12/15/94 CATASAUQUA, PENN." While friends and relatives distributed the posters, Andy invited members of the press to come over and film the broken cellar door before holding an impromptu press conference on his back porch.

Dressed in sweatpants and old sneakers, Andy spoke in a level, even voice with few signs of nervousness. He said it was his belief that Joann had been abducted from behind the house, then forced into her car and driven around to McCarty's parking lot, where the kidnapper switched vehicles. "We think she got as far as putting the child seat down," he said, "and that's where they obviously came up behind her." He admitted he wasn't concerned when he arrived home on Thursday night, but said that when he discovered the break-in and saw the hinge pried away from the basement door, "that's when I started to panic."

Of course, that was not what Andy had told the police, but the press didn't know that. Still, his calm demeanor in discussing the disappearance of his wife and son was unnerving. When asked about it, Andy explained that although he might appear calm and unaffected, that was only because he was exhausted and didn't usually show emotion.

"The way I look at it," he said, "If I lose my edge, I lose the ability to do things for her. There's nobody to do what you have to do."

It was no secret that Andy was under suspicion by the police, but Joann's family both defended and supported him. Peggy told the press that Andy and her sister had a "good relationship" and that she had "no feeling at all that Andy had anything to do with this." Joann's family had directed their anger not at Andy but at the police and their handling of the case—especially their refusal to treat the disappearances as an abduction.

"That's the anger point," Andy said bitterly. "[Joann] obviously didn't kick the door in. She obviously didn't cut the [phone] line. One cop said this happens all the time. This doesn't happen all the time."

The family's fear and frustration were understandable, but many of their actions were not helpful to the authorities. The O'Connors had contacted law enforcement in both Pennsylvania and New Jersey and spoke to any media outlet that would listen. They also had no qualms with condemning the police and their investigation, forcing Catasauqua detective Barry Grube to go on the defensive.

"I don't want to say too much," Grube said, "but based on what we have so far, it certainly is not your typical missing person. There are so many unanswered questions, and it's a little strange. It's very strange."

"You have to understand," he continued, "the family is looking at this emotionally, and they are grabbing at anything. They actually feel if they call all the news media and police departments, this is going to mean their daughter is going to be returned quicker. An investigation takes time. We certainly don't want this to go a long time, but it could go on for weeks, months, or years."

The media perked up at the detective's words. An investigation that might take weeks, months, or even years? Their instincts told them that the Katrinak case was about to evolve into something huge.

3

On December 18, 1994, under intense pressure from both the media and Joann's family, Catasauqua authorities officially relinquished control of the case to the PSP. That same afternoon, officers from both agencies descended on Front Street and proceeded to knock on doors, stop motorists, and interview pedestrians.

State trooper Paul Romanic and detective Barry Grube worked together questioning residents, but most claimed to know little about Andy and Joann. The Katrinaks, so it seemed, were a quiet couple who kept mainly to themselves.

When Grube and Romanic interviewed Dave Wilson again, he told them that in addition to having heard gunshots on the morning of December 15, he had remembered something else that might be important. Two years earlier, during the summer months, he and his girlfriend had witnessed a young woman leaving the Katrinak house. The girl looked as if she'd been beaten and had sat in her car crying for nearly thirty minutes before driving off.

Trooper Romanic didn't question Wilson further about the incident, noting in his report that it had occurred "prior to Andrew Katrinak's relationship and subsequent marriage to Joann Katrinak." That, however, was a mistake. "Two years earlier" would have been the summer of 1992, when Andy was already in a serious relationship with Joann. Who was the woman who looked as if she'd been beaten and sat crying behind the Katrinak house?

In the end, the police could find no one who had seen or heard any-thing unusual on the afternoon of December 15, which did nothing to cast suspicion away from Andy. The Katrinak house sat in the hub of a busy and congested area replete with homes, businesses, and constant traffic—both foot and vehicle. How was it possible for a woman and her baby to simply vanish in broad daylight near the lunchtime hour from such a busy place?

Andy had told the police about several people who mentioned a black truck cruising the neighborhood on the day Joann and Alex disappeared, and Grube and Romanic managed to track down two of those witnesses during their investigation.

GARY ANDERS, an employee of Colonial Landscape, told the officers that between 1:00 and 2:00 PM on the afternoon of December 15—the alleged time of Joann's disappearance—he had been working at the rear of McCarty's parking lot. The Katrinak backyard was in view, but he had seen nothing unusual, nor did he notice Joann's Toyota drive from the back of her house into the parking lot.

When asked about the black truck he mentioned to Andy, Anders looked surprised and then shook his head. He hadn't told Andy about the black truck, he said; Andy had told him. Andy had approached him on Friday morning, December 16, and asked if he had seen a faded black truck driving around the area the day before. Anders told him he wasn't sure, but he may have seen one on Thursday or possibly some other day or even "in my dreams."

The second witness also denied mentioning the black truck first. JOHN TAYLOR said Andy approached him on Friday morning to tell him about his missing wife and son, and in return, Taylor had told him about some tire tracks he'd noticed in the snow behind his building. Although Taylor admit-ted he'd told Andy he thought the tracks had come from a truck, he had not given Andy a description of the vehicle because he had never seen it.

Why had Andy given the impression that others had described the black truck to him, when, in fact, he was the originator of the description?

Joann's tan Toyota had been taken to the PSP impound lot, where, on December 19, 1994, Troopers Ken Coia and Joseph Kocevar began processing it, a job that would ultimately take three days to complete. The vehicle was uncommonly clean, as Trooper Coia would later recall. "The car was immaculate," Coia said. "Probably the cleanest car I've ever been in, both inside and out. Even the undercarriage."

After photographing the vehicle, both men inspected the interior, where they noticed some loose change in the ashtray, a few cassette tapes, and several scraps of yellow paper in a cubbyhole above the stereo. Tucked beneath the driver's seat, they also found Joann's set of car keys.

Using a bright white light, Coia searched the vehicle for hair and fibers. On the driver's side seat back, he discovered a small grouping of six dirty-blond hairs, which, to him, looked like Andy's hair. Turning to Trooper Kocevar, Coia pointed them out and said, "Andy must drive this car."

At the instruction of forensic scientist Dr. Thomas Jensen—who was not a police officer but a civilian working for the PSP—Coia collected the hairs on Post-it Notes—an uncommon collection method never before used—and placed them in an evidence envelope. Coia then handed the envelope to Kocevar, who was in charge of delivering the evidence to the PSP crime lab. Afterward, the two men vacuumed the interior of the vehicle, then sealed it and used super glue fumes to search for fingerprints. Surprisingly, they found none, not even Joann's. Apparently, someone had wiped the car clean of prints.*

Coia and Kocevar's final task was to remove the driver's seat and send that to the state crime lab as well. They fervently hoped that something collected from the car would shed light on the disappearance of Joann and Alex.

---

* Eventually, all the items *inside* the car would also be tested for prints, and three would be revealed: two on Alex's car seat and one on the yellow scraps of paper. Police reports reveal that when the prints were run through the Automated Fingerprint Indexing System (AFIS), one print from the car seat matched a woman in the Philadelphia area. However, by the time of trial, the police would maintain that all three prints came from members of Joann's family—that two belonged to Andy and the third to Joann's sister, Peggy.

Andy had been asked to take a polygraph and readily agreed, so at 2:00 PM, on December 19, 1994, he arrived at the state police barracks in Bethlehem and met with Troopers Robert Egan, Joseph Vasquez, and Lynn Eshleman. For the first time in the investigation, the authorities read Andy his constitutional rights, officially making him aware of the fact that he was a suspect in the disappearance of his wife and son.

Andy was then read the list of questions the police intended to ask, a standard procedure that often unnerves a subject. Afterward, Trooper Eshleman attached him to the polygraph machine, and the examination began.

The test consisted of both relevant and irrelevant questions; those the police deem control questions—name, date of birth, etc.—used to gauge the examinee's reaction when being truthful. The four relevant questions Trooper Eshleman asked Andy that day were:

- Question 3: "Are you attempting to withhold any information concerning the disappearance of your wife and son?"
- Question 5: "Do you know where your wife and son are located at now?"
- Question 8: "Are you attempting to mislead anyone regarding what happened to your wife and son?"
- Question 9: "Did you personally have any involvement in the disappearance of your wife and son?"

Andy answered, "No" to each of the relevant questions, but after reviewing the results, Eshleman determined that he had shown deception on question number three.

Andy was upset to learn this, but he had a ready explanation. When the authorities first searched his house, he had told them that everything in the bedroom was just as he had found it, but that was not true. Before they arrived, he had hidden a vibrator he and Joann used in their lovemaking because he didn't want the police to see it. When the question came up about withholding information, he said his mind had flashed on that, leading him to fail the question.

Rather than question Andy further about that, the police instead asked him about the loosened screws on his basement door. Had they been tampered with? Andy insisted he didn't know but reluctantly admitted that he had told the Catasauqua police that they *had been*. "I wanted them to take the disappearances more seriously," he said.

Not readily apparent was what Andy actually meant by that. Was he admitting that *he* had loosened the screws so the police would take the disappearances more seriously or simply that he didn't know if the screws were loose before December 15 but decided to tell the police that they *weren't* so they would assume an intruder had "tampered" with them?

When asked if there was also tampering in regards to the cut phone line and Joann's vehicle, Andy denied it, but it was a denial the police soon found to be untrue.

When the media discovered that the Catasauqua police had failed to take Joann's car into custody, they chided them for their negligence. At the same time, they praised Andy for having the foresight to preserve evidence by not moving the vehicle. What neither the press nor the public knew, however, was that Andy had not left Joann's car alone that night.

In a subsequent interview with the PSP, Andy would admit that after DeAngelo and Kleiner departed from McCarty's parking lot, he had decided to "play detective" in the car. He thought that "maybe the kidnapper had left his wallet inside," so he opened the driver's side door and sat down, while at the same time Joann's father opened the passenger-side door to take a look as well.

Andy had previously confirmed that the driver's seat was in the right position for Joann to drive the car and that he was capable of driving the car with the seat in that position. Now, however, he insisted that the seat was pulled too far forward for him to fit and that he was forced to sit sideways in the seat, with his legs outside the car. "Every time I tried to swing my legs inside, my knees would hit the dash," he said.

Andy never did find the kidnapper's wallet, he said, but he did notice that the Toyota's red, low-fuel warning light was on and the gas tank was reading below empty. How he could have seen these things—if, as he stated, he never started the car—is unknown.

Regardless, Joann's husband now had a perfect score. Of all the potential crime scenes in the case: the basement door, the cut phone wire, and the abandoned Toyota, Andy had compromised *all three*.

On the morning of December 20, Detective Grube contacted Lieutenant Floyd Henderson of the Randolph, New Jersey, police department to inquire about Joann's ex-husband, Jhared Starr. Henderson was familiar with Starr, and knowing that he lived with his mother, agreed to visit her residence to see if Joann was there.

When he called Grube back later, Henderson told him that Joann was not at Starr's house and that Starr claimed not to have spoken to her in almost three years. Joann's ex-husband had not appeared nervous by the questioning and had provided an alibi for the day of the disappearance. He claimed he worked until 2:00 PM, stopped at a bar for a few drinks, and then went home. Henderson had already spoken to Starr's boss, who confirmed that Starr did work until 2:00 PM on December 15.*

Later that afternoon, Grube received a call from Starr himself, who seemed genuinely surprised to hear that Joann was missing. He said he had not had contact with her in a long time and claimed not to have known that she had married, had a baby, or moved to Pennsylvania.

Grube received another call that day from a New Jersey state trooper named JOHN MALTI. Malti told the detective that his wife, KIM, and Joann's mother, Sally, were coworkers and friends. According to Malti, Sally had allegedly told Kim that Andy had a problem with Alex's crying and was no longer sleeping with Joann. Instead, he was sleeping in the upstairs apartment because he couldn't stand the noise. Sally had supposedly also told Kim that Joann seemed depressed about the baby lately and that she had taken Alex for a weekend to give her daughter a break.

---

* Neither Henderson nor Grube would speak to any of the bar patrons or Starr's mother, however.

It was an interesting tidbit. Perhaps the "perfect marriage" Andy had described was not so perfect after all.

After showing deception on his first polygraph, Andy had been asked to take a second and arrived at PSP Department Headquarters on the afternoon of December 20 to do so. Once again, Troopers Egan, Vasquez, and Eshleman were in attendance, as well as one new addition: state police lieutenant Theodore Kohuth. The situation, so it seemed, was very serious indeed.

Just as before, the men conducted a pretest interview and read Andy the list of questions they intended to ask: essentially, the same questions as before, only formulated in a different manner.

This time, the four relevant questions were:

- Question 3: "Are you now intentionally lying about the disappearance of your wife and son?"
- Question 5: "Are you attempting to conceal the whereabouts of your wife and son?"
- Question 8: "Did you make up any part of your story about the disappearance of your wife and son?"
- Question 9: "Could you right now take me to where your wife and son are located?"

Once again, Andy answered "no" to each question, and once again, Trooper Eshleman noted deception on his results, this time, when their suspect answered "no" to question number eight.

Showing deception on two polygraphs in a row instantly moved Andy up a notch on the suspect scale, but a brutal grilling met with only denials. Joann's husband insisted he had nothing to do with his wife and son's disappearance. He loved Joann, he said. He would never hurt her, and he had no idea where she might be.

It was a stalemate, and the authorities knew it. Before allowing Andy to leave, however, they asked him if he would agree to yet another polygraph, this time conducted by the FBI. Andy, no doubt exhausted and emotionally drained, nevertheless agreed.*

Joann's sister, Peggy, came across to Troopers Egan and Vasquez as very protective of her little sister and fiercely determined to find out what had happened to her. She and Joann were "best friends who shared their thoughts and feelings," Peggy said. They talked several times a week and saw each other regularly, often on Saturdays when Joann brought Alex to New Jersey while Andy worked. Peggy said she last spoke to her sister on Wednesday, December 14, when she called the Front Street house and Joann answered. Her sister had sounded fine, Peggy said, and was looking forward to the upcoming holidays.

The next day, December 15, Andy had called her at 7:30 PM to see if she had heard from Joann. Peggy hadn't, but Andy sounded concerned, so she called her parents to see if they had seen her. When she learned that they hadn't, the family decided to drive to Catasauqua, arriving shortly after 1:00 AM.

Peggy made it clear that she suspected Jhared Starr of being involved in her sister's disappearance. She described him as very abusive and said that Joann confided that the abuse was both physical and sexual. Appalled by these revelations, Peggy had decided to help her sister get out of this "horrible" situation by inviting Starr to lunch one day and informing him that his marriage was over.

When she and Joann then told their father about the abuse, Peggy said, David O'Connor had become so angry that he called Jhared Starr and ordered him to stay away from his daughter. Afterward, Joann moved in with her parents but stayed only a short time before coming to live with Peggy. She was still living there when she and Andy met.

It was obvious that Peggy liked Andy and thought highly of him. She said he treated Joann like a "princess" and she was happy with him. She was sure her sister would not have walked out on Andy without letting someone in the family know.

---

* The results of any future polygraphs Andy may have taken are unknown.

David shared Peggy's feelings. He described his family as "extremely close" and said that Joann was a kind and considerate person who would never intentionally hurt anyone. He recalled finding her car in McCarty's parking lot, "heavily covered with frost" but could not give a time for the discovery because he had been "too upset and not thinking clearly."

Sally's recollections mirrored those of her husband. She told the investigators that Joann had a "great family and marriage and loved her baby very much." There was nothing Joann would not have done for Alex, Sally insisted, and she could not conceive of Joann having left without telling someone.

Andy's mother, Veronica Katrinak, was interviewed again and gave a more detailed account of the day Joann disappeared. She said she awoke at 7:45, watched Mass on TV, and then stripped her bedsheets and carried the dirty linen down to the basement. After lunch, around 1:15, she decided to call her daughter-in-law to see what she and Andy wanted for Christmas. Joann told her she was going shopping that day to buy Andy a new coat, but Veronica, aware that Andy had several coats, told her she didn't think he needed another.

"Hold on," Joann said. After a few seconds, Veronica could hear her moving clothes around in the closet. She knew Joann was using the cordless phone—which later would have its line cut—because the closet was in their bedroom, and the main phone in the living room would not reach that far. Soon Joann came back on the line and told Veronica that she was right: Andy did have several coats.

In the background, Veronica could hear the baby whimpering and, to acknowledge him, said into the phone, "What's wrong? Mommy's not paying attention to Alex?"

"What's wrong, honey?" Joann asked, speaking to Alex. Then, directing the conversation back to her mother-in-law, Joann boasted that the baby had slept ten hours the night before and had already eaten lunch and taken a one-hour nap that morning. It was after this, Veronica said, that Joann invited her to go shopping with them, noting that she wanted to be home by 5:00 PM.

Veronica agreed to go, and Joann, indicating that she was just about ready to leave, told her she'd pick her up in ten minutes and beep the horn when she pulled into the drive.

After the two had hung up, Veronica said, she got ready to go. She put on her coat and shoes, then went down to the basement, brought the laundry upstairs, and folded it. Afterward, she took out the garbage, then came back inside and put the sheets on the bed. Joann still hadn't arrived, so Veronica stood near the living room window watching for her. She stayed there, perched at the window in her winter coat and hat until her husband came home from work at 3:00 PM.

Asked if she were concerned when Joann never showed up, Veronica said she thought it was unusual but just assumed Joann had either changed her mind, decided to go without her, or had come to the house while she was in the basement and left when Veronica failed to hear the horn.

After her husband had arrived home, Veronica said she tried to call her son's house but there was no answer, and the machine (which was attached to the cordless phone) didn't pick up. She tried again a few minutes later but got the same results. She admitted that seemed strange, because Joann always kept the answering machine on, but she didn't become concerned. Nor would she. At least not until later that night when Andy called and told her that Joann and Alex were missing.

4

Rarely is a person's life an open book. Most people have something from their past they prefer to keep hidden, some little secret they tuck away, never intending to reveal. It may be minor (an embarrassing moment, a corrupt idea, a horrible thought) or more serious (an adulterous affair, a hidden addiction, a brush with the law), but whatever it is, it's private to its owner, who takes for granted that it will remain private. For those who become the focus of a criminal investigation, however, that luxury ceases to exist.

One by one, the fears and secrets of crime victims need to be ferreted out, uncovered, exposed, and meticulously examined by complete strangers. It's a sad reality that law enforcement must come to know victims better than anyone else—better even than the victims knew themselves. It's not uncommon for family and friends to put deceased loved ones on a pedestal, but it's an unrealistic vision. No one is perfect. Everyone has a past, and Joann Katrinak was no exception.

She was born Joann Marie O'Connor on October 11, 1968, in the Bronx, New York, the fourth and last child of Sally and David O'Connor. Joann and her siblings, Peggy, David, and Michael, grew up in Hackettstown, New Jersey, in a close-knit and loving family. As the baby, Joann was doted on by both her parents and her siblings.

Joann took after both of her parents in different ways, but her looks were more in keeping with her mother's Italian heritage. As a youngster, she had soft, delicate features and a mop of short, dark curls that eventually evolved into a lion's mane cascading past her shoulders. She also had dark eyes that smoldered behind lush lashes and a brilliant smile that revealed a perfect set of teeth. As a child, she had been cute; by the time she reached her teens, she was a knockout.

Ever conscious of her looks, Joann took great pains with her appearance, but beauty can sometimes be as much a curse as a blessing. Boys were attracted to her and she to them, but Joann often found herself on the receiving end of unwanted attention. Her natural good looks didn't always endear her to other girls, either, some of whom could be petty and jealous.

Her sister, Peggy, would tell the police that Joann was "very spoiled and protected while growing up," as well as "sensitive, trusting, naive, not street smart, and not a good judge of character." But Peggy would also add that her sister could be "rude and flip in her speech to others and inconsiderate of her father's feelings." Like many teens, Joann seemed to have a shaky relationship with her father, who didn't always approve of his daughter's lifestyle.

After graduating from high school, Joann trained to become a cosmetologist, but, according to Andy, soon discovered she was allergic to many of the products needed for a career in hairdressing. Instead, she took a job at the local ShopRite, where she became friendly with a coworker, JESSICA HOWARD, and began dating JASON STERN, a police officer from the nearby town of Washington, New Jersey.

Stern would later tell the authorities about another boyfriend of Joann's, one with a criminal record whom she dated for approximately a year. The relationship was apparently volatile, as after they broke up, the man allegedly assaulted Joann at the Tri-County Fair, causing her to file harassment charges against him.

Stern and Joann's relationship was short-lived, as was her job at ShopRite. In 1989 she abruptly quit and went to work as a teller at United Jersey Bank. Coincidentally, Jessica Howard was also working at the bank, and it was there that she and Joann became close. Another friendly coworker was KIM DESSIN, a woman twelve years Joann's senior.

Fellow employees would describe Joann as an excellent bank teller but a terrible employee. "She was stubborn and defiant," one worker said, "and wouldn't listen to her supervisors. But, that's how Joann was; it was her way or no way." Others recalled an incident where Joann got into an argument with the bank manager and not only began yelling but cursing, too.

"Joann had a bad temper," Kim Dessin would later tell the police.

If not endearing to upper management, Joann's bank customers certainly liked her, especially the men, who often flirted with the pretty new teller. Joann was used to this and routinely shrugged it off, but one customer quickly caught her eye: MARK CASE, a good-looking, divorced father of two. Joann liked Mark, and according to him, she let it be known that she was eager for him to ask her out. Initially, however, Case rebuffed her advances. It wasn't that he didn't find her attractive; it was just that he was nearly ten years older than Joann and their age difference bothered him. But after several weeks of mutual flirting, Joann surprised him with a pair of concert tickets, and he accepted.

After the show, the two began dating regularly, but Case found his new girlfriend peculiar. He would later describe her to the police as a "weekend warrior," a party girl who would "pack a bag every Friday night, tell her parents she was staying with a girlfriend, and then spend the weekend with me." She was also, Case said, someone with few friends and no plans for the future. "She never looked beyond the upcoming weekend."

Case seemed to view their relationship as one of wild times but no real substance. He said he considered both of their behavior to be "appalling and atrocious" at the time but insisted that he recognized it as such, whereas Joann never did. She was a person who had "no conscience and no regrets for her conduct in general."

After dating for about six months, Case claimed he tried to break off the relationship, but Joann didn't want to let him go. He said she called his house repeatedly and showed up there at all hours of the day and night. One early morning, Case told the police, a drunk and angry Joann appeared at his front door and trashed his house.

It was evident that Mark Case harbored a lot of resentment toward his old girlfriend, but his descriptions of her didn't sound that much different from hundreds of other young girls getting their first taste of adulthood and freedom.

Not long after she and Mark split up, Joann began dating another bank customer, Jhared Starr. Starr found Joann pretty and fun to be with. After dating only briefly, Starr proposed, and Joann accepted, but there is evidence to suggest that she was unsure about saying yes. Joann had told one of her friends that she knew the marriage wasn't going to work but had decided to go through with it because the wedding plans were already made.

Jhared and Joann wed on October 16, 1991, but within weeks, the marriage was in trouble and there was already talk of divorce. Starr told the police that Joann drastically changed after they married, but her friends claimed the marriage suffered most because Joann felt "smothered" by her new husband. They said Starr had a habit of calling the bank repeatedly and showing up there unannounced, which irritated his new wife.

Despite their problems, Starr insisted he was shocked to discover that Joann truly wanted out of the marriage and disgusted by how she let him know. It happened just as Joann's sister had described; Peggy took him out to lunch one day and informed him that his marriage was over. Barely five months after they had wed, Joann left Starr and began divorce proceedings.

They say absence makes the heart grow fonder, but not for these two newlyweds. Starr would later tell the police about a fight that broke out when Peggy and Joann came to his house to collect her belongings. When his estranged wife began screaming at him and then throwing things, he ended up calling the police.

After she left Starr, Joann decided to take a vacation and visit with an old friend, MARLEY HAMMER, who had gotten married and moved to Florida. Joann loved it down south, and the two girls had a ball while she was there. They went out, had fun, and spent lazy afternoons sunbathing at the beach. When it came time to leave, Joann didn't want to go, but she had an entire life back in New Jersey and reluctantly returned.

Now single and still working at the bank, Joann moved back in with her parents, but she wasn't particularly happy. Peggy told the police her sister was still angry and found it difficult to live at home, although whether this anger stemmed from her failed marriage or because she was still on shaky ground with her father is unknown. Either way, Joann stayed with her parents only briefly before moving in with Peggy.

Sally O'Connor would later say that Joann tried to rebuild her life, but Jhared Starr wouldn't let her. She claimed that he stalked her daughter by showing up at Peggy's house, an action that upset Sally so much that she threatened to call the police if he did it again.

Joann was friendly with a bank customer named Steve Cryler, a man nearly twice her age, but others at the bank told the police they thought Cryler wanted to be more than just friends with Joann. They said he asked her personal questions that were none of his business and was openly affectionate with her, but they also admitted that Cryler never stalked Joann and she never felt threatened by him.

Joann was well aware of the effect she had on men and routinely shrugged off guys like Steve Cryler, who flirted with her but knew where to draw the line. Some men, however, didn't seem to realize there even was a line, like another of her customers, George Vander.

Vander was much older, married, and the father of several children, but that didn't stop him from brazenly flirting with the young teller whenever he was in the bank. Initially, Joann didn't think too much of the flirting, but when Vander began sending her love letters and then calling her on the phone, she knew she had to do something. Other employees told the police that Joann confronted her customer, told him she was uncomfortable with his behavior, and asked him to stop. Vander apparently got the message, because as far as anyone could tell, Joann didn't seem to have a problem with him after that.

No longer married, Joann began going out again and sometimes traveled to Pennsylvania with friends to visit the nightclubs there. She and her group especially enjoyed a place called the Maingate, in Allentown, where one night Joann met a police officer named Billy Opel.

Immediately attracted to one another, Opel invited Joann to a party at a friend's house, and she accepted. The two left the club together, and Joann ended up spending the night at Billy Opel's house. Although the two began dating after that, Opel considered the affair a casual one. Though he found Joann incredibly attractive, he would tell the authorities that he made a concerted effort not to fall too hard for her. He had the impression that Joann attached herself to men very easily and got bored with them just as quickly. Like Mark Case, Billy Opel viewed Joann as a young girl with no direction in her life. He said she seemed to have no plans for the future and simply lived her life on a day-to-day basis. He never really got to know her, he admitted, adding, "Throughout our entire relationship, we were only together five or six times before the affair just fizzled out."

In early 1992, Joann resigned from her job at United Jersey Bank and went to work in Parsippany, New Jersey, as a secretary at the corporate offices of Six Flags amusement park. Her employers thought highly of her, and she seemed to enjoy her new job, where she got along well with her coworkers.

One Friday in the spring of that year, she, Kim Dessin, and another girl, CINDY SAYER, drove into Pennsylvania to visit the Maingate Club in Allentown. Although Andy would tell the police that he and Joann had met in April 1992, Joann's friends were certain it was May 15. Regardless, it was a fateful trip for Joann: the night she was destined to meet her future husband, Andy Katrinak.

Andy had been born on the south side of Bethlehem, on September 20, 1954, the second and last child of Andrew and Veronica Katrinak. He and his sister, Barbara, had grown up in Salisbury, where Andy attended elementary school at Saint Ursula in Fountain Hill and Salisbury High School as a teen. Tall and broad shouldered, Andy had played football in high school and was active in several clubs, including the sports car club, the Ping-Pong club, and the games club. He was a nice-looking boy, but his severely cropped haircut and heavy, black-framed glasses gave him an awkward appearance. Quiet, perhaps even shy, he was nevertheless well liked by his peers.

After graduating, Andy moved to San Diego, California, where he worked for a time as a professional boxer and began dating a woman named SARA. He and Sara lived together until Andy decided to return to the Lehigh Valley, where he started his own construction company and took a job as an assistant boxing coach at Lehigh University.

His relationship with Sara continued for a time long distance, but eventually the two broke up and Andy began dating a woman named Patricia Rorrer. This too, was a serious, live-in relationship, but it wouldn't last either. Perhaps viewing himself as unlucky in love, Andy would later tell the police that before meeting Joann, he considered himself a confirmed bachelor who would never marry. Joann, however, had changed all that. Instantly smitten, when he asked for her phone number at the Maingate Club, she readily gave it to him.

All week long Joann anxiously waited for Andy to call, but he never did. Morose and disappointed, she returned to the Maingate the following Saturday hoping to bump into him again, and she did. She felt much better when Andy sheepishly admitted he had lost her number and returned to the club for the same reason.

As Andy would later tell the police, it was love at first sight for the couple, and soon, Joann was spending nights at Andy's Catasauqua home.

Three months after Joann and Andy began dating, Josh Bloom was hired to work in the mailroom at Six Flags. Josh was a friendly young man who worked in close proximity to Joann, and as a result, the two grew very close. Joann often talked to Josh about Andy, but he was hardly the only one. Practically everyone who knew her heard about Joann's new love, although some of her friends were not that impressed when they finally got to meet him. There were a few who didn't care for Andy at all, and thought he acted like he was better than everyone else.

Joann, however, appeared head over heels for her new man, and within six months she was already planning a future with him. In January 1993, she gave notice at Six Flags, telling her friends that she intended to move in with Andy and find work in Pennsylvania. Josh was sorry to see her go and took her out for a good-bye lunch before she left. The two promised to keep in touch, and Joann provided Andy's Catasauqua number as a means to reach her.

In February, Joann moved in with Andy and sought employment through a temp agency. They sent her to S&L Plastics, where she was hired to do secretarial work. In keeping with her previous employment, Joann developed a close friendship with a coworker, DEBBIE MARCHEK, and had problems with another, RAY SCONE.

Scone apparently fell hard for the new secretary, and many would describe his attraction to her as a "fixation." Joann let it go, however, perhaps because she viewed her job at S&L as a temporary one. She and Andy were already making plans to marry and move to Colorado, and she didn't expect to be working there long.

Joann had never been to Colorado, but Andy had visited the state several times and had immediately fallen in love with the towering mountains and laid-back atmosphere. He had longed to move there ever since and had suggested it to other women he dated, but Joann was the first to show real enthusiasm for the idea.

On May 29, 1993, Andy and Joann were married in a civil ceremony at the Rose Gardens in Allentown, a popular and well-known wedding spot. It was a lovely ceremony, with Joann looking stunning in her luxurious wedding gown and Andy regal in his tux, but there was no formal reception afterward because the newlyweds couldn't afford it.

Apparently, where finances were concerned, Joann and Andy were very different. Joann was said to be excellent with money and very careful, while Andy was just the opposite. He didn't own the house he lived in and had not been able to qualify for a mortgage only a few years earlier. He also owed the IRS a hefty sum in back taxes.

Joann had kept in sporadic contact with Josh Bloom from Six Flags, and in June 1993, she called to tell him she had gotten married and that she and Andy were considering a move out west. Bloom was surprised to hear this, but Joann seemed serious.

In July, she and Andy contacted a Colorado Realtor, SUSIE STEPPIN, inquiring about land for sale in the Estes Park area. Steppin would later tell the police that the Katrinaks were looking to spend between "fifty and sixty thousand dollars for a parcel of land on which to build a large size residence." Excited by these new prospects, Steppin began phoning the Katrinaks and sending them active listings through the mail.

In August, Josh Bloom called Joann to let her know he was entering the police academy, and Joann told him that she and Andy were making definite plans to move out west.

Having never been happy at S&L Plastics, Joann quit her job in October 1993 and went to work for Guardian Life Insurance. The job was only temporary, however, and after working a few weeks, she was no longer needed. Joann was not upset; being unemployed enabled her and Andy to visit Colorado and look at property. In November, they flew into Denver and rented a car to drive to Estes Park. While there, they rented a room at the Blackhawk Lodge and spent the next week viewing properties with their Realtor.

Steppin would later recall her first impression of Joann as "a very attractive, well-dressed woman, made up with makeup, hairdo, and detailed painted nails." Steppin found it hard to believe that Joann could "possibly be serious about relocating to Colorado," but soon changed her mind when she saw an excited and happy Joann wading through waist-deep snow to inspect potential properties. The couple told her that Andy planned to start his own construction business when they moved and would build their house himself.

Steppin said she didn't think the Katrinaks knew anyone in Colorado, but she did know that they had several long conversations with the managers of the Blackhawk Lodge to discuss discounted long-term rentals, which they would need while Andy built their house.

Steppin also told the authorities that although she had no direct knowledge of the Katrinaks' financial situation, from their appearance, she assumed they'd have no trouble coming up with a down payment. Therefore, it came as a surprise when they told her that the best scenario for them would be to find a seller willing to carry a mortgage. Such a request would limit the number of potential properties available and make Steppin's search more difficult, but she still felt confident that she could find them something satisfactory.

Josh Bloom hadn't spoken to Joann since August, so in December 1993, he called to wish her a merry Christmas and let her know he had graduated from the police academy. Joann congratulated him and then confided that she had just discovered she was pregnant. The baby was due in August 1994.

Bloom was surprised and asked what she planned to do about Colorado.

"We're going to have to push back plans," Joann said matter-of-factly, "because I'm not moving while I'm pregnant."

In January 1994, Joann found employment through the temp agency again, this time working as a secretary for the M. W. Wood Company in Trexlertown. Joann made a good impression on her employers and enjoyed her new job but again found herself dealing with an unwanted admirer. This time, the employee was so annoying and irritating that Joann dubbed him "the little weasel."

Since their return from Colorado in November, the Katrinaks had kept in close contact with their Realtor, and Steppin continued to call them with new listings. Although Joann had told Josh Bloom she didn't intend to move while she was pregnant, she did not tell Susie Steppin. In fact, the Realtor had no idea Joann was even expecting. Neither Joann nor Andy mentioned it, and the couple continued to urge her to find them something as soon as possible, telling her they wanted to relocate by the fall and would make plans to come back to Colorado in February 1994.

It wasn't until just before they were scheduled to arrive in early February that Joann finally called Steppin and told her she was pregnant and that she and Andy would not be coming back to Colorado until after the baby was born.

Joann seemed delighted with the prospect of becoming a mother and took her pregnancy very seriously. She attended all of her doctor appointments, tried to eat a healthy vegetarian diet, and continued to exercise regularly. On August 19 she resigned from her job at the M.W. Wood Company, and ten days later, on August 29, 1994, gave birth to her son, Alex Martin Katrinak.

The Katrinaks brought their little boy home to Front Street, and a few days later, over the Labor Day weekend, Kim Dessin and Cindy

Sayer dropped by for a visit. The two girls stayed only a short time and later told the police that although Joann seemed happy with her new baby, she had also confided that she missed going out with them. She was lonely in Pennsylvania, Joann said, and anxious to move.

Kim and Cindy sympathized with her. They knew that Joann liked to "party hard" in the past, and they realized she was probably not doing much of that anymore. Not with a new baby and Andy, who hardly seemed like the partying type. Both girls would tell the police that Andy seemed bothered by something during their visit. He looked troubled, they said, and remained aloof throughout their stay.

Although family members would insist that Joann did not suffer from postpartum depression, there are indications that she did have a tinge of the "baby blues." Always conscious of her looks, she had gained weight during her pregnancy and was struggling to lose it, and she often complained of having "cabin fever" from being cooped up all the time. She was no longer working, either, so it's likely that the family was feeling the pinch. Although she was collecting unemployment, she received only $187 every two weeks.

Family pressures seemed to frustrate Joann as well. Friends would tell the police that Joann described her mother and sister as "smothering" and complained that Peggy called her daily and her mother almost as often. Everyone, however, was in agreement that the one person who irritated Joann the most was her mother-in-law, Veronica Katrinak. In her statement to the police, Jessica Howard said Joann "couldn't stand" Veronica and that things grew worse after the baby was born. "Every time the baby sneezes," Howard quoted Joann as saying, "Andy's mother expects me to take him to the doctor."

It was no secret that Veronica could be a source of contention for her daughter-in-law. Andy's sister, Barbara, told the police that in her last conversation with her, Joann had described the way Veronica acted around the baby as a "problem." Peggy's husband also told the authorities that Joann didn't like her mother-in-law very much, and even Andy corroborated this when he told the police that Joann could find his mother quite "irritating and annoying at times."

On November 4, Joann took the baby and traveled to New Jersey to have lunch with Jessica Howard. The two girls met at the Inn at Panther Valley and discussed plans to get together just before Christmas. After eating, Joann was to accompany Jessica back to the bank, but on the way there, they ran into Steve Cryler, who was headed to the Inn to have lunch himself. Joann's old bank customer persuaded her to come back to the Inn so they could visit while he ate, and afterward, when Joann arrived at the bank, Jessica asked her what Steve had to say. Joann dismissed the question with a wave of her hand. "Oh, you know Steve," she said, rolling her eyes.

A few days later, Joann phoned Josh Bloom and asked if he'd like to get together for lunch before the holidays. The two decided on December 13, and Bloom said he'd notify their former coworkers from Six Flags to join them at a TGI Friday's restaurant near the amusement park.

On Friday, November 25, Joann's brother, Michael, and his girlfriend, MARTHA, traveled to Catasauqua to pick up Joann for their cousin's wedding. Andy—according to the bride's father—elected to stay behind to babysit Alex and because he was uncomfortable in social situations.

Joann, Michael, and Martha drove to Sally and David's house where they met with other family members and then proceeded to the wedding as a group. Joann had a good time that night and gave no indication that anything was bothering or upsetting her. At one point, she left the festivities to call Andy and see how things were going at home.

After the reception, Joann spent the night in New Jersey, and on Saturday, November 26, Michael and Martha drove her back to Catasauqua, staying long enough to have lunch with her and Andy.

Throughout that fall, the Katrinaks had kept in touch with their Realtor in Colorado and also subscribed to the Estes Park newspaper, which they regularly scanned for any "for sale by owner" (FSBO) properties.

Near the end of November, the couple came upon a FSBO that appeared to be just what they were looking for: a thirty-five–acre parcel of land offered at a reasonable price. They immediately contacted

Steppin and told her they'd be flying out to see the property during the first week of December. They also asked that she set up other properties for them to look at while there.

As November slipped into December, Joann was kept busy with the upcoming holidays. She was excited about Alex's first Christmas and often spoke with Peggy to discuss the family's plans. She also made arrangements to spend time with her old friend Marley Hammer, who was scheduled to return to New Jersey for the holidays.

On December 4, Joann phoned their Realtor, Susie Steppin, and told her that she and Andy would not be coming to Colorado that month. Andy was finishing up a job, Joann said, and they had no one to watch Alex. They hoped to drive out sometime in January.

Steppin was disappointed by the call. She had just come across a "perfect piece of property" that fit all their criteria: a large tract of land offered in a fire sale with an owner who was willing to hold the mortgage. Steppin knew this kind of opportunity didn't come along every day, and she urged Joann to come to Colorado if at all possible. The property would not last long, and the seller was not willing to wait. In fact, he had put a stipulation on the sale; the property had to close on or before December 15, 1994.

Although Joann must have known that such a property was not likely to come around again, she turned down Susie Steppin's offer. They would not be coming to Colorado until January, she said firmly. "If it's meant for us to buy this property, then it'll still be available in January."

On Monday, December 5, Joann drove to S&L Plastics and picked up her former coworker Debbie Marchek. Alex was up front in his car seat, so Debbie hopped in the back while Joann drove to a local Pizza Hut. Debbie recalled how protective Joann was of Alex and how Joann made her stay with him at the table while she went to the salad bar just a few feet away. Only when Joann returned was Debbie allowed to go and make her own plate.

On the evening of December 12, Jessica Howard called Joann to set up a date to get together before Christmas. After chatting for a while, the two finally decided on the weekend of December 17 and 18.

The next day, Tuesday, December 13, Joann traveled to Parsippany, New Jersey, where she met Josh Bloom at TGI Friday's. Shortly after she got there, three of their former coworkers arrived, and the group ordered lunch.

Joann seemed in good spirits and talked about her and Andy's plans to move to Colorado, joking that the main reason she wanted to go was to get away from her mother-in-law. Her tone became more serious, however, when she stated that they would not be going until the latter part of 1995, as she didn't want to move until the baby was older.

Joann passed around pictures of her wedding and noted the weight she had gained during her pregnancy. She said she'd been making a concerted effort to lose it and pulled out a few more snapshots to show that her efforts were paying off. Joann seemed happy and said nothing about any problems with Andy or anyone else, but she did admit that she was glad to get out of the house after being cooped up with the baby so much.

After lunch, Josh and Joann were invited to come back to Six Flags and see everyone. Joann wanted to feed the baby first, and Josh elected to stay with her while she did. Afterward, the two drove separately to Six Flags, arriving around 3:00 PM. Estimates for how long they stayed varied from forty-five minutes to two hours, but everyone agreed that the two left together and that Josh hugged Joann in the parking lot before saying good-bye.

On Wednesday, December 14, Joann spent a quiet, uneventful day at home. She had dinner with her husband, discussed with him her plans to go Christmas shopping the next day and was in bed by 10:00 PM.

On Thursday, December 15, the same day the Katrinaks would have had to close on that "perfect piece of property" in Colorado, Andy awoke early, got dressed, and kissed his wife good-bye. What happened to Joann and Alex after that was anybody's guess.

5

As the police pieced together more and more of Joann's life, two images of the pretty young mother began to emerge. On the one hand, Joann was said to be friendly, sweet, loving, and kind. On the other, the descriptions were more critical. Joann could be wild, headstrong, quick to anger, and at times, even selfish.

Such descriptions, while not uncommon for most young people, could mean that Joann had made enemies in her past. That, of course, could have led to her becoming the victim of a crime. *If*, that is, her disappearance even *was* a crime—and the police were still not so sure that it was. As things turned out, neither were some of Joann's friends.

Many of those who knew Joann thought it *was* possible that she had taken her baby and walked out on Andy. They thought Joann had been deeply embarrassed by her failed first marriage and would have been reluctant to admit another mistake if she had wanted to end this one too. Steve Cryler thought it possible, and so did Kim Dessin and Cindy Sayer.

Marley Hammer told the police that when she initially heard about Joann's disappearance, her first thought was of Mark Case. Joann often talked about Case, Marley said, and if she left Andy to go back to him, embarrassment would have forced her to keep it quiet.

Of course, Joann had not gone back to Mark Case, but he, too, thought she had probably taken off on her own, and he told the police he didn't think it would take her long to find another guy. Joann could be a "cold and uncaring person with little regard for anyone she might be hurting," Case said.

Was Joann the type of person who could just walk away and never look back? It seemed possible, as even Peggy told the police that her sister "never had an overwhelming emotional commitment to any of her men, and was never deeply distressed when her previous love affairs ended."

Joann's family had focused their suspicions on Jhared Starr, and initially, Starr sounded like a good suspect. The PSP had dealt with enough angry husbands to know their typical reaction when a wife left, especially if she began seeing another man, and technically, Joann had still been married to Starr when she met Andy. As investigators began delving into the couple's relationship, however, the picture of Starr as an abusive ex-husband stalking his beautiful ex-wife began to lose credibility.

Starr had denied ever physically abusing Joann, but he recalled one incident when Joann had grabbed *him* by the neck with such force that the police showed up and escorted her from the house. Even more troubling was the fact that Joann had confided in no one—other than her family—about Starr abusing her. Not even her new husband.

Andy told the police that Joann admitted that Starr yelled a lot and had pushed her on occasion, but she never actually said he beat her. In fact, what Joann had told him was that she left the marriage because she felt she *would* be abused if she stayed. At the same time, she told others that she was leaving Starr because the two of them couldn't get along or because he was lazy and spent a lot of time doing only the things he wanted to do. Peggy's husband didn't believe Starr ever abused Joann either, but he did tell the police that Joann would get angry because Starr sat around the house drinking beer all day while she worked. Most of those who knew Joann said they thought the marriage had ended because Joann was bored with the situation and missed going out and having fun.

There were other things that didn't fit with Starr being a wife beater. He had enlisted the aid of a priest to help save his marriage, and there was no indication that he had ever tried to contact Joann after their divorce became final. In fact, their divorce had been granted by default because Starr failed to show up for the hearing.

Was Joann's marriage to Jhared Starr abusive, or had she embellished the horrors of it to justify leaving after only five months?

Though there were those who continued to suspect Joann's first husband, others were focusing their suspicions on her second. Cindy Sayer told the police she thought Andy had something to do with Joann's disappearance, and Jessica Howard reported a bizarre encounter she and her husband had with him only three days after Joann and Alex disappeared.

At that time, Jessica and her husband made a trip to Catasauqua to offer Andy support, only to find him lounging on the couch, watching a football game. Jessica's husband said he felt distinctly uncomfortable when it began to seem as if the game were more important to Andy than his missing wife and son. He would later describe Andy's behavior as "strange, unemotional, and suspicious," and Jessica would tell Steve Cryler, "Andy's taking Joann's disappearance unusually easy."

Others had noted Andy's lack of emotion too. Not only had it been reported on in the press, but several of the Katrinaks' neighbors had mentioned it to the police early in the investigation. One man described Andy as unusually composed when speaking of his missing wife and son, with "only a small amount of distress in his voice." Another said Andy seemed upset, "but not a whole lot," and still another said, "He looked a little collective [*sic*] for someone who just lost his wife and son."

Although the authorities knew that people reacted differently in stressful situations, all of these descriptions only added to their frustration. The case had become a guessing game. They had several suspects but didn't even know if they had a crime. They had a family who insisted Joann would never leave on her own and friends who were just as adamant that she would. They had an ex-husband who might, or might not, have been abusive, and a present one who displayed suspicious behavior. And they had a missing young wife and mother who might, or might not, have made enemies in her past. Joann's temper couldn't just be discounted, especially because several people had mentioned her short fuse and sometimes rude behavior. Coworkers had described her yelling and cursing at her supervisor. Mark Case claimed that she trashed his house. Jhared Starr said she screamed at him, threw things, and grabbed him by the neck with such force that the police had to be called. Peggy said she could be "rude and flip in her speech to others, and inconsiderate of her father's feelings." Even Andy, who was reluctant to say anything negative about his wife, did tell the police that Joann was a "typical Italian woman" who didn't hide her emotions but let him know whatever was on her mind.

Was it possible that Joann had offended or angered the wrong person?

———————

Despite the unanswered questions, the police knew they had to follow the trail wherever it led, and it seemed always to lead back to Andy.

His insistence that an abduction had occurred behind his home left many people to wonder how such a thing could have happened, especially in broad daylight, near the lunchtime hour, from such a busy street.

That question had been troubling from the start, but now, having learned more about Joann's reputation, it seemed to beg an answer even more. Andy's wife didn't sound like some meek and mild wallflower who would just timidly follow along. In fact, she sounded like one feisty and determined woman who would have fought like a mother bear if she believed she or her baby were in danger. If someone *had* abducted the Katrinaks, why was there no sign of it?

In going over Andy's statements, the police noted a number of inconsistencies. For instance, Andy sometimes said he left for work at 6:00, sometimes 6:15, and at other times 6:30. In one interview, he claimed he called Joann's sister twice on December 15, in another, it had only been once. Sometimes he said he called Peggy first and his mother second; other times he reversed the order of the calls.

He told the police he was unconcerned when he found his house broken into but then told the press just the opposite. He said he searched all over the neighborhood for Joann, yet he failed to find her car sitting right next door. Despite having lived in the Front Street house for the past four years, when asked if he searched the canal located only yards from his back door, Andy denied knowing the canal existed.

These were little things, true, but still troubling, and there were some big things that Andy needed to explain as well. Like the fact that he had shown deception on not one but *two* polygraphs and had compromised not one, not two, but *three* potential crime scenes: the basement door, the cut phone line, and Joann's car.

For the police, all of this suspicious behavior tallied perfectly with the known statistics, that most crimes committed against a wife or child are perpetrated by a husband or parent. Regardless of his denials, until the police could clear him or develop a stronger suspect, Andy would remain the focal point of their investigation.

In an effort to establish Andy's alibi, the police spoke to both his father and his good friends Lauren and Jim Brenner, at whose house Andy had been working on the day Joann and Alex disappeared.

Neither Brenner could give a time for Andy's arrival; Jim had already left for work, and Lauren could say only that both Andy and his father were there when she left the house around noon. Jim said when he arrived home shortly after 3:00 PM, only Andy was still there, and he invited him to stay for dinner. Andy had declined, however, saying he and Joann had plans to shop for a Christmas tree that night.

Andy had left around 6:00 PM but called the Brenners at 10:00 to ask if Lauren had heard from Joann. Lauren hadn't and was concerned when she learned that Joann still wasn't home. At 11:00, Lauren called Andy back to ask if there was any news, but of course there was not.

Andrew Katrinak Sr. told the investigators that he arrived at the Brenners' house around 9:30 on the morning of December 15 and found Andy already there. The two had worked together until approximately 2:30 when Andrew left, leaving Andy behind to finish up. When Andrew got home, he found his wife standing at the window wearing her winter coat. She said she was waiting for Joann, who was supposed to have picked her up hours earlier but never arrived. Andrew suggested she call Joann, and when Veronica said she already had, he told her to try again. Veronica did, but the phone just rang and rang.

Andrew thought Joann had probably just changed her mind, and his wife seemed to agree because she took off her coat and the matter was soon forgotten. When Andy called later that evening to say that someone had broken into his house and Joann and Alex were missing, Andrew said, he and his wife hurried over to their son's house, arriving around 10:00 PM. Joann's family was already there, Andrew continued, and the police had already come and gone. When Andy then showed him the basement door, he recalled the outer piece of plywood being completely detached and lying on the ground.

"I assumed whoever broke in intended to get in that way until he saw the second piece of plywood inside," Andrew said. "Once he realized that wouldn't work, he just popped the lock from the hasp and went in that way."

Whether Andy's father was questioned further about his recollections is unknown, but much of what he told the police could not possibly have been true:

- Andrew claimed he arrived at his son's house around 10:00 PM to find that the O'Connors were already there and the police had already come and gone. But Andy didn't call 911 until 10:40 PM and the O'Connors didn't arrive in Catasauqua until after 1:00 AM. Furthermore, the O'Connors stated that when they arrived at Andy's house, the elder Katrinaks were not there.
- Andy's father claimed that when he saw the basement door, the plywood was detached and lying on the ground, but no police

officer even noted the loosened screws then, let alone the plywood being completely removed.

- Gary DeAngelo, one of the officers who responded to Andy's third 911 call at 5:30 AM, testified that he looked at the basement door and saw the hasp "loose in nature," but he said nothing about loosened screws.

- Detective Barry Grube was the first officer to make note of the plywood on the basement door when he accompanied Andy to the house the following morning. Grube stated that he observed the screws partially backed out, but not removed, and the plywood still attached to the door.

All of this points to the screws having been tampered with *after* DeAngelo inspected the door at 5:30 AM on the morning of December 16.

One week after Joann and Alex disappeared, the case remained a mystery, frustrating investigators. The police had interviewed scores of people, tracked down countless leads, searched numerous places, administered several polygraphs, and spoken with everyone who had ever known Joann, Alex, or Andy, all to no avail.

On the afternoon of December 22, PSP captain Robert Werts and FBI special agent Bob Reutter held a press conference to ask for the public's assistance.

Although the police were still reluctant to call the case a kidnapping, Werts did stress, "We are not ruling anything out. There is a possibility that this investigation will take us through a rather broad spectrum, from her walking away voluntarily to an abduction. We are not closing the door on anything."

When asked about suspects, and in particular, Andy Katrinak, Werts insisted that they hadn't ruled anyone out but added that they had nothing to suggest Andy had been involved.

"Let me put it this way," Werts said, "at this point, we don't have any information that would make him a quote-unquote suspect."

When the questioning turned to the subject of polygraphs, and specifically whether Andy had been administered one, Special Agent Reutter stepped forward. He acknowledged that it was routine for the FBI to ask for polygraphs in investigations such as this, but he declined to comment on whether Andy had taken one or not.

Later that evening, when reporters reached Andy at home, he too sidestepped the subject of a polygraph. Omitting the fact that he had already taken two—and shown deception on both—Andy simply said, "I've agreed to take one whenever they want to give me one."

———————

The authorities had determined that both Joann's purse and Alex's diaper bag were missing, and on December 22, Andy described for them what Joann kept in each.

In the diaper bag, she carried: a baby bottle, an extra can of powdered formula, a spit-up diaper, baby diapers, a blue plastic telephone that Alex used as a pacifier, and a small white hinged box that contained wet wipes.

Interestingly, although Andy seemed to know exactly what was inside the diaper bag, he was unable to describe what it looked like on the outside. When he told the officers that the bag was powder blue with a caricature of a teddy bear on it, his mother interrupted to contradict him. The diaper bag, Veronica said, was black and white checked with matching straps. She knew because she had bought the bag herself.*

Andy described Joann's purse as "rather new, flat black in color, with brown markings and long shoulder straps." And, just like with the diaper bag, he seemed to know exactly what she carried inside: a checkbook with a brown suede cover, a long light-brown wallet, a pack of Trident sugarless chewing gum, and a tube of Blistex lip balm.

Again during this interview, Andy's times varied for certain events. Now, he claimed he awoke about 5:00 AM because Joann was feeding the baby, made his lunch, and left the house between 7:00 and 7:15. He

———————

* Veronica was correct. The bag was black and white checked.

stopped at a restaurant, had coffee and a donut, and then drove to the Brenners', where he met his father.

He described returning home to find his family gone, his house broken into, and, much later, Joann's car. Then, around 5:00 or 5:30 AM, he said he walked over to McCarty's bar and noticed the owner cleaning up inside. He tapped on the window, startling the man, and after being let in, questioned the barkeeper about his missing family. McCarty said he hadn't seen Joann the previous day, and Andy gave him a photo of her and Alex before he left. From there, Andy claimed he walked next door to Wint Casket Company and questioned some employees just arriving for work, again leaving a picture of his missing wife and son before returning home. Then, Andy said, "later that morning," when he tried to use the cordless phone, he discovered the phone line had been cut.

The police didn't get a chance to ask Andy about the many discrepancies in this sequence of events, as Andy terminated the interview citing a prior engagement. Before he left, however, he began describing what Joann would have been wearing on the day she disappeared: a gold wedding band on her left ring finger, a Helbros Countdown watch on her left wrist, light blue jeans, size seven black shoes, a tan leather coat, her contact lenses, and long, dangling earrings.

It was quite a detailed description for someone who had claimed to have last seen his wife undressed and still in bed.

When local newspapers ran a picture of Joann, it prompted a flurry of phone calls to the PSP, some of which seemed promising. One such call came from an elderly gentleman named BEN STAN, who had witnessed an incident on the train tracks behind the Katrinak house on the afternoon of December 15, 1994.

Around 4:00 PM, Stan found himself stuck in traffic on the Race Street Bridge, and while sitting idly, he noticed two people—a man and a woman—walking down the railroad tracks. The woman was short, with long brown hair, and wore black slacks and a leather coat. She was carrying what looked like a blue baby blanket or sleeper bundled up against her chest. The man was husky, sporting a long beard, and seemed to be urging the girl further down the tracks. He was pulling her along, Stan said, and the girl, who looked frightened, kept glancing back toward the bridge, a pleading look on her face.

When traffic began moving, Stan lost sight of the couple, but when he saw the picture of Joann Katrinak in the newspaper, he recognized her as the woman he had seen on the tracks that day.

The story was interesting because, according to Andy, Joann would have been wearing a leather coat and carrying Alex in a blue, sack-type garment. The police immediately investigated. On December 21, the day before Andy's latest interview, they conducted a search of the area, beginning at the back of Andy's house and moving toward the canal, then proceeding up to the railroad tracks and down to the banks of the Lehigh River. They found several things, but for some reason, decided not to take any of them into evidence.

Trooper Joseph Kocevar found a woman's purse but discarded it because "it didn't have the brown markings Andy had described." (Why the trooper would have relied on any description Andy gave is unknown. He had already proven himself to have an unreliable memory.) Kocevar also found a baby diaper but ignored that too because it looked as if it had been there for more than six days. The most interesting find, however, was a rag that appeared saturated with blood. Kocevar had the rag photographed but declined to take it into evidence. When later asked about this decision, the state trooper became defensive.

"If you look at the picture, it looks like it's a fresh rag full of blood, believe me," Kocevar said. "Well, I examined it, and I determined that it wasn't blood, and I discarded it. I made the call, and as far as I was concerned, looking at what I saw, I didn't feel it was blood."

Perhaps it wasn't blood, but having it analyzed in a lab would have conclusively proven it either way.

Ben Stan was not the only one who thought he saw Joann after her picture ran in the paper; police received dozens of potential sightings of her. Joann was supposedly spotted hitchhiking on a lonely road, sunbathing on a beach, traveling on an airplane, and shopping in a mall. The missing mother seemed to be here, there, and everywhere.

One sighting that sounded promising came from a woman named SHERRY STORM. On Tuesday, December 20, 1994, Storm saw a very attractive woman come into a convenience store in the township of Whitehall. The woman was in her early twenties, slim, with dark, shoulder-length hair, and wore a reddish patchwork jacket. While she shopped, a man also came into the store, bought a soda, and then went back outside to stand near a dark-colored van parked out front. Storm described the man as white, clean-shaven, and in his late thirties. He had short brown hair combed to one side and was wearing jeans and a jean jacket. After only a few minutes, the man came back inside and stood at the front door, keeping his eye on the woman shopping but often glancing back toward the van.

The woman bought one hundred dollars' worth of groceries—unusual at a convenience store—and also a child's toy.

Storm said the man was strange and left the door only to come to the counter and pay for the woman's purchases. He also seemed nervous and looked like he didn't want to be there. Later, when Storm saw a picture of Joann, she was convinced that Joann was the woman in the store that day.

The authorities took the sighting seriously—seriously enough to sit down with Storm and create a composite sketch of the man—but Andy did not. He told the media that Storm's sighting of Joann was "total garbage."

The prior engagement Andy mentioned when he terminated his interview with the PSP on December 22 was actually another interview, this time with the FBI, and again, discrepancies cropped up in his story.

Andy now shaved two hours off the time the Catasauqua police responded to his call and at least an hour off the arrival time of the O'Connors. He told the FBI that the police arrived around 8:30 when in fact, it was 10:42, and the O'Connors between 11:30 and midnight, although they claimed they didn't arrive until after 1:00 in the morning. Andy also said his parents showed up while the police were at his house, or shortly after that, although the O'Connors claimed the elder Katrinaks were not there when they arrived.

Andy now recalled finding the portable phone dead shortly after they found Joann's car but claimed he didn't discover the cut line until sometime "between 8:00 and 9:00 AM" on the morning of December 16. In fact, the police had responded to the cut phone line at 5:30 AM.

Andy also provided the FBI with a new potential suspect, a man named FRANK ALONZO who had once threatened to "get him." Going on to explain, Andy said his old girlfriend, Patricia Rorrer, had lived with Alonzo after she and Andy broke up, and one night in early 1991, after she and Frank fought, Patty had showed up at Andy's house bloody, disheveled, and looking like "she'd been hit by a bus." Both of her eyes were blackened, and blood was gushing from a nasty wound on her forehead.

Shocked, Andy took Patty to the hospital, where she received treatment and several stitches. Then, because Andy had no phone at the Front Street house, he took her to a pay phone, so she could call her mother. Afterward, he helped Patty file a complaint with the PSP and agreed to accompany her back to Alonzo's house to collect her belongings. When the two of them arrived, Andy said the police were just placing Alonzo under arrest, and as they escorted the handcuffed man across the lawn, Alonzo suddenly turned to Andy and screamed, "Somewhere down the road I'll get you for this."

Months later, Andy claimed he received a threatening phone call from a man he suspected was Alonzo, but that had been years ago and he had neither seen nor heard from the man again.

After investigating the incident, the police would come to learn that Andy's story about Frank Alonzo's threat was a complete fabrication. Though it was true that Alonzo had beaten Patricia Rorrer and she had turned to Andy for help, Andy never laid eyes on Frank Alonzo that night. Alonzo had been arrested and taken away before his girlfriend even left their house.

6

Christmas arrived ten days after Joann and Alex disappeared, and for the Katrinaks and O'Connors, it was undoubtedly an agonizing time. It was Alex's first Christmas, a day that should have been celebrated with happiness and joy but instead was consumed by fear and pain.

One week later was New Year's, and that seemed only to make things worse. Now Joann and Alex had been missing since *last year*. It was a devastating realization that got harder to bear with each passing day.

For Joann's mother, not knowing what happened to her daughter and grandson was torture. Sally would later tell a journalist that she would talk to her daughter every night, asking Joann for some kind of sign so she could be found. The pain of Joann and Alex's disappearance was excruciating, but Sally never gave up hope that one day they would be found alive.

Shortly after the holidays, Peggy told the FBI that for several weeks before she disappeared, Joann had complained of receiving hang-up telephone calls. When she hit *69 in an attempt to find out who was calling, a recorded message told her that the calls were coming from outside the calling area. Peggy added that she, too, had recently received some hang-up calls.

Andy informed the police of something he had forgotten as well. Joann had told him her ex-husband, Jhared Starr, was a member of a motorcycle club and wore "colors." He also remembered Joann saying she felt uncomfortable with Starr's biker friends and kept her distance because they did not accept her.

Interestingly, several people in Andy's neighborhood had mentioned seeing a motorcycle gang in the area around the time Joann and Alex disappeared.

With a new year stretching before them, the police had high hopes they would finally solve the Katrinak case, and initially, it looked like they might.

The composite sketch of the man seen in the Whitehall convenience store with a woman identified as Joann Katrinak began to get results. Several people called the PSP to say the sketch looked remarkably similar to a man named SIMON GRAY.

Gray was a bus driver who owned a dark-colored van, and the police found him to be an intriguing suspect. Although he was older than the man described by Sherry Storm, he did bear an uncanny resemblance to the composite sketch she had helped create. He also had a criminal record and an alarming background. Twenty years earlier, Simon Gray had been implicated in the abduction and murder of a young woman from a New Jersey shopping mall.

Gray adamantly denied being involved in Joann's disappearance and dismissed his trouble in New Jersey as nothing significant. The police had questioned him, he insisted, only because he happened to be at the same shopping mall when the victim disappeared. The authorities, however, knew there was more to the story than that.

In 1980, Gray was picked out of a photo lineup and arrested for the New Jersey woman's murder. Although subsequently indicted for the crime, the police dropped the charges before trial.

Gray claimed he had worked on December 15, but his work schedule could have left him free during the critical time the police believed Joann had disappeared. When they asked if he'd be willing to take a polygraph, Gray declined, citing his prior trouble in New Jersey. He did allow them to search his van, however, which netted nothing in the way of clues.

Days passed, and then weeks, and still investigators were no closer to finding the missing Katrinaks. For the family, it was distressing to see interest in the case begin to wane.

For the first thirty days after the disappearances, people inundated the small town of Catasauqua. "You couldn't walk outside without seeing a local cop, state trooper, or FBI agent," one resident said. "Every place you went, reporters would stop you and shove a microphone in your face. Then one day, everybody was just gone."

By February, most of the investigators had moved on to other cases, and with nothing new to report, the media moved on to other stories as well. After the case dropped from the headlines, the public soon forgot about it too.

For the Katrinaks and O'Connors—as well as those investigating the crime—there was no forgetting and no moving on. Joann and Alex were never far from their thoughts. The "ABDUCTED" posters bearing their images still hung all over town, but they were faded and tattered now.

Desperate to keep his family in the public eye, Andy began contacting television stations, even enlisting the aid of the FBI in contacting the hit series *America's Most Wanted* in the hope that it would air details of the case. When Lehigh Valley Crime Stoppers offered a $1,000 reward for information on the crime, Andy's parents added $10,000 to the coffer, but none of it brought results.

By the end of February 1995, Andy began contacting psychics. They, of course, were happy to help. According to police reports, one insisted the bodies of Joann and Alex were hidden in a lake in New Jersey, while another said two men and a woman from a "southern state" were involved in the disappearances. Newspapers reported that Andy had received a sketch from a psychic showing a balding man allegedly involved in Joann's disappearance and was circulating it among area businesses.

In March, another psychic told Andy that Joann and Alex were in Good Pine, Louisiana, so Andy called state trooper Robert Egan, who in turn contacted a detective in the LaSalle Parish Sheriff's Office. Although the Louisiana detective attempted to find the location the psychic provided, he soon discovered that her description applied to hundreds of places in the area.

Rather than be deterred, the detective's words motivated Andy. He had endured Christmas, New Year's, Valentine's Day, and Saint Patrick's Day without his wife and son. All these "first" holidays for the baby and he had shared none of them with him. Now, Easter was fast approaching.

At the end of March, neighbors saw Andy packing up a trailer in preparation for a long trip. He told them he was going to Louisiana to search for his missing family, unaware that he had chosen the worst possible time to leave.

———————

Palm Sunday, April 9, 1995, dawned mild and pleasant, just the type of weather people look forward to after being cooped up all winter. Farmers can read the signs of spring better than anyone, and they take the hints of the season very seriously. After lying dormant under heavy snow, the rich soil carries its own aroma, and for JIM KOVACK, the smell was telling him it was time to get his fields ready to plant.

Kovack worked as an airline pilot, flying for American Airlines, but he lived on a farm that had been in his family for years. Located in Heidelberg Township, approximately fifteen miles from Catasauqua, the Kovack farm was a large spread consisting of dense woods and low-lying fields.

Despite the beautiful weather, the forecast was calling for heavy rain later in the day, and Kovack decided to get his plowing done before the storm came in. Around 10:30 AM, he climbed aboard his tractor and began tilling the rich, soft earth.

On his third pass around the field, he pulled the nose of the trac-tor into the brush, intending to back up and turn around, and that was when he noticed the heap of trash lying in the woods. Kovack sighed, then shook his head in disgust. It wasn't the first time someone had used the property as a garbage dump, and he knew it wouldn't be the last, but he was getting damn sick and tired of it.

In an effort to curb the illegal dumping, Kovack had begun picking through the trash, aware that people often left behind envelopes and bills that still bore their names. Now, as he idled down the tractor and got off, Kovack was hoping to find such incriminating evidence again.

Walking into the woods, he could clearly see the color blue, but he couldn't make out what it was. As he approached the bundle, he suddenly stopped and cocked his head. He thought he was looking at a scarecrow wearing blue jeans and a bright blue top, but who in the world would throw away a scarecrow way out here?

Jim Kovack would later say his brain was not processing what his eyes were seeing. As he moved closer to the pile, he was taking in the sight, but his mind was reeling as it desperately tried to prevent him from seeing it. He saw boots, blue jeans, arms, hair, a face.

Dear God, the farmer thought, panic gripping him. *It's not a scarecrow. It's a body.*

After a moment, fear and adrenaline took hold, and Jim Kovack broke and ran. The only thought swirling through his mind was that he needed to summon help.

———————————

Trooper Thomas Mase was the first officer to arrive at Kovack's farm and, because neither man thought the police cruiser would make it through the field, Kovack used his truck to drive him to the scene.

As the two men walked into the woods, Mase asked, "Is that a blue blanket on the body?"

Kovack peered closer and then nodded. "Yeah," he said. "It looks like a blue blanket."

Mase continued walking, then suddenly stopped. "I know who this is!" he cried excitedly. "That's not a blue blanket. It's the baby's blanket sleeper, and the baby is in there."

Jim Kovack felt his stomach turn. He knew as well as the trooper did that this had to be Joann Katrinak and her baby boy. As Mase radioed for help, Kovack, his plowing forgotten, returned home where he could watch the activity unfold from his house.

The second officer to arrive at the scene was Trooper Joseph Vasquez, who had initially entered the case on December 18 but was reassigned to a different one in February. Although a thin layer of leaves covered the bodies, Vasquez could see that Joann was lying on her back with knees bent, her right leg tucked slightly behind her left. Her right arm was thrust out at a forty-five-degree angle, her left, bent at the elbow allowing the hand to rest on her chest. Glittering in the afternoon sun was her gold wedding band, still adorning her left ring finger.

She wore a waist-length, brown leather jacket, and black hiking boots. Her gray Mickey Mouse sweatshirt was pulled up to her bra, and her blue jeans, unbuttoned and unzipped, were pulled down below the right hip, revealing a pair of red satin panties.

Just as Andy had described earlier, Joann was wearing blue jeans, long, dangling earrings, and a Helbros Countdown watch on her left wrist that still displayed the time it had stopped: 3:50. Joann's gorgeous hair remained a tangle of rich dark curls, but time and the elements had ravaged her once beautiful face.

On the left side of her stomach lay baby Alex, his arms stretched out, his legs dangling off to brush against the ground. Yellow-tufted pajamas could be seen poking from the cuffs and collar of his fuzzy blue sleeper, perfectly matching the tiny socks he wore on his feet.

The body site, located 200 feet northwest of the intersection of Best Station and Saegersville Roads, was not readily visible but not particularly isolated either. Positioned along Saegersville Road was the field Kovack was tilling, and separating the field from Best Station Road was a narrow strip of woods approximately 250 feet wide. It was within this small strip of woods that the bodies of Joann and Alex were found. The area where the bodies lay was accessible from two points: an old railroad bed off Saegersville Road that cut through the small patch of woods or an old logging trail off Best Station Road that led into those same woods. Either access point would have been dangerous for a killer looking to dump two bodies.

To come in from the logging trail would require parking a vehicle in a pull-off on Best Station Road and risking someone seeing or remembering it being parked there. Despite Heidelberg Township being in the "country," Best Station Road was still frequently traveled by motorists. Bringing the bodies in off Saegersville Road would have been only slightly less risky. The railroad bed was not groomed for vehicular traffic and may have required a four-wheel-drive vehicle to maneuver. It was also regularly used, even in winter, by joggers, horseback riders, and ATVs, again leaving someone vulnerable to a possible sighting.

Shocked by the discovery, Trooper Vasquez did a cursory walk through the scene, keeping his eyes peeled for anything out of the ordinary. There was no sign of a murder weapon or Joann's missing brown purse, but near the left side of her head lay Alex's black-and-white-checked diaper bag, and farther on, his baby bottle, its dinosaur cap nearly buried in fallen leaves. Fifty feet to the east Vasquez felt his stomach knot as he stared at a blue rattle shaped like a telephone, Alex's favorite toy.

When Trooper Ken Coia arrived, he and Trooper Mase secured the area with yellow crime scene tape, and within an hour Jim Kovack's open field resembled a small parking lot. Vehicles were haphazardly parked all over the place: state police cars and unmarked FBI sedans, an ambulance, a fire truck, the coroner's van, and more. Soon, the top brass arrived as well: PSP's Lieutenant Theodore Kohuth and Captain Robert Werts, Deputy Coroners Jeff Perrault and Scott Grim, and later that afternoon, District Attorney Robert Steinberg. There was no doubt the case was going to explode into something huge, and, mindful that the investigation might one day come under scrutiny, they wanted things done right.

In viewing the bodies, officers noted something unusual: three foreign objects that resembled pieces of fingernail resting on Joann: two on her bicep and the third, much larger, lying on her chest. This nail fragment had a ragged edge, as if torn from its owner, and appeared to have a piece of flesh flecked with dried blood still attached. Had the killer left a sample of blood and tissue at the scene? Carefully, the three pieces of fingernail were removed from the body and placed in separate evidence envelopes.

After the victims had been pronounced dead and the police had photographed their bodies, everyone stood in silence while the coroner removed Alex from his mother's stomach. He was so tiny and so fragile that several of the state troopers—all hardened detectives—had to hold back tears. Alex was lying skin to skin with his mother, and as the two were carefully separated, the baby's tiny head left a perfect indent in Joann's flesh. After gently laying both mother and son on a white sheet, the bodies were wrapped and concealed in the same body bag.

Partially hidden beneath Joann's body, investigators found a gold bracelet, broken in half, a cigarette butt, and nearby, a piece of gray duct tape. As numerous troopers stayed behind to process the scene, others began gearing up for a task they were dreading: notifying the families.

At 7:30 PM, a Hackettstown, New Jersey, police officer knocked on the O'Connors' door. Joann's mother answered, and instantly knew why he was there.

"You've found them," Sally whispered.

As the officer nodded, Joann's mother, perhaps finally allowing the weight of the prior four months to descend upon her, broke down and wept.

As much as anyone might try to prepare for the worst, one never really can. A death like Joann and Alex's would cut a searing pain, unlike anything her family had ever known. The shock, the grief, the horror of it all was enough to take away their breath and leave them weak in the knees. It created an overwhelming feeling of helplessness.

Peggy would later say that it was her father who took Joann and Alex's death the hardest. He was never the same, and the family worried about him. Their concern would turn out to be justified: David O'Connor would not live long enough to see anyone brought to justice for the murder of his daughter and grandson.

Things were no better at the Katrinak house. Andy wasn't even in Pennsylvania. He was still down in Louisiana following up on the psychic's tip.

Andy was staying in a campground, so there was no way to call him. Pennsylvania authorities contacted the Louisiana State Police and asked for their assistance in notifying him. When they finally located him, they put him in touch with the Pennsylvania State Police in Bethlehem, who told him the search for his missing wife and son was over.

Andy was distressed to find that he couldn't get a flight home until the next morning. After spending a sleepless night, he flew into the Lehigh Valley International Airport on April 10, where his father waited. There, in the middle of the airport, the two men held each other and wept.

———

The *Allentown Morning Call* reported that a fully decorated Christmas tree still stood in the O'Connors' living room, Joann's parents having vowed not to take it down until the police found the missing pair. Now, back in New Jersey, Sally and David finally took down their tree. They packed away the tinsel and the lights, the carefully wrapped ornaments, and the festive red bows—everything except for one solitary decoration: a small needlepoint ornament that Joann had made for her mother.

After holding the ornament for a long time, Sally finally got up and walked slowly across her living room. Carefully, she hung the ornament on the picture window where she would see it every day, a reminder of the love she shared with her lost little girl.

7

State troopers would spend more than fifteen hours combing the woods where the bodies of Joann and Alex were found. It was an arduous task; as some officers used rakes and metal detectors, others searched on their hands and knees, gathering evidence from amid dead leaves, broken tree limbs, and rotted debris. Everything they found was bagged, labeled and sent for processing at the state crime lab, but they found no murder weapon, no shell casings, no footprints, and no fingerprints.

What they did find, however, were several hairs entwined within the fabric of Alex's diaper bag, one of which was long, blond, and remarkably similar to those found on the driver's side seat back of Joann's car.

The Katrinak murders sent shock waves through the small town of Catasauqua and devastated local law enforcement. Many of the investigators had children of their own, and the appalling nature of the killings led several to request assignation to the case.

The brutality of the crime was almost too much to comprehend, leaving local citizens outraged and afraid. Most had believed Joann and Alex would be found alive, and their deaths left the town reeling.

Before the panic could even begin to settle, Joann's family and the public at large were dealt another shattering blow by the autopsy results.

Forensic pathologist Dr. Isadore Mihalakis determined that Joann had been shot once in the face and bludgeoned about the head at least nineteen times. Her body also bore defensive wounds—a severely bruised shin and fractured left middle finger—indicating that she had fought hard for her life.

Although her clothing was in disarray, the pathologist found no visible signs of sexual assault, nor any traces of semen, but this was not surprising. Any biological fluids left behind would have long dissipated.

Mihalakis could not say whether Joann was shot first or beaten, but each of the wounds had actively bled, indicating she was alive when she received both. He listed the manner of death as a homicide, and the cause as a bullet wound to the face and blunt force trauma to the head.

There were no injuries to the baby: no wounds, no signs of violence, and no clear indication of how he had died. In Mihalakis's opinion, Alex had either been suffocated or simply left to die of exposure.

The medical examiner's findings brought a swift response from the public. There were loud and angry demands that the killer of Joann and Alex be found and found fast. For law enforcement, the pressure was on, and it would continue to grow daily.

———

For those investigating the case, Joann's wounds seemed peculiar. Why were there two separate modes of attack? If the killer had a gun, why revert to bludgeoning the victim?

Trooper Joseph Kocevar thought he might know the answer. He had once worked a similar case, where the victim was shot once and then severely beaten. In that case, the killer's gun had jammed, and he had reverted to using the weapon to beat his victim to death. Could the same thing have happened here?

———

Everything collected at the crime scene was sent to the PSP lab and examined by Dr. Thomas Jensen, who had already processed the evidence found in Joann's car. Between the car and the body site, the police recovered hundreds of hairs, but Jensen focused on only eight: six from the seat back in Joann's car and two from the body site, one found on Alex's diaper bag, and the other discovered in what the police termed "forest litter."

In comparing the eight hairs, Jensen noted a number of similar characteristics and something else: the hairs appeared darker near the base. Could the hairs have been chemically dyed? Because men rarely dyed their hair, Jensen wondered if the hairs could have come from a woman.

Concentrating on the six car hairs, Jensen first separated them into two groups of three. He mounted the first three individually on glass slides and left the remaining three unmounted in order to conduct testing on them. All six hairs measured approximately eight inches long, and though no visible roots were noted, Jensen did see what he thought was dried blood on the distal end of one.

There was another hair found at the crime scene, one that, for unknown reasons, Jensen paid little attention to: *a human hair found in Joann's right hand.*

Despite the fact that this hair must have come from the last person Joann had contact with, Jensen apparently didn't feel it was important. He failed to examine it, photograph it, measure it, or even note its color—perhaps because, as he later testified, this hair showed no similarities to the eight already recovered.

Authorities collected hair samples from Joann's husband, other family members, and friends for comparison, but none of the hairs matched.

In trying to determine if Joann had any connection to Heidelberg Township, where the killer had left her body, state troopers decided to drive Andy out to the area to see if he recognized anything.*

Andy sat in the back seat of the cruiser, unfettered, and gazed out the window. He watched the passing landscape but remained quiet as

---

* Police have actually given two versions of this part of their investigation. In one, the happenings occur in an interview at Andy's house, in the other, the police drove Andy out to the crime scene area. I've chosen to rely on the second version as they recalled it.

the officers' anticipation began to wane. Was there any reason Joann would be out here, they asked? Did she or Andy know anyone who lived in the area?

Andy glanced around, then shook his head. He didn't know anyone out here, he said, and he was sure Joann didn't either.*

The troopers were disappointed as they headed back to town. The idea that they might never solve this case was beginning to take hold, and that was something none of them were willing to accept. Then suddenly, Andy piped up from the backseat.

"You know," he said, "I do know someone who's familiar with this area. A woman who used to keep horses out here. She managed a horse stable nearby."

Feeling a jolt of excitement, Trooper Kocevar asked Andy the name of the stable, but Andy couldn't remember. He could give them directions to it, however.

"OK, go ahead," Kocevar said.

As Andy began to describe how to get there, Kocevar felt the hair on the back of his neck stand on end. *My God*, he thought, *he's leading us right to the bodies!*

"Who is this woman?" the trooper asked.

"Her name's Patricia Rorrer," Andy answered. "She's the same person Joann argued with just before she disappeared."

When, on the morning of December 16, 1994, Andy first mentioned his old girlfriend, Patricia Rorrer, he described her as someone who occasionally went through periods of depression, adding, "When she's in these states, she sometimes calls me." In fact, Andy continued, Rorrer had called his house on December 12, only three days before Joann disappeared. He hadn't spoken to her, but Joann had, and she was decidedly unhappy about the call. She told Rorrer not to call their house again before hanging up on her.

---

* In fact, Andy did know someone who currently lived in that area, a woman whom he would later describe as one of his best friends, but for some reason he failed to mention her to the police.

At the time, investigators had been skeptical of Rorrer as a suspect. The call sounded trivial and the crime not the type commonly perpetrated by a woman.* When they also learned that Rorrer didn't even live in Pennsylvania but more than five hundred miles away in North Carolina, they were even more doubtful. She had moved down south long ago and had not had a romantic relationship with Andy Katrinak in nearly five years. It seemed ludicrous to think that she would drive all the way to Pennsylvania to murder two people she had never even met, all over a petty hang-up call.

In fact, so dubious were the police then that they didn't even bother to contact Patricia Rorrer—not until an FBI agent answered the phone at Andy's house and found her mother, Pat Chambers, on the other end.† It was December 21, 1994, six days after the disappearance, when Pat Chambers called to see how Andy was holding up. Told that Andy wasn't there, police then asked Patty's mother if she'd agree to an interview over the phone, and she said yes.

Pat Chambers said she knew Andy well because he and her daughter had lived together for many years and, although she admitted he could sometimes have a temper, she described him as "basically a decent person, incapable of hurting anyone." She did recall one time when he had either hit or pushed her daughter, but she didn't believe it was anything serious and the two had remained friendly after they broke up. They'd kept in touch through letters and phone calls, Pat said, "until about a month ago" when her daughter told her she called Andy's house, and Joann answered. Patty had said Joann was upset by the call and told her not to call their house again before slamming down the phone. After that, Patty said she wasn't going to call Andy anymore.

When asked to speculate on what might have happened to Joann, Pat Chambers admitted that she thought Joann had left on her own, and she suspected she knew why. Her daughter had lived with Andy for

---

* An FBI profiler had judged the likely offender to be a male, someone familiar with the Katrinak family and their habits, the town of Catasauqua, and the body site.
† Like Andy and his father, Patty and her mother share the same first name. To avoid confusion, Patricia Chambers will be referred to only as "Pat" throughout the book.

five years and never used birth control, yet she'd never gotten pregnant. Neither had any of Andy's other live-in girlfriends.

"I've always wondered if Andy were even capable of fathering a child," Pat Chambers said.

It was an explosive statement; if Alex wasn't Andy's child, that could provide a strong motive for murder. Knowing the lead needed to be followed up immediately, the FBI first requested a semen sample from Andy and then made arrangements for agents in North Carolina to interview both Patty Rorrer and her mother.

The PSP did not consider Patty a suspect; they wanted her to help them build a case against Andy. The teletype sent to the FBI in North Carolina asked them to "determine if Patricia Rorrer has any knowledge of Andy Katrinak's ability to conceive children, and also determine her opinion regarding his potential for violence."

The next day, December 22, North Carolina FBI agents Dwight Ayers and William Bradbury questioned Patty Rorrer at her mother's house. While Bradbury interviewed Pat, Ayers spoke with Patty and noted in his report that she appeared genuinely concerned for Joann and Alex.

The interview was casual. The fact that Ayers was there to build a stronger case against Andy was evident to both Patty and her mother.

"The entire interview was about Andy," Patty said. "Every bit of it."

Patty told Ayers she had no knowledge of Andy's ability to father children, other than the fact that she had never gotten pregnant with him. But she did remember that Andy once told her he didn't want kids and wasn't even sure he could have children.

Like her mother, Patty couldn't conceive of Andy being capable of murder. Although they would argue at times, she claimed there were only two instances when Andy ever displayed violence. Once he had pushed her down on a bed, and another time he attempted to backhand her but she raised her leg to stop him and his hand hit the bottom of her foot, injuring his finger.

Questioned about the phone call with Joann, Patty readily admitted it had happened but denied it occurred on December 12. She'd called Andy's house on December 7, more than a week before Joann and Alex disappeared, and yes, she admitted, Joann had told her not to call the house again before hanging up on her.

In the last few minutes of the interview, according to police records, Ayers asked Patty her whereabouts on the afternoon of December 15, and Patty told him that she had bought grain for her horses and stopped at a local gas station to inquire about some lost keys. Because Patty wasn't a suspect in the crime, Ayers didn't bother to check out her alibi, nor did the PSP ask him to.

Now, nearly four months later, authorities wondered if that had been a huge mistake. There was no evidence that a woman wasn't involved, and Patricia Rorrer fit all the necessary criteria. She was familiar with Catasauqua, the Front Street house, and the area where the killer left the bodies. More important, she had been involved in an argument with Joann only days before she disappeared.

For police, that made Patricia Rorrer a viable suspect in the case, and someone they would need to learn as much about as possible.

8

Patricia Lynne Rorrer was born on a blustery winter day—January 24, 1964—in Phillipsburg, New Jersey, the youngest child of Robert Rorrer and Patricia Celia Mills. Although Bob and Pat each had children from previous marriages, Patty would be raised as an only child and never share a close relationship with her half-siblings.

The Rorrers took their little girl home to a small farm in Asbury, New Jersey, where Pat kept a slew of animals, a passion she would pass along to her youngest daughter. Pat considered all her animals "pets," but even she knew she had far too many for their tiny farm. She longed for a place large enough to keep them, and after years of pleading, Bob finally relented and moved his family to a rented one hundred-acre farm in the town of Whitehouse Station. Bob could easily afford it; he was a machinist who made a good living. Bob told his wife she could raise as many animals as she wanted, with one exception. "No elephants," he said with a grin.

Pat later laughed that she took her husband's words to heart and soon the large farm was bursting at the seams with everything except an elephant. There were goats, sheep, chickens, rabbits, carrier pigeons, pigs, dogs, cats, and horses—always horses.

Pat loved horses, and Patty, having been around them since the day she was born, loved them too. Pat rode with her when she was an infant, holding her daughter securely in front of her, but only a few short years later, Patty was riding on her own. She was a natural and skilled horsewoman who developed a deep and passionate love for her animals.

Patty was a pretty girl, shy and quiet, and at times very lonely. She had no brothers or sisters at home, and although she had friends who lived in town, she was often busy with farm chores and had little time for socializing or play. At school, she felt awkward, not only because she was a "farm girl," but also because she was tall and thin and towered over most of her peers. Rather than view her model-like assets as a blessing, Patty found them embarrassing.

Pat's mother and brother both lived in North Carolina, and the Rorrers would travel there every Fourth of July for vacation. Each time they did, the family would pester them to move down south, but Bob regularly begged off. He had a good job in New Jersey, and Pat had her animals. Besides, they had good friends up north, especially their best ones: Telly and Ellie Fiouris, a couple who were closer to them than siblings. Pat's family scoffed at Bob's excuses, insisting that family was more important than friends.

In 1978, while the Rorrers were in North Carolina for the Fourth of July, the talk once again turned to their moving, and Bob cracked a joke meant to appease. Looking around, he pointed to a little house at 1251 Wilson Road, in the small community of Linwood, and said with a laugh, "I'll tell you what. If that house ever goes up for sale, I'll buy it, and we'll move here."

Sure enough, on their return home, the Rorrers saw a "For Sale" sign planted in the front yard of the little house on Wilson Road. Pat gave her husband an incredulous look, and Bob, staring in disbelief, simply shrugged his shoulders. "Maybe it's an omen," he said.

Not long after that, Patty came home one day to find her mother packing up the house.

"What's going on?" she asked.

"We're moving to North Carolina," Pat told her daughter.

Moving to North Carolina? Patty was stunned. She was fourteen years old and just about to start the eighth grade, but no one had told her anything about their plans to move.

Patty found Linwood strange and worlds away from New Jersey, where she had always lived. Everything was so different—from the terrain to the accent to the weather—and some things were downright frightening.

Only weeks after they arrived, a hurricane hit, and Patty had to help her panicked parents batten down the house. Then, during her first week of school, a blaring alarm sent all the children rushing out of the classroom.

"What's going on?" Patty asked a student next to her.

The boy looked at her as if she were daft, before mumbling, "It's a tornado drill."

A tornado drill? Patty remembered having fire drills in New Jersey but never a tornado drill. It was a frightening thought for a young girl who had spent her entire life surrounded by trees and mountains.

The very next week, an anonymous voice came over the loudspeaker at school and announced an early dismissal. Not wanting to appear stupid again, Patty said nothing, but she soon discovered that this was a common occurrence. She had loved missing school for snow days in New Jersey, but down here, they sent you home if it got too hot. It was all so *weird*, Patty thought.

Shortly after the Rorrers settled in North Carolina, Bob began complaining about not feeling well. He was weak and tired, he said, and it burned whenever he urinated. When he began passing blood in his urine, he figured he had a bladder infection and saw a doctor who prescribed some antibiotics and sent him on his way.

Back in New Jersey, Telly and Ellie Fiouris found they missed their friends dearly, and soon they, too, purchased property in North Carolina. The Fiourises did not move down south full time, but they visited often, and both couples were happy to be spending time together again.

A month passed, and Bob's health did not improve. He was still taking antibiotics, but they didn't seem to help. Pat finally convinced him to see a different doctor, who immediately sent him for additional tests. X-rays of his stomach revealed a tumor the size of a football in his bladder, and Bob underwent emergency surgery to have it removed.

After completing a round of chemotherapy and radiation, his doctors sent him home cautiously optimistic about his prognosis.

By late fall, things had pretty much settled back to a normal routine in the Rorrer house. Patty was beginning to acclimate to North Carolina, and Pat had made several new friends. Then one day in November, after Bob had been outside pruning some rose bushes, he came inside the house limping and complaining of a searing pain in his legs.

"I must be getting arthritis," he told his wife, dropping onto the couch. "My legs ache like a rotted tooth."

Pat gave him some Tylenol, but the soreness didn't ease. In fact, it grew worse. After several days of this, Bob knew something was wrong and called his doctor. Subjected to a battery of new tests, when the results came in, the news was not good. The cancer had spread to his bones, and Bob Rorrer was dying. The news was a devastating blow for Patty but even more so for her mother, who was about to lose the love of her life.

Bob's cancer moved swiftly. As his illness progressed, doctors advised Pat to put him in hospice, but Pat refused, determined to care for her husband at home. It was a courageous decision, but it created an atmosphere that weighed heavily on her young daughter. Patty could hear her father in the bedroom, moaning and writhing in pain, and it terrified her. She felt incredibly helpless, and, as her mother spent more and more time caring for her father, incredibly alone.

Patty was only fourteen and going through the most traumatic experience of her life. She didn't understand why this was happening. All she knew was that life as she had always known it was quickly fading away, and she felt powerless to stop it. "Uncle" Telly and "Aunt" Ellie were there, but they had little time for her. Their concern lay with their dying friend and his grieving wife.

The Rorrers could not have asked for more loyal and devoted friends than the Fiourises, and Bob Rorrer knew that. One day, shortly before the end, he grasped Telly's hand and pulled him close.

"Promise me you'll take care of my girls," Bob whispered.

Telly, grief-stricken by the loss of a man who was more a brother than a friend, nodded his head and began to cry. "I will," he said in his thick Greek accent. "I promise."

It was a promise Telly Fiouris would go above and beyond to keep.

On January 24, 1979, Patty turned fifteen, and nineteen days later, on February 12, Bob Rorrer died in the little house on Wilson Road, having lived there less than a year. Patty and her mother were inconsolable. They buried Bob two days later, on Valentine's Day, February 14, 1979.

Had it not been for Telly and Ellie, Pat didn't know if she would have survived the death of her husband. The two stayed as long as they could, helping her with the settling of Bob's estate, but eventually, they had to return to New Jersey, leaving Patty and her mother to face their loss alone.

Life went on, but it became more and more difficult in the little house on Wilson Road. Pat found herself not only consumed with grief but also facing the loss of her husband's income. Bob had made a good living, and without him, the money soon ran short, as did Pat's patience with a teenage daughter. She and Patty argued often, seemingly about everything: from school and friends to who was going to do the dishes and clean up the house.

Patty's entire world was in chaos, and she hated how everything had changed. She needed her mother, but it felt like her mother didn't have time for her anymore, and it hurt.

Pat, who was dealing with her own pain and grief, probably didn't realize how deeply her actions affected her daughter, but they did affect her. Sometimes Patty thought her mother would have been happier if it were she who died, rather than her father.

It wasn't long before Patty found someone to help her through her pain: JAKE SUMMERS, the brother of a friend. Jake was three years older than Patty, but she didn't care. She met him at a school dance when he came to drop off his little sister. The dance was for younger kids, but Jake, attracted to Patty, stayed for the duration just to be with her. From that moment on, the two were a couple.

Patty found Jake cute, smart, and understanding. He seemed to be the only person who could identify with what she was going through. She viewed him as her best friend, her confidant, and the one person capable of taking her mind off her troubles. Patty was in love, and Jake told her he loved her too.

The two youngsters spent all their time together, but when Patty finally brought Jake home to meet her mother, Pat was not happy. Although she liked Jake well enough, Pat thought Patty was too young to date, and she let her daughter know she didn't approve. Patty was upset. She loved Jake, but she loved her mother even more. Tired of the constant fighting and bickering, she eventually acquiesced to her mother's demands and ended the relationship, but things did not improve at home. She and her mother still fought, and Patty still felt very much alone.

Money problems continued to plague the household, and Patty heard about them often. At sixteen, she decided to drop out of high school and help her mother with the mounting bills. She took a job waitressing tables, but still wanting to get her diploma, she also enrolled in night classes at an extension program offered by her school. It was there that she met the brother of another friend, a young man named Charles "Gary" Gabard.

Gary worked as a landscaper, and at twenty-five, was nine years older than Patty. Today, she has trouble remembering what even attracted her to him. "He was nothing like Jake," she said, a thoughtful look on her face. "I think he was just a distraction from all the upheaval in my life."

Despite their age difference, she and Gary hit it off and soon began dating. Gary found Patty pretty and fun to be with, and Patty found him a wonderful escape from her troubles at home. Her mother didn't like Gary and begged Patty to break off the relationship, but this time, her daughter refused.

Patty had no idea why her mother cared so much; after all, she had a new man in her life too, a fellow by the name of Ray Chambers. Patty liked Ray, and she didn't begrudge her mother seeing him. But she figured if Pat could get on with her life, then so could she.

After dating for only a short time, Patty asked her mother to sign papers so she and Gary could marry. Pat looked at her daughter as if she'd lost her mind and immediately refused. Patty, upset and undeterred, packed her bags and moved in with Gary, despite her mother's protests.

In January 1982, Patty turned eighteen and no longer needed her mother's permission. She and Gary traveled to South Carolina where they got married in a little wedding chapel along the way.

Gary would later tell the police that the marriage was a mistake and that he and Patty were just a couple of dumb kids who had nothing in common. No one would argue with that, but it hardly mattered then. Patty had just discovered that she was pregnant.

Patty and Gary's marriage was tumultuous from the start. Gary would later tell authorities that Patty was cold and always looking for a fight, and it was true that the couple argued often. The pressure of having to grow up so quickly certainly contributed to that, but Patty claimed their problems went far beyond immaturity.

"My husband was abusive," she said, "both mentally and physically. He was always putting me down and telling me I was dumb, stupid, and ugly. He belittled me constantly, and sometimes he could be violent. We would fight, and people would call the police. They showed up at our house several times."

On August 19, 1982, Patty gave birth to her first child, a son she named Charles Robert Gabard, in honor of her husband and her father. Charlie was a beautiful baby, but he brought added stress to an already delicate situation—and so did Patty's mother.

Pat doted on Charlie, coddling and cooing over him, and it seemed a baby was just what she needed to get over the loss of her husband. For Gary, however, Patty's mother soon became an unwanted interference. He was frustrated by her presence and complained that she was always around.

Both Patty and Gary had full-time jobs, and much to Gary's consternation, Pat always babysat for Charlie while they worked. He was annoyed that Patty wouldn't use daycare, but Patty just shook her head when asked about this.

"We were broke," she said, "*and I mean broke*. It was crazy to pay for daycare when my mother was willing and able to babysit Charlie for free."

Years later, after Patty's arrest, Gary was quick to label her an unfit mother. Patty neglected their son, he said, and seldom wanted to hold him. In the next breath, however, he seemed upset—even jealous—that Patty was too possessive of Charlie.

"The baby was more hers and her mother's than mine," Gary lamented.

Less than a year after they wed, the Gabard marriage was already crumbling.

The only thing not in dispute regarding Saturday, November 20, 1982, is the fact that something happened to little Charlie Gabard.

According to Gary, after working a twelve-hour shift, he and Patty picked Charlie up from her mother's house and drove home. Patty put the baby down for a nap and, exhausted, she and Gary went to bed as well. Hours later, Gary said Patty awoke and went to check on Charlie, returning after a lengthy absence with a dazed look on her face. She told her husband that something was wrong, at which point he leaped out of bed and rushed into the baby's room. There, Gary said he found his son blue and not breathing. He immediately began CPR while Patty went to call not the ambulance but her mother.

Patty, however, insisted that Gary's story is a complete fabrication. "It never happened," she said, shaking her head. According to her, Charlie had been fussy all day, so she put him down for a nap, and after a while, went in to check on him. He was fussing in the crib, so she rolled him over and rubbed his back. He seemed to be going back to sleep, so she left him alone in the room, tidied up the house, and then called her mother.

"Thanksgiving was on the coming Thursday, and we had plans to go shopping to get our turkeys. I called my mother to ask what time she wanted to go, and she said I should come over then. I told her it'd be a bit because I'd have to wake up Gary and see if he'd watch Charlie or at least feed him while I got ready. I went into the nursery before waking him, and I saw immediately that Charlie wasn't breathing, but he was not blue. I screamed for Gary from the nursery, and he came in and tried to do CPR but he was panicked and said he forgot how.

I called 911 first, and then I called my mother and told her what had happened. The volunteer firemen were there in minutes, and they did CPR until the paramedics arrived."

An ambulance rushed Charlie to the hospital, but it was too late. Little Charlie Gabard was dead. An autopsy revealed that the baby had died from sudden infant death syndrome (SIDS), but even today, thirty-four years later, Patty has a hard time accepting that. "I swear Charlie looked at me as the paramedics took him out the door," she says, breaking into tears. "That's why I refused to believe he was gone at the hospital."

The Gabards took their little boy home and buried him in a nearby cemetery. Most of those who knew Patty—with the exception of Gary—insist she took Charlie's death very hard. Even those who clearly did not like her agreed that she never got over it. People described Patty as "walking around like a zombie, sobbing uncontrollably" at Charlie's funeral.

Even Andy Katrinak would tell the police that Patty grieved for her lost little boy, but Gary Gabard saw it differently. He told the police that Patty seemed more upset when one of her dogs died than when her son did.

After the baby's death, things went rapidly downhill for Patty and Gary. Their fighting increased, and the end of their marriage loomed. Patty said that one day, an irate Gary smashed out the headlights and windows in her car before holding a shotgun to her head and threatening to kill her. Only weeks later, the two fought again, a violent row that finally convinced Patty to leave. According to her, she and Gary were outside arguing at Gary's mother's house. Patty was standing on the lawn and Gary on his mother's porch, which had a railing around it. Patty apparently said something that pissed Gary off, because all of a sudden he was "jumping over the rail in what could only be described as a flying karate kick. He hit me squarely in the chest and sent me flying." Dazed and in pain, Patty lay on the ground for a while, unable to breathe.

Eventually, the couple went home, but Patty's chest felt like it was on fire, and she was still having trouble breathing. Gary went to bed, but

Patty was up all night in severe pain. Her breath was coming in wheezing gasps, and her chest throbbed every time she breathed. By early morning, even Gary looked alarmed and immediately took her to the emergency room where doctors determined she had a fractured sternum.

"When they asked at the hospital what happened," Patty said, "I told them I fell. I always covered up for him, *always*, but they didn't believe me. They knew what happened."

Years later, Gary would deny that he ever abused Patty and insist that their marriage ended because his wife was having an affair. Patty, however, shook her head at the idea. "Pull the medical files," she said with a shrug. "It was actually the sheriff who convinced me to leave. He told me if he arrested Gary he'd bail out by morning, and if I stayed, Gary was sure to kill me one day."

Patty's mother had been seeing Ray Chambers for several years, and it was Ray who secured a car so Patty could flee back to New Jersey. Her Aunt Ellie and Uncle Telly still lived there, and Patty went to stay with them. She had no plans to settle there permanently; she just wanted some time to grieve for Charlie and decide what she was going to do with her life. But being in New Jersey was a welcome relief. Things were calm there. There was no fighting, no fear. Patty coped well, began to gain weight, and according to her, finally saw her marriage for what it was.

"I was in an abusive relationship," she said with a shrug. "I didn't see it that way until I got out."

Patty had taken a thirty-day leave of absence from her job, but when the time was up, she realized she didn't want to leave. Throughout the summer and fall of 1983, she continued to live with Telly and Ellie and kept herself busy working two jobs. During the week, Patty worked in the office of a welding company, and on weekends she waitressed at a nearby restaurant. It helped keep her mind off Charlie, and she needed the money to start a new life of her own.

One day while glancing through the newspaper, Patty saw an ad placed by Mutual of Omaha Insurance. They were recruiting new agents, and on a whim, she applied. After passing the necessary test to get her license, Patty was hired to sell insurance out of their Flanders, New Jersey office, working on commission. She did quite well and had soon saved enough money to get a place of her own.

Slowly, Patty began putting the pieces of her life back together. She rented an apartment not far from Telly and Ellie, made new friends, and even went out a few times with a local police officer, DAN MIT- TEN. She saw her aunt and uncle, but they were busy too, having just purchased a new restaurant in Bethlehem, Pennsylvania. The Fiourises named their new venture Smiley's and soon had a thriving little business on their hands.

"Things were going well for everyone," Patty remembered. "I was doing great, Mom was fine down in North Carolina, and Telly and Ellie were enjoying their new diner. And then Ellie got sick."

Only months after buying the restaurant, Ellie Fiouris learned she had cancer. Patty had watched her father die of that same deadly disease and immediately offered to help.

The Fiourises were grateful, and so, in late 1983, while still keeping her job at the insurance company, Patty also began working part-time at Smiley's. And it was there that she met a good-looking regular customer named Andy Katrinak.

Patty found Andy pleasant and attractive, and though the two would joke and flirt whenever he was in the diner, she assumed he was married. Then, one day in the spring of 1984, another customer asked them why they didn't go out.

Andy smiled, and Patty giggled. "I would," she said, "if he wasn't already married."

Andy looked surprised and then started to laugh. "I'm not married," he said. "You want to go out sometime?"

That same weekend, they had their first date.

Patty liked Andy, and he seemed to like her too, but she told him she wouldn't be able to see him much because she had some medical issues that needed attending. She had injured her back in a car accident in 1983 and was scheduled for tests and rehab at Hahnemann Hospital, where doctors told her she'd need to stay for roughly two weeks.

Admitted to the hospital nearly one hundred miles away, Patty didn't expect to see Andy until she was released, but he surprised her by making the two-hour drive just to visit. It was an impressive move. No other man had ever done anything like that, and it raised Andy's status considerably in Patty's eyes.

As he would later do with Joann, Andy treated Patty like a princess. He wined and dined her, took her to fashionable and expensive restaurants, and introduced her to a world she had rarely seen. He was kind, considerate, and overly generous with his compliments, telling her often that she was beautiful and special. It was foreign treatment for Patty, who had only Gary Gabard to compare him with.

"I was twenty years old and just coming out of an abusive relationship," Patty remembered, "and here was this older, good-looking, successful business owner showering me with all this attention. It was pretty overwhelming. Gary had put me down for so long. He really had convinced me that I was dumb, stupid, and ugly, and I had a hard time believing Andy's compliments. It took me a long time to accept them."

Patty was hardly dumb, stupid, or ugly. In fact, she was tall, shapely, and very attractive. The landlord of her apartment was an older man named CARL BRYCE, who owned not only rental property but also a photography shop. Bryce was attracted to his new tenant but hardly chivalrous in how he let her know. He suggested Patty allow him to do a nude photo layout of her, assuring her that she could make "big bucks" doing so. Patty turned him down flat, but Bryce didn't give up that easily. Occasionally, Officer Dan Mitten, the cop she had dated and was still friendly with, would stop by Patty's apartment while on his rounds, and of course, Andy visited her there as well. One day, when neither man had been there, Patty's landlord confronted her outside her apartment.

"When's it going to be my turn?" Bryce asked.

"Excuse me?" Patty said.

"Well, you're fucking the cop, you're fucking that blond guy. When's it going to be my turn?"

When Patty told her boss at the insurance company what had happened, he grew concerned. "Does your landlord live in your apartment building?" he asked.

"No," Patty said. In fact, he lived a considerable distance away.

"Pat, the guy's a stalker," her boss said. "If he doesn't live there, how does he know who's visiting you? He must be watching you."

Patty realized she was in trouble and considered moving back to North Carolina, but Andy didn't want her to go. Instead, he came to her rescue by suggesting she move in with him. Patty agreed, and after requesting a transfer to work out of Mutual of Omaha's Allentown office, she moved into Andy's rented duplex in Bethlehem during the fall of 1984.

Patty's love of horses had never waned, and she owned several while living in Pennsylvania. Andy didn't seem to mind; in fact, he indulged her passion. When her beloved mare died not long after Patty moved in with him, Andy surprised her with a new filly he bought from a woman named SANDY WALKER.

Walker managed the Silver Shadows Stable in Heidelberg Township, and Patty decided to board the filly there until she could make other arrangements. On her first visit to the stables, however, she discovered that Sandy was also boarding a beautiful stallion, and soon the two women had worked out an arrangement. Patty would show and condition the stallion in exchange for free board for her filly.

Patty loved spending time at the stables. She was a country girl at heart who dreamed of one day owning her own horse farm. Neither she nor Andy was happy in the duplex, and after settling a lawsuit stemming from her 1983 car accident, the two decided to look for a place of their own. They knew they couldn't afford a farm in the country, but Andy was a contractor and Patty quite handy herself. They hoped to find a fixer-upper that they could remodel and flip for a decent profit.

After months of searching, they finally settled on a place in a desirable neighborhood near Andy's parents. At only 550 square feet, the house was little more than a cottage, and it needed a ton of work, but it had real potential. Patty was excited about the possibilities, but when she and Andy approached the bank to apply for a mortgage, she was stunned to find that Andy couldn't qualify for a loan. At first, she thought it had to be a mistake. Andy's lifestyle certainly didn't indicate any financial problems. But Patty soon discovered it was no mistake. Andy's credit was so bad that he couldn't even qualify for a credit card, let alone a mortgage.

Patty, however, had sterling credit, and the bank agreed to loan her the money as long as Andy's name was not on the loan. It was a lot to consider. Not only would they need to borrow money to buy the house, but they would need to borrow funds to renovate it too. Patty and Andy discussed it and decided that while technically, Patty would own the property by herself, in reality, the house would belong to both of them, and so would the bills. The bank allowed Patty to roll a construction loan into the mortgage, and in October 1987, she purchased the house on Savercool Avenue, and she and Andy began renovating it.

———————

Back in North Carolina, Patty's mother had married Ray Chambers, and when they decided to purchase their own place, Pat offered to sell Patty the little house on Wilson Road. If Patty would give her $10,000 down and take over the monthly mortgage payments, Pat Chambers would sign the house over to her as soon as it was paid off. Patty didn't want to lose the last tangible link she had to her father, and besides, it was a good deal. There weren't that many years left to pay on the mortgage and those payments were a paltry $150 a month, but she would still have to take a loan for the $10,000 down payment.

Again she and Andy discussed it and decided that they could use the Wilson Road house as a rental property for added income. By the time everything was said and done, the couple found themselves saddled with three separate mortgage payments totaling nearly $1,000 a month.

Patty and Andy went to town on the Savercool house. They added a second floor, put up oak beams in the living room, and gutted the kitchen. They installed new carpeting and ceiling fans, erected a garage, built a stone wall, and lined the front with a stone facade.

"What a nightmare," Patty recalled with a laugh. "Don't get me wrong; it was a lot of fun. I remember we'd order pizza and spend late nights fixing the place up, but it was hard work, and we were both exhausted."

Never before had Patty been doing so well. She was the sole owner of two properties, and even with the three mortgage payments had maintained such a good credit rating that she was able to lease a brand-new car, which she added to Andy's insurance policy. She had also enrolled in real estate classes, got her license, and went to work for Century 21. But at home, things were gradually falling apart.

"It wasn't anything specific," Patty said. "It was a combination of things." The remodeling was nowhere near complete, but they had no funds left to finish it. Andy had underestimated the cost of the job, and even after Patty threw in the remainder of her lawsuit money, it still wasn't enough.

"Andy's work was slow at the time, too," Patty recalled, "and his business wasn't doing well. That made him moody and miserable."

As the relationship deteriorated, Patty began spending more and more time at the Silver Shadows Stable with her horses. When Sandy Walker decided to leave the farm, Patty jumped at the chance to rent it herself, and things improved slightly at home. Andy came by the stables often, helping Patty repair fences and build a riding ring, but it wasn't enough. By late 1988, there was little communication between the two, and they were no longer sleeping in the same bedroom. Eventually, needing some space to decide where the relationship was going, Patty rented an apartment and moved out, leaving Andy behind in her Bethlehem home.

Patty began dating someone else, but she and Andy had a long history, and neither was ready to end the relationship for good. Andy wanted her to come back home, and after about a month, Patty did. But nothing changed. The relationship still wasn't working, and they continued to sleep in separate bedrooms. By 1989, although they were still living together, they were little more than roommates, living separate lives and dating other people.

"I wanted to leave," Patty said, "but leaving for me wasn't as easy as it sounds. If I left, I would be solely responsible for *three* mortgage payments: one on the Bethlehem house, one on the North Carolina house, and the one on the $10,000 down payment I gave my mom. All three of them were solely in my name. As long as I was living with Andy, at least, he was paying his share of the bills."

Although Andy denied it, Patty was sure he was seeing a girl named DONNA LONG, but she barely even cared. She had met someone as well: Frank Alonzo, whom she eventually began dating.

Patty fell hard for Frank, and the more the two saw of each other, the more she wanted to be with him. It was Frank who became the deciding factor in her decision to end her relationship with Andy for good, but there was still the problem of the three mortgage payments she couldn't afford by herself.

Andy's name was not on the Savercool house, but Patty considered the house half his and was more than willing to split any profits with him. Patty suggested that one of them stay in that house and make the mortgage payments while the other left and made the mortgage payments on the North Carolina property. Andy liked the idea and opted to stay in the Savercool house where he promised to make the mortgage payments and continue working on the renovations to get the house ready to sell.

With her mortgage problems finally solved, Patty took up residence with Frank Alonzo, in a trailer set up next door to his mother's house, but she kept in close contact with Andy. Not only was he still living in her house, but, according to her, each month she would drop money off for him to pay her portion of the car insurance. Frank was jealous of Andy and unhappy with the situation, but there was little he could do.

Six months after moving in with Frank, Patty totaled her new leased car when she swerved to miss a deer and ended up hitting a tree. Calling Andy's insurance agent, she joked, "Well, I missed the deer but killed the tree."

The agent didn't laugh. In fact, he didn't say anything for several moments. Then, quietly, he said, "Pat, you're not insured. That policy was canceled months ago."

Patty didn't know what to say; she was stunned. According to her, she had been giving Andy money every month for her share of the insurance. *What the hell was going on?* She immediately called Andy, but he didn't answer and continued calls to the Savercool house met with the same results.

Within days of this occurrence, Patty received a phone call from the loan officer at the bank who told her he was "glad he found her," as her mortgage was six months in arrears and the bank was about to foreclose.* This time, Patty was beyond stunned. Andy had promised to make the mortgage payments and had sworn that he had. There had to be a mistake.

"That's impossible," Patty said.

Only it wasn't. The loan officer told her that there had not been a payment made on the house in the last six months and that in order to save it, she would need to come up with seven months of payments.

Seven months of payments? That was more than $5,000! She didn't have that kind of money, and thanks to Andy, she didn't even have a car to get to work anymore. This time, Patty went directly over to the house on Savercool, where Andy tried to placate her with an offer from his father to buy the house and pay off the mortgage.

Although the renovations were nowhere near complete, the house was still worth considerably more than Patty owed on it, but when she mentioned this to Andy, he balked. His father wasn't willing to negotiate, he said. He'd pay off the mortgage, and that was it.

Assuming that Andy and his father planned to finish the remodeling and sell the house for a hefty profit, Patty refused. She was dismayed, distraught, and madder than hell. "I'll let the bank take it before I'll do that," she said, storming out of the house.

All of a sudden, Patty's life was in a tailspin. She was being held responsible for the leased car that wasn't covered by insurance, the bank was foreclosing on her Savercool property, and she could kiss her sterling credit rating good-bye.

After weeks of watching her mope around, Frank suggested that they move to North Carolina. Patty still owned the house on Wilson

---

* Patty had not thought to notify the bank when she moved out of the Bethlehem house. Her accident enabled the bank to finally obtain her new contact information.

Road, and they could start over there. Patty, wanting to get away from Pennsylvania and Andy Katrinak, jumped at the suggestion.

Meanwhile, with the bank about to foreclose on the Savercool property, Andy needed to find a new place to live, so he moved into the house at 740 Front Street in Catasauqua owned by his father and sister, Barbara. The house was a two-family, so while Barbara, a recent widow, moved into the upstairs apartment, Andy took up residence in the downstairs.

In North Carolina, Frank found work as a welder, and for a while, things went well for the couple. But Patty and Frank's relationship was a stormy one, and they argued often.

"Frank was the nicest guy you'd ever want to meet," Patty said, "except when he was drinking. And Frank liked to drink a lot." Within six months of their move, the relationship was over. Frank moved out while Patty remained alone in the little house on Wilson Road.

As amazing as it seems, Andy was still a part of Patty's life. Apparently feeling bad about what had happened, he called her several times to apologize and ask her forgiveness. He sounded sincere, and little by little, Patty forgave him.

Asked about this today, Patty appeared embarrassed. "I was so young and so naive and so *stupid*," she said, shaking her head. "I should have cut all ties with him after what he did, and I would have, if he hadn't have kept calling me. I never would have called him—I couldn't call him. He didn't have a phone at the Front Street house."

Regardless, after Patty forgave Andy, the two resumed their friendship through letters and the occasional phone call. One day, after Andy had called, Patty mentioned that his work was slow in Pennsylvania, and her aunt, sitting nearby, offered to bring him down to North Carolina to do some work for her. Patty passed along the message the next time they talked, and Andy accepted. When he got there, although he didn't stay with Patty, the two of them saw each other and talked.

In December 1990, Patty received a call from Frank Alonzo, who was living back in Pennsylvania. Though their relationship had been troubled, Frank missed Patty, and he invited her to come and stay with him over the new year. Patty was not seeing anyone at the time and decided to accept. There, Frank asked if she would be willing to come back and try again, and Patty said she'd think about it. After returning home, Patty did think about it. She'd found no one special in North Carolina and, realizing that she missed Frank too, decided to give the relationship another chance.

Bringing her horses along, Patty arrived in Pennsylvania during mid-January 1991 and moved back into Frank's trailer, boarding her animals at a nearby stable.

Things went well for the reunited couple until the weekend of Saturday, February 9. That night, the two attended a party where there was heavy drinking and loud music. Patty was not feeling well and told Frank she wanted to leave, but he was having a good time and ignored her. Annoyed, Patty eventually left on her own and went home, where she soon dozed off on the couch.

She awoke later to find a drunk and irate Frank screaming at her. He was furious that she had left the party and accused her of embarrassing him in front of his friends. Patty snapped back that she hadn't done anything wrong, and then shouted, "You're acting crazy."

"And that really pissed him off," she said.

Frank lashed out and struck her, and Patty, frightened by his fury, ran next door to his mother ROSE's house. Frank was in hot pursuit, and just as Patty reached Rose Alonzo's door, Frank grabbed her by the shoulder, spun her around, and punched her in the face. She went down, dazed, her left eye immediately beginning to swell, her right blinded by blood that gushed from an open gash on her forehead. Rose Alonzo, hearing the commotion, soon came outside, and Frank, perhaps realizing he had gone too far, quickly retreated.

Inside the house, Patty made a move to call 911, but Frank's mother stopped her, telling Patty she would take her to the hospital herself. Patty didn't argue, but she did tell Rose she wanted to call Frank and let him know they were going. When she picked up the phone, however, Patty dialed 911.

The ambulance arrived first, but the paramedics refused to enter the house until the police had cleared the scene. Inside, Patty held a pile of blood-soaked rags to her face, trying to staunch the flow of blood. When state troopers finally arrived, they took one look at her and immediately placed Frank Alonzo under arrest. The paramedics put Patty in the back of the ambulance, but before they could leave, an angry Rose Alonzo appeared and started screaming at Patty to get her car off her property. Afraid Frank and Rose might do something to the vehicle, Patty disregarded the paramedics' advice and hopped out of the ambulance.

Driving away, she suddenly realized she didn't know anyone in Pennsylvania anymore other than Andy. She knew how to get to Catasauqua because she had once worked with a girl who lived there, so she drove around the town until she found 740 Front Street.

At 2:00 AM on the morning of February 10, 1991, Patty knocked on Andy's door. Shocked to see her "looking like she got run over by a bus," Andy immediately took her to the hospital. There, doctors stitched up her forehead and noted that she had two black eyes, a cut above her right one, and a swollen nose.

Worried about her stuff, Patty asked Andy to accompany her back to Frank's house to pick up her belongings. He agreed, and afterward, because he still didn't have a phone, Andy took her to a pay phone so she could call her mother.

Andy offered to let her stay at the Front Street house, and Patty did for a few days before moving to a women's shelter in Reading. When her wounds healed, she rented a room in Kutztown and took a job at a local car dealership. She wanted to return to North Carolina, but she needed to save enough money to take her horses with her, and it was not until May that she was able to do so.

That August, Andy called Patty to give her his new phone number.

"Wow," she said, laughing, "you've finally got a phone. You're really moving up in the world."

Andy laughed too, but he didn't bother to tell her he had put the phone in *her* name.

Sometime after Labor Day, Patty called Andy to tell him about a big roofing job in North Carolina, and Andy decided to put a bid in on it. His offer was accepted, and this time, when he came down south, Patty allowed him to stay with her in the little house on Wilson Road. Within days, their relationship had resumed. Not only were they sleeping together, but they also began making plans for Andy to move to North Carolina permanently. He would need to return to Pennsylvania first, to finish one last job, but in the meantime, he had business cards printed up for his new North Carolina business, Oakwood Construction, using Patty's address and phone number as his contact information.

Andy stayed in North Carolina for an entire month, but once he was gone, Patty began having second thoughts about him coming back.

"I just wasn't sure I still felt that way about him," she said.

The two continued to write and call each other, but Patty didn't mention her doubts. Instead, she vacillated. She cared about Andy, but did she still love him enough to want to spend the rest of her life with him? When she realized that she didn't, she finally worked up the courage to tell him.

"I don't know if I want to go through all that again," she wrote. "We seem to work better as friends than as lovers."

According to her, Andy didn't seem upset; in fact, he told her that he had expected her to say as much. Though the romance was over, the two stayed friendly and continued to keep in touch. That November, Patty received a Thanksgiving card from Andy and a Christmas card the following month. In January 1992, he sent her a New Year's card and a birthday card. It seemed unusual, and she called him up to ask about them. "What's next, a Saint Patrick's Day card?" she joked.

Sure enough, in March, she opened her mailbox to find another card with a note inside: "Here's your freaking Saint Patrick's Day card," Andy wrote. Perhaps Patty was right that the two of them worked better as friends, because they even made tentative plans to vacation at Virginia Beach, Virginia, that spring. Before that could happen, however, Patty met someone else at a horse show, a man by the name of TIM SELLERS.

Not long after Patty met Tim, Andy called her to say he wouldn't be able to go to the beach, and Patty told him she couldn't go either. "I'm seeing someone," she said with a laugh. "We're practically engaged."

"Really?" Andy said, "I've met someone too."

"Oh, yeah," Patty replied, "Who?"

"Her name's Joann O'Connor."

When Patty began dating Tim Sellers, she was unaware of the many problems that plagued his life. She was attracted to him because he was good-looking, charming, and shared her love of horses, but Tim Sellers was also a heavy drug user and drinker, as well as a convicted felon with a hair-trigger temper. In the beginning, however, he hid these unsavory characteristics well.

Patty was no angel; she liked to party, too, but to a much lesser extent than her new boyfriend. Clearly, Tim's partying was way out of control. He not only drank to excess, but he smoked weed as if it were tobacco and had a strong attraction to crack cocaine. The first time Patty caught him using hard drugs, she threatened to end their relationship, and a repentant Tim promised to stop. To his credit, he did try, even agreeing to seek counseling, but it did little good.

"He could not let go of the drugs," Patty said, shaking her head, "and his drinking made things worse. Tim was not a pleasant drunk."

He was jealous, too, and after he had learned about Frank and Andy, he was jealous of both. It bothered him that Patty still talked to her two old boyfriends, but it was Andy whom he seemed to resent the most. Later, Tim would tell the police that when Patty drank and the two of them fought, she would take out Andy's picture and cry over it.

Patty smiled when she heard this and shook her head. "I never cried over his picture," she said, a gleam in her eye, "but when I was mad, I knew how to push Tim's buttons."

Another way Patty found to irritate her new lover was to compare him with Andy. "She wanted me to be like Andy," Tim later testified. "She said I ought [to be more] like this man was to her. He was good to her. She wanted me to be good to her. We would fight a lot and fuss."

Indeed, the couple fought fiercely, their shouting matches rattling the windows in the little house on Wilson Road and beyond. Sometimes their brawls even led outside to the front yard where neighbors would gawk as the two screamed at each other. Tim had a fiery temper and could be physically violent, but he rarely was to Patty herself.

The police would later portray Patty as a literal street fighter, a brutal woman who settled her differences with her fists. Those who actually knew her, however, claim that Patty's hard exterior was just an act.

"She would put on a tough front," her friend Kathy Barber told me. "But she was all talk and no action. She had a tough life, you know. But I never saw any violence where Patty was concerned."

One day, about a year into Patty and Tim's relationship, Tim came home, and the two drove to a nearby convenience store. On the way, Patty realized that her boyfriend was high, and the two began arguing. By the time they reached their destination, the fight had increased and then spilled out into the parking lot. Infuriated, Tim suddenly bent down, picked up a brick and threw it at Patty's truck. The brick smashed into the windshield, creating a spider web of cracks, before bouncing across the hood and falling to the ground. When Tim made a move to retrieve it, Patty ran over to a pay phone and called his counselor, who instructed her to call 911.

When the police arrived, Tim began screaming that he threw the brick in self-defense because Patty was trying to run him over with the truck. The police placed him under arrest and took him to Thomasville Medical Center, where doctors tried to calm him enough to draw blood for a drug screen.

Patty knew her boyfriend was using, but even she was shocked by what the blood test revealed. Tim Sellers tested positive for crack cocaine, Xanax, marijuana, alcohol, and Valium. Tim's counselor gave Patty an option; she could either have him arrested or committed, and Patty chose commitment.

A judge ordered Tim sent for treatment at Dorothea Dix Hospital, where Patty signed him in and then picked him up four days later when doctors released him. Tim was laughing as he climbed into the truck and told her he could get drugs in the rehab center easier than he could on the streets.

After returning to the little house on Wilson Road, the couple began arguing again. Tim was mad that Patty had called the police, and she, in turn, was disgusted with his drug use. Only days later, the two attended a horse sale, and halfway through it, Tim disappeared. Patty found out later that he had called his brother, asked him to meet him there, and then took off with him when he did.

Patty was ambivalent about the relationship. She cared about Tim, but she was not stupid enough to think he would ever change. Two weeks after he disappeared, he sheepishly showed up at her front door asking for another chance. Against her better judgment, Patty allowed him to come back on one condition: there would be no more drug use. Tim promised, and, in an effort to stay clean, took a job that required mandatory drug testing. It was in Gastonia, seventy miles away. The two agreed he would stay in Gastonia during the week and come home only on weekends.

Patty had not heard from Andy in almost a year, so in early 1993, she called the Front Street house to say hello, and Joann answered. Andy came on the line a few seconds later, and the two chatted for nearly half an hour. Andy sounded happy, and Patty was glad for him. A few months later, she called again, and Andy told her he and Joann were in bed watching television. Andy sounded giddy, and an amused Patty asked when the two were getting married.

"Hold on," Andy said, apparently turning to Joann. "She wants to know when we're getting married."

Patty heard Joann laugh and then say, "Tell her tomorrow."

"She seemed real friendly," Patty said of Joann, "real nice." After chatting for another twenty minutes, she and Andy said good-bye and hung up.

Patty did not talk to Andy again for almost a year, but she had little time to think about him or anyone else, including Tim Sellers. Her passion for horses had metamorphosed into her whole world, and she had little time to dedicate to a relationship. She had become deeply involved in the sport of team penning, a fast-paced rodeo event, and was concentrating almost entirely on that.

The sport required three horseback riders to separate three specific cattle from a herd of thirty. Afterward, they had to direct the three cattle through a ten-foot pen opening while holding the other twenty-seven animals at bay. Patty had a real knack for the sport and was good enough to qualify for several events, but the preparation was intense. She needed to condition and train her horses daily and, at least two or three times a week, she was showing them as well. It took a lot of dedication and hard work, but Patty didn't mind; she loved it.

"Horses had always been a big part of my life," she said, "and at that time, they had become my whole life."

By 1994, they had also become her career. Not only was she renting and managing another horse farm, Riverwood Stables, but she had also started a small photography business. On weekdays, Patty would visit different daycare centers, dress the kids in little cowboy and cowgirl outfits, and take their picture on a pony she brought along.

Andy and Patty usually spoke about once a year, and in April 1994, she called the Front Street house on a whim, and Andy answered. He immediately told her that he had some big news: he and Joann had gotten married.

"No way," Patty said, surprised. "The bachelor getting married? Next thing you'll be telling me is that you have a kid, too."

"Well," Andy said, "she is pregnant."

Later, Andy would tell the authorities that Patty's entire attitude changed after that. "She became very quiet and moody," Andy said.

Patty admitted she probably was initially speechless. "At first, I was shocked. I knew Andy was close to forty years old and had never been married, never had children. So yeah, I was a little shocked by the news, but I was glad for him." She insisted she was not upset or angry, and because the two spoke for another twenty minutes, it seems unlikely that she was.

It was spring again, and Patty's life was incredibly hectic; winter had put her behind on everything. The stables needed cleaning and repair, her horses needed additional exercise, and she was working to build her photography business. She had little time for socializing or fun and regularly begged off any invitations to go out. In August, however, two friends refused to take no for an answer. She needed to get out, they said, and they were taking her.

Reluctantly, Patty agreed to go and was glad she did. Her friends took her to Cowboys Nitelife, a country and western bar located in the town of Kernersville, about thirty-five miles from Linwood. Cowboys was a private club, requiring its customers to purchase a membership and sign in each time they visited. It was a popular place where people came to dance, drink, and socialize.

Patty had a great time at Cowboys and decided to purchase a membership for herself. Soon, she became a regular at the club on weekends, where she made several new friends, including SETH ALDEN and JAKE BEAMER.

Seth was the complete opposite of Tim Sellers: a US Marine Corps reservist with a bright future, Seth was good-looking, stable, secure, and drug-free. The two danced, and it soon became apparent that Seth was interested in her.

"We should go out sometime," he said.

Patty stopped in mid-move and drew back. "How old are you?" she asked.

"Twenty-two," Seth answered.

Twenty-two! Patty thought. *Ten years younger than me.* She shook her head and said with a laugh, "I don't think so. You're awfully young."

Seth laughed too, but he seemed unconcerned by their age difference. He was interested in her, and everyone in the club knew it. Although flattered by his attention, Patty didn't take Seth's crush seriously.

Not long after she began going to Cowboys, Patty found herself in a heap of trouble when an officer with the SPCA charged her with animal cruelty in relation to her horses, an accusation Patty adamantly denied. "I would never hurt my animals," she said with conviction. "Never. I loved those horses more than anything at the time."

Patty was convinced that the charges were nothing more than a personal vendetta, as the officer who filed them, DARLIE PETERS, not only knew Patty but was related to her through marriage. Peters accused Patty of neglect and described her horses as "nothing but skin and bones." Although Patty believed the charges had nothing to do with her animals, she did have an old and blind stallion whose health was failing through no fault of her own. "He wouldn't eat," Patty said, "but Darlie's charges had nothing to do with that. She never liked me, because her husband was interested in me before they got married. He used to send me flowers."

Darlie had been working for the SPCA for only five months at the time, and when she and Patty got into court, the judge appeared skeptical of the abuse charge. He didn't confiscate Patty's horses or levy a fine, but he did order her to retain grain receipts and produce them upon request.

Patty was humiliated, but she did as the judge ordered. She would keep her feed receipts and show them to an officer when he came by to check them a few months later. Afterward, Patty asked if she needed to keep the receipts he had already seen, and the officer told her, no, only future ones from that date on.

In order to dedicate more time to training and showing her horses, Patty gave up the twenty-seven-stall barn at Riverwood Stables and pastured her horses in several different locations. By then she owned nearly a dozen, and she knew she could not keep them all. She heard about a horse auction in Quakertown, Pennsylvania, and decided to put four of her horses in the sale. Although she and Tim were no longer a couple, he had not disappeared from her life. After their breakup, he had begun taunting her by entering and competing against her in horse shows. It seemed childish to Patty, and perhaps Tim realized that it was because one day when they ran into each other, he spoke kindly to her. Mentioning the sale she was planning to attend in Quakertown, Tim offered to accompany her to help handle the horses. Patty thought he was offering because he felt bad about everything that had happened, and needing the help, she accepted.

On October 9, 1994, she and Tim left North Carolina, pulling a horse trailer behind her van. Patty sold one of the horses at the sale, and the two returned to North Carolina the next day. Tim went back to Gastonia, but a few days later, he called Patty and asked if she would pick him up. She agreed, but when she got there, he was high on drugs, and for her, that was the last straw. She ended her relationship with Sellers for good and immediately did something that was sure to enrage her old boyfriend.

Tim Sellers was hardly a choir boy—he had been arrested and convicted of several crimes in the past and was facing pending criminal charges again, this time for selling stolen horses. In fact, the police had arrested both Tim *and Patty* in connection with the thefts, although the charges against Patty were quickly dropped. Those against Tim were not, and now, when the police approached Patty again, she agreed to cooperate with the investigation.

Less than a week after returning from Quakertown, Patty received a second court summons from Darlie Peters, this time charging her with animal abandonment. Peters claimed Patty had pastured one of her horses without the landowner's consent, and the summons ordered Patty to appear in court for a hearing in a few months, on December 12, 1994.

Patty couldn't believe it. She was reminded of the old saying—when it rains it pours—and she wondered why all of this was happening to her. Between Darlie Peters, her arrest for the horse thefts, and her long association with Tim Sellers, her reputation suffered severely. Residents regarded Sellers as trouble, and much of that trouble sloughed off onto Patty. For many, the fact that she stayed with Sellers for so long proved that she was just like him. Convinced that if the police arrested her, she must be guilty, people began to shun her. Tim didn't help matters when he began telling anyone who would listen that Patty was in on all the thefts and only cooperating with the authorities to avoid jail time herself.

The gossip continued, and it grew more scathing with each passing day. Patty couldn't be trusted. She was an animal abuser, a thief, and a liar. Rumors soon spread that she not only starved her animals but beat and whipped them too. There were horror stories from those who boarded their horses with Patty of her mistreating the animals. Patty was deeply hurt and embarrassed by what was happening, but there was little she could do.

She worked at rebuilding her reputation, and slowly, things began to improve. Having finally shed Tim Sellers from her life, Patty began spending more and more time with Seth Alden, the young marine she met at Cowboys. Despite the age difference, which still concerned her, she found they had a lot in common, and she enjoyed his company. Soon, they were spending every weekend together at the club.

Other than the gossip, Patty had little to complain about in her life. She remained devoted to her horses, loved her photography work, and was excited about her new boyfriend. That fall, she also received some fantastic news. She and her team penning mates had qualified to compete at the US Nationals in Guthrie, Oklahoma. It was quite an achievement for three amateurs; in order just to qualify you had to be in the top 30 percent of riders from New York to South Carolina.

Patty couldn't wait to call everyone and tell them the good news. On October 31, she called Frank Alonzo and two of her old coworkers from Century 21. She also called Andy's house, but no one answered and she didn't leave a message.

Excited about going out west, Patty decided to learn how to line dance and signed up for lessons at Cowboys Nitelife. JERRY BOGAN, the dance instructor, held classes every Thursday night from 7:00 to 8:00 PM, and afterward, Patty would meet Seth inside the club, where they'd stay until closing.

Patty was scheduled to leave for Oklahoma on December 1, so she was distressed when her van began making a bad clicking sound in late November. At the time, she owned three vehicles: a Ford Thunderbird, a Chevy Blazer, and the Dodge van, but neither the Blazer nor the Thunderbird was running. The van was hardly reliable either—in fact, Darlie Peters would describe all of Patty's vehicles to the police as "run down and unable to pass inspection"—but the van was the only vehicle Patty had running and the clicking sound worried her.

She knew what the problem was; the universal joint was going bad. She had replaced the part in the past and knew that the added stress of using the van to tow her horse trailer was the problem. She could still drive the vehicle with a bad U-joint, but the moment she went over thirty-five mph, it began to vibrate and shake nonstop. Patty was upset; she was due to leave for Oklahoma in just a few days and she needed the van. But she was scraping pennies just to make the trip, and there was no way she could afford to get it fixed.

Luckily, one of her teammates offered to give her a lift, and on December 1, 1994, the two of them left North Carolina, pulling a trailer loaded with three horses.

At finals, Patty's team worked in perfect unison to separate the three animals they needed to pen while driving off the others. Incredibly, their team won first place in their division, which was no small feat. Patty and her two teammates stood proudly, shoulder to shoulder, to receive their award and have their picture taken.

Arriving back in North Carolina on December 5, Patty could not wait to start telling people about her exciting win. During the next two days, she called virtually everyone she could think of: her family, friends, relatives, coworkers, even casual acquaintances, to brag about her accomplishment.

On December 7, she called Frank Alonzo and gave him the good news, and at 7:32 PM she called Catasauqua to tell Andy. Patty had not talked to him since she learned he and his wife were expecting a child, and she was anxious not only to tell him about her win but also to find out whether they had had a boy or a girl.

Patty listened as the phone rang on the other end, and then she heard Joann answer.

"Is Andy there?" Patty asked.

"Yeah, hold on," Joann said. There was a brief pause, and then she came back on the line. "Who is this?" Joann asked.

Andy, who was sitting on the couch at the time, would later describe the events this way: when Joann answered and he heard her say hold on, she turned toward him with the phone held out. As he began to get up, however, Joann placed the phone back to her ear and asked, "Who is this?"

"Pat," Patty replied, unprepared for the anger that word unleashed.

"Why the fuck are you still calling him?" Joann shrieked. "Andy's happily married, and we have a new baby."

Taken aback, Patty tried to respond, but Joann did not want to hear it. "We don't want you to call here anymore," she shouted before slamming down the phone.

At the other end, Patty stared at the phone in her hand, the dial tone buzzing loudly. She said she was not angry over Joann's rant but more amused.

"My first thought was 'Wow, somebody's uptight about the new baby,' and my second was 'Who else can I call to tell about my win?"

Patty does admit, however, that Joann had gotten her point across. "I had no intention of ever calling the Katrinak house again. I figured

Joann would tell Andy about the call, and if he wanted to talk to me, he'd call." Afterward, Patty continued calling others to tell them about her win, and, according to her, the conversation with Joann was soon forgotten.

Five days later, on December 12, Patty appeared in court on the animal abandonment charge and won her second victory. Not only did the judge throw out the case, but apparently believing Patty's claim that the charges were a personal vendetta, he chastised Darlie Peters and ordered her to "refrain from having any contact with the defendant." To celebrate, Patty went out to lunch with a friend and then drove to her mother's house to tell her the good news.

"I remember thinking to myself that things were finally looking up," Patty said. They were. She had won the team penning competition and her court case, had laid to rest her problems with both Darlie Peters and Tim Sellers, was making great strides in rebuilding her reputation, and was excited about her future with Seth Alden. Although not officially a "couple" yet, she and Seth met every Thursday, Friday, and Saturday night at Cowboys. She was looking forward to seeing him on the coming Thursday, December 15, because they had not seen much of each other over the past two weeks. She had been away at finals on the first weekend of December, and Seth had been away at reserve training on the second. Patty missed Seth, and she was anxious to see him.

Other than being broke—the trip to Oklahoma had set her back weeks, and it was winter, so she was not working with her photography—Patty had no reason to complain. Things were going well for her, and her mood was happy and upbeat.

She remembered staying home on Tuesday, December 13, to wrap Christmas presents and decorate her house for the upcoming holidays. On Wednesday, December 14, she bought gas at Gaines Gas Station and then stopped at the Exxon station to buy kerosene. While there, she discovered a problem with the pump: the numbers would not clear from the last purchase. She went inside and told the woman behind the counter, who seemed perplexed; the pump was working fine on the digital reading inside.

On Thursday, December 15, the day Joann and Alex disappeared, Patty said she went to the Welcome Milling Company to purchase grain for her horses—her normal routine—and chatted with the grain dealer, Leroy Rouse, about the upcoming holidays. While there, she realized that she was missing the key ring that held the key for her van's gas cap. Assuming she left it at Gaines's the previous day, she drove back to the gas station and inquired about it, but the station owner hadn't found it nor had anyone turned in a key ring.

Patty returned home around 4:30 that afternoon and noticed her neighbor, Joyce Reagan, getting her mail. Patty waved, then went inside and called her mother, mentioning that she was going to Cowboys later that night. She still had to feed her horses, and left again to do so. Her previous supply of feed was not yet exhausted, so she didn't bother to unload the new grain, which put off a strong, sweet odor in the vehicle.

Returning home, Patty showered, changed, and left for Cowboys at 5:45. Dance class was not until 7:00, but Cowboys was thirty-five miles away, and she couldn't drive fast because of the bad U-joint in her van. It was a real inconvenience, but Ray Chambers had promised to replace the part over the coming weekend.

At the club, Jerry Bogan taught dance class, and afterward Patty hung out with Seth and Jake until Cowboys closed at midnight. The three left the club together and walked over to Patty's van, where Seth stood at the window talking to her. Jake hung back to give the couple some space until Patty started the van and discovered her heater wasn't working. When Seth walked around to the passenger side, opened the door, and removed a panel from her glove box, Jake walked up to the open driver's side window but quickly stepped away.

"Ugh, what is that smell?" he asked, wrinkling his nose.

Patty didn't know what he was talking about until she realized it was the fresh grain in the back of the van. Jake spoke to her for a minute or two but then shook his head.

"That smell's making me sick," he said. He asked Seth for the keys and told him he'd wait for him in the truck.

Seth was about to leave anyway; all he'd had to do was jiggle a few wires, and Patty's heater began blowing hot air. The couple said goodnight, knowing they would see each other at the club the next day, and then each drove away.

Patty got home around 1:15 and went to bed shortly after that. Sometime later, the sound of the ringing telephone woke her, and she fumbled to reach it in the dark. As soon as she picked it up, she heard her mother's voice say, "So you are home."

Bleary-eyed, and still half asleep, Patty glanced at the clock and saw that it was 3:02 AM. "Where else would I be at 3:00 in the morning?" she mumbled.

"Andy just called," Pat Chambers said.

"Andy who?" Patty asked. There were two Andys whom she rode horses with, and she assumed it was one of them.

"Andy from Pennsylvania," Pat answered. "His wife and baby are missing, and he called down looking for you."

Patty, beginning to come awake, asked why he hadn't called her.

"He said he lost your number."

"Well, how did he get yours?"

"I don't know," her mother said, "but I have to call him back."

"I'll call him," Patty said, getting ready to hang up.

"No," Pat Chambers said, "I'll call him. He told me to call him back because he didn't want his wife coming home and finding him on the phone with you."

"Why?" Patty asked.

"Because of the fight you had with her on Monday."

"What fight?" Patty asked. "I didn't have a fight with his wife on Monday. That was last week. I had court duty on Monday."

"Well, I don't know," Pat said, "but he wants me to call him back."

Although Patty thought it was strange, she said OK and hung up, figuring that either her mother or Andy would soon call her, but no one did. Wide awake now, she got up and turned on the television, then tidied up a few things still waiting for the phone to ring. Around 5:30 AM she saw lights on in the house next door and knew her neighbor, Joyce Reagan, was awake. Joyce knew Andy from the times he had come to North Carolina, and wanting to talk to someone, Patty called her. Joyce, however, was getting ready for work and told her she didn't have time to talk.

Exactly one week later, on December 22, 1994, the FBI interviewed Patty and her mother in North Carolina. They did not consider Patty a suspect then, but four months later, when a farmer discovered the bodies of Joann and Alex Katrinak in the woods in Heidelberg Township, that feeling completely changed. From that point on, the police would focus their investigation on Patricia Rorrer to the exclusion of anyone else.

9

Andy had been the prime suspect in the disappearance of his wife and son literally right up to the moment their bodies were found; all of a sudden, he wasn't. It seemed strange, since everything that troubled the police about Andy before the bodies were discovered was still troubling after they were found. Despite that, once the authorities set their sights on Patty Rorrer, they never focused them elsewhere again.

When the PSP realized—more than four months after the FBI initially questioned her—that no one had ever checked Patty Rorrer's alibis, they asked FBI agent Dwight Ayers to interview her again. At the same time, they began a discreet inquiry into her and her background.

With the arrival of spring, Patty was again busy with her horses, team penning, and her photography. Several times Ayers stopped by her house, but he never found her home and repeated phone messages went unanswered. Finally, on the morning of April 27, 1995, the FBI agent arrived at her house early in the morning, just as Patty was getting ready to leave. Dressed in western garb, Patty spoke to him through the screen door, explaining that she was on her way to a photo shoot and could only talk a minute.

Later, Ayers would say that Patty's attitude had changed. No longer eager to help, she was now defensive and evasive and refused to invite him inside.

When asked about this, Patty shook her head. "I didn't invite him in because I was already late, but I'll admit I was upset by that point. People had told me the police were asking questions about me and about where I was the night Joann and Alex disappeared. I'd answered all their questions before—cooperated with them—and now here they were, four months later, asking the same questions. If they had checked out what I told them back then, they would have known where I was."

There was another reason Patty's attitude had cooled; she had also learned that the police were asking questions about her son, Charlie, and insinuating that she might have killed him. "I was *really* upset by that," Patty said, "and I told Ayers about it. Do you know what he said to me? He said, 'Well that was a long time ago. You should be over that by now.'"

Stunned by the callous remark, Patty had asked him if he had children, and when Ayers replied that he did, she said, "Well, you certainly never lost one. Because if you had, you would know it's something you *never* get over."

Despite her anger and the agent's description of her as being uncooperative, Patty went on to answer Ayers's questions that morning. When asked where she was on the day of the disappearance, she told him that she purchased grain at Welcome Milling and then stopped at Gaines Gas Station to look for her keys. Later that evening she said she went to Cowboys, where she saw "Jake and the dance instructor, Jerry."

In comparing her December 22 interview with this one, the PSP noted that Patty had not mentioned Cowboys, Jake, or the dance instructor in the earlier one. Patricia Rorrer, so it seemed, had changed her story. Still later, when Seth Alden's name surfaced as an alibi witness, the police were even more convinced. According to them, Patty hadn't mentioned Seth in any of her earlier interviews.

"That's simply not true," Patty said matter-of-factly. "I mentioned Cowboys in all of my interviews, and I mentioned Seth, Jake, and Jerry in all but the first."

Going on to explain, Patty said that when the FBI first interviewed her and her mother on December 22, 1994, they were each questioned by different agents. "I talked to Ayers, and mom spoke to Agent Bradbury.

As soon as they arrived, I mentioned to Bradbury that he looked familiar, and he said I did too. We tried to figure out where we knew each other from, and when he said he lived in Kernersville, which is where Cowboys is, I figured I knew him from there. But Bradbury said no, he'd never been to Cowboys. I told him he should go because it was a great place and that I was a regular there every Thursday, Friday, and Saturday night."

This conversation was not part of the interview, Patty said, but just general conversation when the agents first arrived. Afterward, Ayers questioned Patty in the kitchen, and Bradbury spoke to her mother in the living room.

"The whole interview was about Andy," Patty said, "the entire thing. Right up until the end, when Ayers told me that Joann had disappeared sometime on the afternoon of December 15 and then asked me where I was at the time of the disappearance. So, I told him where I was that afternoon, buying grain and stopping at Gaines Gas Station. He never specifically asked me where I was that night, but since we'd just had that conversation about Cowboys and I'd told them I was there every Thursday, Friday, and Saturday night, I assumed he knew I was there *that* Thursday, the day Joann and Alex disappeared."

Years later, at Patty's trial, Ayers would confirm her story. He remembered the conversation about Cowboys, he said, but admitted he had not included it in his report.

"The whole thing went over my head because I didn't know what Cowboys was," Ayers testified. "I had only been in North Carolina for three months."

Ayers also admitted that he "spent maybe five minutes on Patty's alibi and only in the last ten minutes of the interview. Her alibi wasn't that significant to me," he said.

While it was true that Patty had not mentioned Seth, Jake, or Jerry Bogan on December 22, she insists that she mentioned all three in every single interview after that.

"I didn't mention anyone from Cowboys during the December 22 interview," Patty said, "because Cowboys wasn't discussed after that initial conversation when the agents first arrived. But I know that when

I talked to Ayers at my house in April, I told him I was at Cowboys with my *boyfriend*, Jake, and Jerry, the dance instructor. I think now that Ayers thought Jake was my boyfriend and that I was talking about two people rather than three."

Although Patty says she tried to explain this to the police, they were not buying her explanation. To them, Patricia Rorrer was a liar who had changed her story and was now "defensive and evasive" in her attitude.

———————

Within days of her April 27 interview with Agent Ayers, Patty received a call from PSP trooper Robert Egan asking for another interview.

"I wanted to help," Patty said. "I wanted to show them that I had nothing to do with these murders, but I *was* getting worried."

Still, Patty agreed to the interview but on one condition: she wanted it to take place in the presence of a lawyer. Bill Fritts was not a criminal attorney, but he had done work for Patty's family in the past, and Egan agreed to question her at his office.

On May 4, 1995, Patty and her mother arrived at Fritts's office and met with Troopers Robert Egan and Lynn Eshleman. Fritts, apparently not realizing the seriousness of the situation, was not in attendance, nor would he be for any of the interview. When Egan asked Patty if they could question her alone, Patty declined. Without an attorney present, she wanted her mother there.

Before the questioning began, Patty had a stipulation: she did not want to talk about anything she'd already discussed with the FBI. She'd given them her alibi not once, but twice, and she was tired of it. Egan agreed, but Patty went on to rehash everything anyway. She again told them about stopping at the gas station and buying grain, only now she also added that she talked to her mother and saw her neighbor, Joyce Reagan, outside her house later that afternoon.

She described going to Cowboys that Thursday night and again on Friday, telling the troopers that she remembered that particular Friday because several people had asked her what was wrong. She had told them she'd barely slept the night before because she had bad news from up north—an old boyfriend's family had disappeared.

She admitted she hadn't thought the disappearances would turn out to be anything serious and had assumed Joann and Alex would return shortly. She even remembered joking with a few people at the club, telling them, "Don't forget I was here last night in case I ever need an alibi."

Egan asked her when she was last in Pennsylvania, and Patty paused for a moment, trying to remember. Although she had been there six months earlier at the horse auction with Tim Sellers, Patty insists that trip never crossed her mind.

"I wasn't thinking about Quakertown. I was thinking about the last time I was in the Allentown/Bethlehem area, and I told them it was a long time ago, probably in 1991."

Egan, aware of the October trip, immediately made note that he had caught her in a lie.

Regarding the Silver Shadows Stable she managed in Heidelberg Township—a farm located only two miles from the body site—Egan wanted to know where Patty rode her horses when she worked there. Patty told him she rode near the stables and in a cornfield across the street but denied riding the nearby trails or on the roads themselves.

Throughout the interview, Pat Chambers had become more and more uncomfortable. Patty may not have realized that the two state troopers suspected her but her mother did, and Pat had a hard time controlling her anger. Egan was annoyed with Patty's mother, later saying she often answered questions for her daughter and "basically disrupted the interview."

During a break in the questioning, Bill Fritts's secretary told Patty and her mother that the police were outside inspecting their vehicles and taking pictures of them. For Pat Chambers, that was the last straw. When she returned to the room, she lit into the two state troopers, accusing them of trying to frame her daughter and informing them that the interview was over.

As the PSP investigated Patty in Pennsylvania, the Davidson County Sheriff's Office in North Carolina was doing the same, and soon, Patty's past came back to haunt her.

People repeated and expanded on the rumors that had spread after her troubles with Darlie Peters. Patty was untrustworthy, an animal abuser, a thief, and a suspected barn burner. She was also known to pass bad checks, skip out on paying other bills on occasion, and sometimes, she could be downright mean and nasty. She had allegedly once pulled a knife on a man in a bar and had assaulted a woman outside of Cowboys Nitelife.

No one seemed to have a problem bad-mouthing Patty now. If they'd been skeptical of Darlie Peters's initial charges, this new investigation seemed to prove that Darlie had been telling the truth. And Patty Rorrer, now suspected of two brutal murders, was apparently far worse than anyone ever imagined.

Patty shrugged when asked about this. "Look," she said, "I've done some things in my past that I'm not proud of. But I didn't do half the stuff people accused me of doing, and I'm certainly no murderer. All those negative feelings towards me stemmed from my relationship with Tim Sellers and my problems with Darlie Peters. The PSP just added fuel to the fire."

Despite what people were saying, the police knew that Patty had no criminal record, and they could find no history of violence in her background, either. Nothing, really, other than the story of her assaulting a woman outside of Cowboys Nitelife.

When asked about this, Patty smiled, indicating it was hardly an "assault" at all. According to her, she and Seth were in Cowboys one night when another girl began flirting with him. They'd all been drinking, and although Patty let the flirting go for a while, the girl soon became totally obnoxious.

"She was all over [Seth]," Patty said, "dragging him onto the dance floor and gyrating against him, and I finally told her to back off and she did."

Patty thought that was the end of it, but later, when she left the club, she claimed the girl was waiting for her and cold-cocked her with a punch to the face.

"I fought back," Patty admitted, "and someone in Cowboys called the police."

According to her, the girl took off before the police arrived, but Patty was still there, disheveled and bleeding from a split lip.

"They put me in the back of their squad car and took details of the incident. I'm not proud of what happened, but it happened," she said with a shrug. "They charged me with drunk and disorderly, and I pled guilty and paid a fine."*

Police found only one other blemish on Patty's record: a shoplifting charge from March 1995. Patty insisted this was an accident rather than a theft. One item, amid many in her shopping cart, had slid down into her purse, and she hadn't realized it. Regardless of her explanation, she was convicted of the charge and sentenced to one year of probation.

It frustrated authorities that the only real trouble Patty had ever been in was petty and minor, because it made it that much more difficult to convince people that she might wake up one day as a monster, capable of savagely murdering a tiny baby and his young mother.

While many of those questioned had nothing of relevance to say about Patty initially, when the police made it clear they believed she was the killer, some of those same people began to add to their stories or change them.

Andy's good friends Lauren and Jim Brenner did. The Brenners had known Patty when she dated Andy, and both were asked about her during their initial interviews. At that time, neither had anything significant to say. However, when suspicion eventually focused on Patty, both Lauren and Jim suddenly remembered something of great import. They said that on December 13, 1994, Andy had worked late at their house and mentioned that Patty and Joann had argued on the phone "the night before." But that wasn't all. Lauren also said that as she and

---

* When the PSP tracked down this woman, she confirmed that she threw the first punch outside of Cowboys that night.

her husband discussed the call with Andy, Joann telephoned their house and mentioned Patty's call as well.

The problem with this story was that Andy never said anything about working late at the Brenner house on December 13, nor had he ever told the police about discussing Joann and Patty's argument with them. Lauren later testified that she considered the argument to be "very important," yet she waited months after Joann disappeared to tell the police about it. Why hadn't she told them earlier? Why hadn't she told them as soon as Joann vanished?

The Brenners insisted that they *had* told the police about the call early in the investigation, claiming they had told either Trooper Egan or Trooper Kocevar about it on December 16, 1994. That was not possible, however, since Egan didn't become actively involved in the case until December 17, and Kocevar not until December 19. The Brenners had been interviewed by Trooper Michael Gownley on December 23, 1994, and again on January 12, 1995, but when Patricia Rorrer's name came up, neither mentioned the phone call. Nor did Troopers Kocevar or Egan recall hearing about it before May 1995.*

Another person who recalled something important after Patty became a suspect was JILL SARNEY, a young girl who knew Patty from the Silver Shadows Stable in 1989.

Jill was only eleven at that time but lived near the stables, and in exchange for work, Patty let her board her horse there for free. When Trooper Egan interviewed Jill on October 18, 1995, she told him that she and Patty would occasionally go riding together and agreed to show him and Trooper Kocevar where they rode.

The trio proceeded to the Silver Shadows Stable, where Jill told them that she and Patty would sometimes ride in open fields and nearby trails or on Harter Road, Saegersville Road, and Best Station Road. Of

---

* Nor did Joann apparently tell anyone else about the call. She didn't mention it to Jessica Howard when they spoke on the evening of December 12, nor did her sister, Peggy, say she mentioned it when they spoke on December 14. Joann also didn't mention it to Josh Bloom, her friend from Six Flags, in whom she appeared to confide quite often. Joann had met Josh for lunch on December 13—supposedly the day after the argument—at which time Bloom said Joann was in good spirits and didn't mention anything or anyone that was bothering her.

course, Saegersville Road and Best Station Road were both near the body site, but Sarney didn't mention actually riding into the woods where the bodies were found. In fact, Trooper Egan noted in his report, "Sarney did not have any current information on Rorrer or the Katrinak investigation."

One and a half years later, however, when Egan interviewed Sarney again on March 27, 1997, she told the state trooper something very different. Now Jill said that she and Patty would ride their horses on the old railroad bed and pass right by where the killer had left Joann and Alex. She also added that sometimes they would veer off the railroad bed and ride on the old logging trail—the trail that led directly to the bodies.

Like Lauren and Jim Brenner, Jill Sarney had added to her story after Patty became a suspect, and Jerry Bogan, the dance instructor at Cowboys, would change his. When first questioned, Bogan stated that Patty was present for dance class "every Thursday night in December," but after repeated questioning by the PSP, Bogan was suddenly not so sure. Now he said that "from the second week of December until the second week of January" he didn't know whether Patty was at the club or not. "She may have been," he said, "but I can't say what day or dates she was there."

Others, however, refused to change their stories. Patty's neighbor, Joyce Reagan, wasn't questioned until July 26, 1995, but she told Trooper Kocevar that she normally saw Patty every day—which made it highly unlikely that she would not have noticed if Patty were away for any length of time. Joyce was also the one who looked after Patty's animals whenever Patty did go away, marking each time on a calendar, which she handed over to Kocevar.

Joyce claimed that Patty was happy in December 1994 and that things were going well for her. When Patty returned from Oklahoma, she had invited Joyce to take a dance class with her at Cowboys, and although Joyce couldn't be positive of the date they were supposed to go, she'd narrowed it down to only one possibility: Thursday, December 15. She told the officer that during the first two weeks of December she was busy planning a wedding, so she would not have agreed to go then, and the last two weeks were Christmas and New Year's. The only week she would have considered going was the week of December 12, and since dance classes were held only on Thursday nights, the invitation had to be for December 15. Joyce had initially told Patty she would go but then changed her mind because she had to work on Friday and didn't want to get home late.

Joyce also recalled Patty's phone call to her in the early morning hours of December 16. She said Patty had called somewhere between 5:30 and 6:00 AM to tell her about Andy calling her mother, but Joyce was getting ready for work and couldn't talk so had not learned any of the details.

When Kocevar finished interviewing Reagan, he was quick to note that she could not substantiate Patty's alibi for December 15, 1994. Technically, that was true, but a close look at the time frame casts doubt on Patty being the killer.

The distance between Andy's house in Catasauqua and Patty's house in North Carolina is five hundred and ten miles, a conservative driving time of nine hours. The police believed the killer had used Joann's car to commit the crime and then returned it to McCarty's parking lot, so the important question is: What time was Joann's car left in the lot?

Although no one knows for sure, there were many people in the area who never noticed Joann's car sitting there.

- Colonial Landscape employee Gary Anders was in the lot between 9:30 and 9:45 PM on December 15, 1994, and did not notice Joann's car at that time.
- Both Andy's and Joann's families claimed they "searched all over the neighborhood," and stopped vehicles on Front Street, but they did not notice the tan Toyota either.
- Officers Kicska and Kleiner were at Andy's house between 10:42 PM and 11:00 PM when Andy gave them a description of Joann's car. Yet neither of them noticed the vehicle sitting next door.

If the vehicle *was* in the lot at these times, how could everyone have missed it? It was sitting only 150 feet from Joann's house, yet no one discovered it until nearly 3:00 AM on the morning of December 16. In examining the car, the police recovered no fingerprints, which indicated that whoever left it there had first wiped it clean of prints, a task that would have taken additional time.

Both the police and the prosecution knew the time frame was a problem, and they went to great lengths to find people who were willing to say Patty had bragged about making the trip to North Carolina in as little as seven hours. It's doubtful anyone could have made the trip in that short amount of time; to do so would require a continuous, nonstop speed of 73 miles per hour. Besides that being impossible, is it likely that having just killed two people, Patty would have risked a speeding ticket racing back to North Carolina?

Joyce Reagan was not the only one who attempted to verify Patty's alibi. AUDREY BRUSSELS, the woman from the Exxon station, handled more than one hundred customers a day and was not questioned until May 1995. Not surprisingly, she told the police she couldn't remember if Patty was at the station on December 14, 1994, but she did recall experiencing problems with the kerosene pump and a woman coming in to tell her about it. How could Patty have known about the pump problem if she hadn't experienced it firsthand?

Patty's grain dealer, Leroy Rouse, was first interviewed in April 1995 and described Patty as a pleasant, talkative, and friendly person who usually bought her grain on Thursdays. Rouse remembered Patty coming in sometime before Christmas, possibly the week before, and the two of them discussing the upcoming holidays.

The police and prosecution would always maintain that Patty did not purchase her grain on December 15 but one week later on December 22. Leroy Rouse, however, said he thought Patty was there "the week before Christmas," not three days before. He also described her as "talkative," yet she mentioned nothing about the missing Katrinaks despite having told numerous people about their disappearance, even those she barely knew. Last, Patty and her mother's interview with the FBI took place on December 22, and surely she would have mentioned that to Rouse.

It seems more likely that the grain *was* purchased on December 15, and that Patty mentioned none of these things because she did not yet know that Joann and Alex had disappeared.

Michael Gaines from Gaines Gas Station, had the same problem as
Audrey Brussels; he handled scores of customers every day and couldn't
say exactly when Patricia Rorrer was in looking for her keys. He did
recall her coming by and inquiring about them, however.

For the police, the fact that none of these witnesses could say they
positively saw Patty Rorrer on December 15, 1994, meant that she was
not in North Carolina on that date. And, if she were not in North
Carolina, then she must have been in Pennsylvania murdering Joann
and Alex.

In truth, the police were negligent in not trying to verify Patty's alibi
sooner. Apparently, they were so wrapped up in building a case against
Andy that they couldn't be bothered investigating a long shot down in
North Carolina. It was a huge mistake on their part and one that would
cost Patricia Rorrer dearly in the end.

Michael Gaines summed it up best when he asked the police, "Why
didn't you question me about all of this when it happened?"

10

Despite the mistakes, the PSP continued to try and build a case against Patricia Rorrer. In questioning those at Cowboys Nitelife, they could find no one—other than Seth and Jake—who was willing to say that Patty was definitely in the club on the night of December 15, but they could find no one to say she wasn't there, either. As with all her alibi witnesses, those from Cowboys couldn't remember that long ago. She might have been there, they said, or she might not have. They just didn't know.

Although disappointed, the police had discovered something else that proved to them that Patty Rorrer *was not* at Cowboys on that particular Thursday night. Her name didn't appear on the sign-in sheets for December 15, 1994.

State law mandated that any member of a private club must sign in, so for authorities, no signature for Patricia Rorrer meant Patricia Rorrer was not there. Though several of the club's employees agreed, far more scoffed at the notion, including JOE PERRY, the club's owner.

"It wasn't unusual for people to get in without signing the sign-in sheets," Perry said with a shrug. "You try your best, but it happens."

Signing in at Cowboys was especially lax on Thursdays when the doors opened early for dance class. Signing in was not required at that time, nor were the sign-in sheets available to sign until sometime after dance class began. If those at class planned to remain in the club afterward, they were supposed to go back outside, get in line, and then sign in, but few ever did.

The way the club was set up made it difficult to know whether people signed in or not. Only one person manned the booth in the vestibule, and that person was responsible for several tasks: checking membership cards, collecting fees, making change, stamping hands, and checking coats, which required hanging up garments and collecting a separate fee.

The sign-in sheets were set out on a counter beyond the booth, and the rule was, after a person paid, he or she was to move forward and sign in. The setup made it difficult for the person in charge to see whether people were signing the sheets or not, and often when the club was busy and the line backed up, people didn't bother to wait. Instead, they simply bypassed the sign-in sheets and went into the club. No one ever stopped them, and no one ever went back to check and see if they had signed in or not. It wasn't that big of a deal.

Beyond the sign-in sheets was the door leading into the club. This door too was manned by only one employee who checked hand stamps and clicked a "clicker" to count each customer. Police would later determine that the clicker count didn't always tally with the signatures, proving that people often went into the club without signing in.

Tom Bellings, a North Carolina private investigator, found it absurd to think that Patty wasn't in the club simply because her name wasn't on the sign-in sheet. Bellings had conducted surveillance at Cowboys on numerous occasions and had witnessed many patrons entering the club without signing in. "Especially," Bellings said, "if they were young, pretty and female," just like Patty Rorrer.

State law also mandated that you sign in with your legal name, but Bellings had once signed in as Richard Nixon and no one questioned it. He had also noticed people signing in with just their initials or nicknames and sometimes nothing more than a scribble.

The fact that Patty's name didn't appear on the sign-in sheet was hardly proof that she was not there, but club employees may have been reluctant to admit that. To do so would be an admission that they were violating North Carolina law by not following proper sign-in procedure, which could subject the club to a hefty fine and possible investigation by the state Alcohol Beverage Control.

Piecing together the evidence they had gathered, the police had come up with a theory for the crime. They believed it all began on December 12, 1994, when Patty called Andy's house and Joann hung up on her. That action had sent Patty into such a fit of rage that within hours of the phone call, she was in her van and headed for Pennsylvania, hell-bent on murder. For the next two days, Patty stalked the Katrinaks, driving past their house, ascertaining their movements, and taking note of the family's routine. By the morning of December 15, she was ready to act.

When Andy left for work that morning, Patty broke into the house and hid in the basement until she heard Joann on the phone with her mother-in-law, making plans to go Christmas shopping. After Joann had hung up, Patty cut the phone line, followed her and Alex outside, and at gunpoint, forced her terrified victims into the tan Toyota. Then, ordering Joann to drive, she led them to Heidelberg Township, walked them into that lonely patch of woods, and killed them.

Convinced that the hang-up call had triggered the crime, authorities hit a major snag when they finally pulled Patty's phone records. There was no call to the Katrinak house on December 12, 1994, only one on December 7, just as Patty had said.

The police assumed Patty had called from somewhere else, and undeterred, they subpoenaed the phone records of everyone Patty knew: her mother and other relatives, her boyfriend, her friends, her acquaintances, and even Telly Fiouris in New Jersey, all to no avail. There was no call placed to the Katrinak home on December 12, 1994, from any phone accessible to Patty. Though frustrating for authorities, it wasn't a total loss. Their investigation had revealed something else on Patty's phone bill; from December 12 through December 15, there were no long-distance calls made.

There were several long-distance calls just before December 12 and more beginning on December 16, but none from the 12th through the 15th. The missing calls indicated to the police that Patty was not home during that time, which meshed perfectly with their theory; Patricia wasn't home during those four critical days because she was in Pennsylvania murdering the Katrinaks.

On June 2, 1995, police attached a recording device to Andy's telephone and asked him to place a call to Patty in the hope that she would say something incriminating.

Andy phoned his old girlfriend, and Patty answered. "Well, hello, stranger," Andy said. His voice, devoid of anger, was soft and casual—almost intimate.

"Hey," Patty replied, her tone weary and cautious.

Each of them knew that Patty was the prime suspect by then, and Andy wasted no time getting right to the point. "When did you call Joann?" he asked.

"Hell, you'd know that better than me," Patty said. "I don't know, a week or two before . . ."

Andy said he thought it was only a few days, but Patty disagreed and offered to pull her phone records "to pinpoint it." When he then suggested that the phone call between her and Joann was an argument, Patty denied it.

"She said not to call anymore, and I didn't think anything of it," she said, pausing for a moment. "I think you know that I don't have a temper like that, to do anything like that. If I was going to have that kind of fight for you, I think I would have had it a long time ago and not waited until after you got married and had a kid. That's long gone, over with."

Well, Andy said, the police were claiming they had proof that she was in Pennsylvania when Joann and Alex disappeared.

"They said I was up there?" Patty asked, her tone incredulous. "That's funny. They haven't checked any of my alibis down here. I was at a dance class at a club the night they disappeared. I was not up there anywhere near that time, and I have more than enough witnesses on that."

"Then why do the police think you did it?" Andy asked.

Patty said she had no idea. "If they had went to these people the first time they talked to me, I mean, it would have been very simple. But no. Now they wait months and months and months later." She was tired of the suspicion, Patty added, and unhappy with the FBI knocking on her door. "They've been a pain in the butt, is what they've been," she said. Nor was she pleased with them delving into her son's death. They were asking questions about Charlie and implying that she might have hurt him, which in their minds, made her capable of hurting another baby as well. "I just told them they're barking up the wrong tree, and they need to find out who the hell done it, and stop."

Near the end of the call, Patty told Andy how hurt and disappointed she was that he "might think I had something to do with this. I hope they find who done it," she added.

Police had heard a lot about Patty's old boyfriend Tim Sellers, and they were eager to talk to him, but when Trooper Egan contacted North Carolina authorities, what he learned was alarming.

North Carolina investigator Roger Page told Egan, "Sellers is one of the worst criminals in the area and one who's done everything short of murder." He was a known burglar, Page continued, "with numerous arrests for stealing guns that he would then sell or trade for dope." Page believed Tim Sellers was "quite capable of murdering somebody" or assisting in the same, and added, "He hates the police and will not cooperate with them unless he's in trouble."

Despite this description, the PSP—and later, the prosecution— seemed to believe every word Tim Sellers had to say.

Patty did have a gun, Sellers told Trooper Egan, a little .22 Jennings semiautomatic that she purchased at a yard sale when they were still together. It was a small gun that fit in the palm of her hand, and Patty kept it with her all the time. The two used it to target practice, sometimes in Patty's backyard, sometimes elsewhere, but the weapon was "a piece of junk," Sellers added, and had a tendency to jam after the first shot was fired, rendering it useless to fire again until you cleared the chamber.

Asked when he had last seen the .22, Tim Sellers grinned before saying, "When me and Patty broke up and she was pointing it at my head."

Although ballistic experts couldn't determine whether the bullet that killed Joann had come from a rifle or a handgun, it *had* come from a .22-caliber weapon. No one had forgotten Trooper Kocevar's theory for the two modes of death: that the gun had jammed and the killer was then forced to use the weapon to bludgeon Joann to death. Sellers's story seemed to substantiate that theory, which was enough for the PSP. At their request, Detective Tony Roberson of the Davidson County Sheriff's Office went to court and secured a search warrant for the little house on Wilson Road.

On July 28, 1995, Patty was outside on her porch talking to her neighbor, Joyce Reagan, when she suddenly saw a squadron of police cars coming down the street. The cars turned in at her house, as she knew they would, and Detective Roberson walked over and asked Joyce Reagan to leave. Patty had been on her portable phone earlier and was still holding it as Roberson waved a paper in her face.

"I have a search warrant for your house, Patty," Roberson said.

Patty accepted the warrant and asked what he was searching for.

"A .22-caliber handgun."

"I don't own a .22," Patty said.

"What about the one you bought at the yard sale?"

Patty shook her head. "I don't have it. That gun disappeared back in the summer. Tim Sellers took it."

According to Patty, not long before she had Tim committed to the detox center, she had noticed several things missing from her house, including cash, a shotgun, and the little .22 Jennings. Patty knew Tim was using again, and she suspected he was stealing the stuff to sell or trade for drugs. It would not be the first time, as the PSP had already learned from the North Carolina authorities.

It was evident that Roberson didn't believe her, and for the first time, Patty was overcome by a terrifying fear. *My God*, she thought, *they honestly believe I drove up to Pennsylvania and killed Joann and her baby.*

"So you don't deny owning a .22?" Roberson asked.

"No," Patty replied, enunciating each word, "I don't deny I had a .22, but I don't have it now. Tim took that gun back in the summer."

Roberson instructed her to stay outside and then began directing his detectives on where to search. Patty stood on the porch, her face wet with tears of fear and frustration. It seemed no matter what explanation she gave for any of this "so-called evidence," the police didn't believe her. She didn't know what to do. She was angry, upset, and scared, not only because of the investigation but also because she had recently discovered she was pregnant with Seth Alden's child.

Suddenly realizing she still held the phone, Patty quickly dialed Bill Fritts's number, the attorney at whose office Trooper Egan had questioned her previously. Fritts was not in, so she asked his secretary to find him and have him get back to her.

"It's important," Patty said. "The police are here searching my house."

Pat Chambers, who knew nothing about the search, was on her way to Patty's house when she saw the cop cars parked all over the place. Rushing to her daughter, Pat asked if she'd called Fritts.

"I tried, but he's not in," Patty said. "I left a message for him to get back to me."

Pat Chambers was angry as she watched the officers carrying things out of her daughter's house. *Where the hell was Patty's lawyer? Didn't he know this was serious?* Taking the phone from her daughter, Pat turned it on, intent on calling Fritts herself, but there was no dial tone. She clicked the phone off, then turned it on again but got the same result.

"I glanced around," Pat Chambers later said, "and I saw Trooper Egan smiling at me."

"Do you have the phone off the hook?" she shouted at him, furious.

Pat said she heard Egan mumble, "She don't need a lawyer," before he turned toward the door and yelled, "Put the phone back on the hook."

As soon as Egan said this, the phone in Pat Chambers's hand began to ring. Bill Fritts was on the other end, and he sounded upset. "What the hell is going on over there?" the lawyer asked. "I've been trying to call you."

Detective Roberson's version of events went like this: As the search continued, Patty went and stood under a shade tree. She was reading the search warrant, and when she saw Roberson come outside, she called him over.

"I don't own a gun," Patty said, "I never owned a gun."

"You want to talk about it?" Roberson asked. "Let's go over to the car." The two proceeded to the detective's car, where Roberson took a seat behind the wheel and Patty sat on the passenger side.

Again, Patty said, "I don't own a gun. I've never owned a gun."

According to Roberson, he then called Trooper Egan over, and Egan took a seat in back, directly behind Patty. For the third time, Roberson said their suspect repeated, "I don't own a gun. I've never owned a gun."

Patty denied she ever told the police she never owned a gun, and in this instance, at least, Trooper Egan agreed. At trial, he testified that although he was present in Roberson's patrol car during the conversation, he did not recall Patty saying anything about a gun.

In the end, the search netted absolutely nothing. Although police confiscated a number of weapons from the house, each was determined to belong to Seth Alden.

It was maddeningly frustrating for the PSP officers, who were certain they had their killer in their midst but were unable to prove it.

11

When Troopers Joseph Kocevar and Ken Coia initially processed Joann's car on December 19–21, 1994, they found a small grouping of six blond hairs on the seat back of the driver's side seat. Now, at the Pennsylvania state crime lab, Dr. Thomas Jensen was working closely with those six hairs.

He labeled the six hairs collectively as the "3E" hairs, measured them, and then examined them under a microscope. Jensen's reports note no hair roots on any of the six, but they do note a reddish substance on the frayed end of one. Next, Jensen separated the six hairs into two groups of three; the first three he mounted on individual glass slides, using Norland Optical Adhesive to create a permanent mount, and the other three he left unmounted and sent to the FBI for testing. These three unmounted hairs were received by Dr. Harold Deadman of the FBI on July 12, 1995. Deadman then relabeled the three unmounted car hairs Q1, Q2, and Q3.

Like Dr. Jensen, Dr. Deadman examined the hairs under a microscope and also noticed the reddish substance but noted no hair roots. Apparently, with no roots to DNA test, Deadman decided to swab the outside of the three hairs to determine what the reddish substance was. The results were startling.

The reddish substance proved to be blood, but Deadman also found that each of the three hairs contained a mixture of DNA, indicating several contributors. Deadman could not rule out Joann or Alex as possible sources for the DNA, but the major contributor was someone else, an unknown subject.

DNA was relatively new science in 1994. Few people had ever heard of it, and fewer still understood it. Today we know that a mere speck of blood, semen, or saliva can be DNA tested and matched to a donor by astronomical odds, but it was not that way in 1994. At that time, it took large samples of material to test for DNA, but scientists had no large samples in the Katrinak case.

The mixture of DNA found on the three unmounted hairs from Joann's car indicated contamination to Dr. Deadman. So, on October 13, 1995, he returned the three unmounted hairs to the PSP, telling them of the contamination and informing them that he had conducted no other DNA examinations on them.

———————

Less than a month later, on November 8, 1995, North Carolina investigators procured a search warrant to obtain hair and blood samples from Patricia Rorrer. Detective Chris Coble and Deputy Denise Chisgar drove Patty to Lexington Memorial Hospital, and on the way, Patty sat in the backseat, reading the search warrant out loud. When she came to the section describing the hair from Joann's car as being dirty blond in color, Patty turned to Detective Coble.

"Dirty-blond hair?" she said, sounding dumbfounded. "Who has dirty-blond hair? Does my hair look blond to you?"

Indeed, it did not. Patty's hair was dark. It always had been. But Coble had seen a picture of Patty taken in Oklahoma only weeks before the Katrinaks disappeared, and although Patty was wearing a hat in the photograph, the ends of her hair appeared to be blond.

At the hospital, Patty, heavy with pregnancy, sat crying as doctors drew two tubes of blood and plucked a number of hairs from her head. Curiously, it seems that neither the medical personnel nor the police bothered to note the number of hairs they took, even though it was standard procedure to do so. For instance: Andy provided twenty hair samples,

Lauren Brenner fourteen, and Debbie Marchek four, but no report lists the number of hairs the police took from Patricia Rorrer. Their failure to document a count on Patty's hair samples would make it impossible to account for what became of each of those hairs in the future.

North Carolina investigators placed Patty's blood and hair samples in an unsealed envelope and handed them over to Troopers Egan and Kocevar. Egan and Kocevar then hand-delivered Patty's blood and hair to Dr. Jensen back in Pennsylvania on November 10, 1995. Dr. Jensen first selected fourteen of Patty's hairs "at random" and mounted them in Norland Optical Adhesive, "exactly" as he had mounted the three hairs taken from Joann's car. Next, he compared Patty's hair to those found in Joann's car and noted a number of similarities, but there were differences as well.

- The hairs from Joann's car were blond, while Patty's were dark brown.
- In December 1994, Patty wore her hair in a tight, curly perm, but nowhere is there any reference to the hairs found in Joann's car being curly. Joann's hair, which was not as curly as Patty's, is often referred to as curly in reports.
- The hairs from Joann's car measured approximately eight and a half inches long, but, as evidenced in the photo, Patty's curls hung below her shoulders and undoubtedly would have measured much longer than eight and a half inches if pulled straight.

Visually, Jensen thought the hairs from the car looked dyed, so he decided to test Patty's samples to see if she had dyed her hair in the past. Treating two additional hairs of hers with methylene blue, Jensen concluded that Patty had subjected her hair to bleaching action at one time. The problem was, Jensen never bothered to test or determine if the hairs found in Joann's car actually were dyed. If the hairs in the car were natural blond hairs, then Patty could not have been the one to leave them.

Despite this, Jensen felt he could not exclude Patricia Rorrer as a possible source for the hair found in Joann's car.

After coming to this conclusion, Jensen dried two samples of Patty's blood on patches and sent one, along with three of her unmounted hairs, to the FBI. Once again, Troopers Egan and Kocevar hand-delivered this evidence on November 16, 1995.*

Meanwhile, in an attempt to determine who had contaminated the three unmounted hairs from Joann's car, the FBI requested a saliva sample from Dr. Jensen. Jensen sent the sample, along with more of Patty's hair, to Dr. Deadman on January 17, 1996.

In an FBI report dated May 6, 1996, the PSP finally learned who the culprit was that contaminated the hairs found in Joann's car: Dr. Thomas Jensen, the PSP's own forensic scientist.

Incredibly, Jensen had used his bare hands to stretch out and measure the hair and in the process had contaminated them with his own DNA.

The May 6 report is interesting for another reason. It notes that the FBI planned to run additional tests on the unmounted hairs from Joann's car. This seems strange, because:

- The FBI was no longer in possession of these hairs, having returned them to the PSP due to the contamination now attributed to Dr. Jensen
- At the time the hairs were returned, the FBI informed the PSP that they had not conducted any additional DNA testing on the hairs, presumably because of the contamination
- There is no evidence—no PSP or FBI report—to indicate that these three unmounted hairs from Joann's car were ever sent back to the FBI
- Nothing indicates why the FBI would *want* these hairs back, since they would still have the same contamination issues for which the bureau rejected them in the first place.

At the time, though, the FBI was experimenting with a new investigative tool called mitochondrial DNA. Unlike nuclear DNA, which is

---

* It should be noted that hand-delivering evidence is not a normal procedure. According to the FBI, most investigators send their evidence via FedEx delivery. This not only ensures an unbroken chain of custody on the evidence but also makes it virtually impossible for anyone to tamper with that evidence.

present in the nucleus of each cell, mitochondrial DNA is located outside a person's cell and in much greater quantity. Nuclear DNA comes from both parents, while mitochondrial DNA comes from only an individual's mother.

The preferred method of DNA testing in 1996 was restriction fragment length polymorphism, or RFLP. However, a large sample was needed to test that way. If one didn't have a large sample—as police didn't in the Katrinak case—they could use polymerase chain reaction, or PCR, which simply copied a small amount of either nuclear or mitochondrial DNA over and over until the DNA became large enough to provide a profile. There was a problem with this method, however. PCR didn't just copy a person's DNA. It copied everything on the sample, including any contamination it might contain, and it's possible that the hairs found in Joann's car had been contaminated in multiple ways:

- Dr. Jensen had contaminated the hairs
- Andy may have contaminated the hairs when he sat against them in Joann's car
- David O'Connor had also opened Joann's car that night, but to what extent he compromised it is unknown
- The hairs were collected on Post-it Notes, a nonsterile and unsanitary collection method*

---

* Dr. Jensen had contaminated the hairs through touch DNA. Post-it Notes could be vulnerable to this type of transfer contamination as well. A perfect example of this occurred in Germany in 1993 when the police found they had a rare criminal on their hands: a female serial killer. The unidentified woman had been linked to more than forty crimes, including six murders, through DNA found at the crime scenes. Through dogged investigation, police finally discovered their female serial killer, only she wasn't a killer at all or even a criminal. She was simply a woman who worked in the factory where the cotton swabs used to collect evidence were made. Inadvertently, she had been contaminating the swabs with her own DNA for years. Today, of course, we also know that sneezing, coughing, or simply speaking can also contaminate evidence by leaving that person's DNA on an item.

In September 1996, the FBI opened a fledgling mitochondrial DNA lab under the auspices of Dr. Joseph Dizinno. Dizinno had been working with mitochondrial DNA since the 1980s, but this would be the first time he began implementing it into his case work.

Despite there being no evidence that the PSP ever returned to the FBI the three unmounted and contaminated hairs from Joann's car, somehow Dr. Dizinno allegedly came into possession of these three hairs. Like Dr. Jensen and Dr. Deadman before him, Dizinno first examined the hairs under a microscope and made no note of any roots.

Apparently, because there was no root to perform nuclear DNA testing, Dizinno's only option was to try and test the hairs for mitochondrial DNA. Extracting a tiny sample from one of the hairs, Dizinno used PCR to amplify it, copying the DNA—and anything else on the sample—until it was large enough to provide a profile. After comparing the mitochondrial results to a DNA sample of Patricia Rorrer's blood, Dizinno found that he could not exclude her as a source for the hair found in Joann's car.

Dizinno then mounted the three unmounted car hairs and sent them back to Dr. Deadman. Deadman, who had already examined the hairs, seen no roots, and returned them to the PSP because of the contamination, now miraculously discovered a "forcibly removed hair root" on one of the three hairs.

Excited, Deadman cracked the cover slip, used a solution to dissolve the mounting medium, and, after cutting a small section of the root material, placed it in a glass tube. He then added a gelatin substance and exposed the hair to an electric field, enabling him to extract a DNA sample from the hair root. Using PCR to amplify it, Deadman soon had a sample sufficient for a nuclear DNA test.

Despite what the police, the prosecution, and the media all reported, the nuclear DNA results *did not* match Patricia Rorrer. The report merely states, "Patricia Rorrer is a potential contributor of the DNA recovered from the root portion of the Q1 hair by the odds of one in thirty-seven thousand." In fact, those low odds were just a guess on Deadman's part. At trial, he would testify, "The probability of going out and selecting someone that's unrelated to the source of the hair but who

Joann and Alex Katrinak.

Andy Katrinak.

The back of the Katrinak house, from which Joann was allegedly abducted, as it appears today. The vegetation is much heavier now than it was in 1994. *Courtesy of Sherry Sparks, photographer*

The Katrinaks' basement door, with the plywood covering the missing window. *Courtesy of Sherry Sparks, photographer*

A view of Colonial Landscape (left) and the Katrinak house (right). Joann's car was found parked approximately where the double doors are. *Courtesy of Sherry Sparks, photographer*

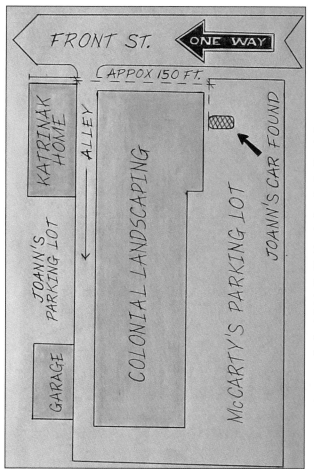

An aerial sketch of the Katrinak house and surroundings. The description of Joann's vehicle backed into the second space, with its wheels turned toward Front Street, indicates that it was driven into McCarty's parking from around the back of Colonial Landscape and not off Front Street. *Sketch by Joe Malinowski, courtesy of the artist*

The woods where Joann and Alex were found. *Courtesy of Sherry Sparks, photographer*

A 1992 aerial view of the body site. X marks the approximate location of where Joann and Alex were found. *US Geological Survey, via Google Earth*

LEFT: Patricia Rorrer, 1999. *Courtesy of Patricia Rorrer*

RIGHT: Patricia posing after winning the team penning nationals, December 1994. *Courtesy of Patricia Rorrer*

LEFT: Patricia and her mother, Pat Chambers, 1999. *Courtesy of Patricia Rorrer*

RIGHT: Patricia's father, Bob Rorrer, in 1978, when he was already ill. *Courtesy of Patricia Rorrer*

LEFT: Patricia Rorrer and her "uncle," Telly Fiouris, 2000. *Courtesy of Patricia Rorrer*

RIGHT: Patricia and her step-pop, Ray Chambers, 2000. *Courtesy of Patricia Rorrer*

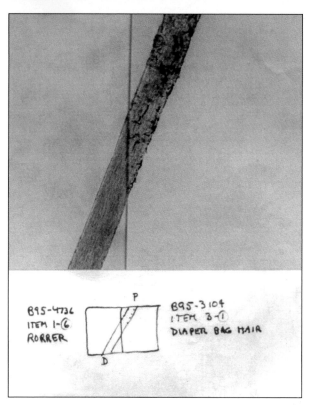

Evidence photo: Rorrer hair sample on the left, diaper bag hair on the right. *Courtesy of Patricia Rorrer*

Evidence photo: close-up shot of the fingernail found on Joann's chest. *Courtesy of Patricia Rorrer*

The Lehigh County Courthouse. *Courtesy of Sherry Sparks, photographer*

Prosecutor Michael McIntyre.

Patty with her good friend Kathy Barber, October 2016. *Courtesy of Kathy Barber*

Patty interviewing with Investigation Discovery's *Murder in Lehigh Valley* correspondent Keith Morrison, October 2016. *Courtesy of Patricia Rorrer*

would have the same DNA type as the owner of the hair, is, in my best estimate, one in thirty-seven thousand."

One in thirty-seven thousand. By today's standards, where it's not uncommon to see odds in the billions and even trillions, Patty's odds are pitifully unconvincing. How many other people would "match" the hair found in Joann's car? In 1994, in Lehigh County alone, there were more than three hundred thousand people—nearly ten other "matches." In Pennsylvania, there were more than twelve million people—nearly 325 "matches." How many in the United States? How many in the world?

It took two and a half years after the discovery of those six hairs in Joann's car for Dr. Deadman to match them to Patty, and in all that time, no one had ever seen a root on any of those hairs. Three of the country's top forensic scientists—Dr. Jensen, Dr. Deadman, and now Dr. Dizinno—had looked at those hairs, studied them, examined them, compared them, and looked at them some more, and not one report from any of those scientists ever noted a hair root on any of those hairs. *Not one.*

There obviously were no roots on the hairs found in Joann's car, and the fact that Dr. Dizinno tested them for mitochondrial DNA proves it. Had there been a root, he would not have had to use that method.

So was it just a coincidence that no one ever noticed a root until after the police secured samples of Patty's hair? Or is it possible that somehow Patty's hair was mislabeled as a hair from Joann's car and DNA tested against her own blood?

———

The police would not receive the DNA results linking Patty to the crimes until May 30, 1997. By then, two and a half years had passed since Joann and Alex went missing, and in that time much had changed.

By January 1996, Andy had packed up his belongings and moved to Colorado, just as he had always dreamed of doing, but it seems he failed to inform the police of his move. According to a report dated March 13, 1996, Trooper Joseph Kocevar learned about Andy's move from Veronica Katrinak. When Kocevar asked for her son's new contact

information, however, Veronica was not anxious to give it to him. Kocevar noted in his report that "subject reluctantly gave the officers [Andy's]
new address and phone number, explaining that he wished to maintain his privacy." Apparently, Andy wanted to "maintain his privacy"
even from the police who continued to search for the killer of his wife
and son.

That same year, the O'Connors were dealt another tragic blow when
David O'Connor passed away on April 27, 1996. Joann's father had
never gotten over the death of his daughter and grandson, and their
murders had taken a heavy toll on his health. For the family, David was
yet another victim of the same predator who had killed Joann and Alex.

Things had changed for Patty as well. She had gotten engaged to
Seth Alden, and in early 1996 had given birth to their daughter, HOLLY.

Patty took a job as a salesperson at a North Carolina car dealership
after Holly's birth and became known as a responsible employee, well
liked by both coworkers and customers. Her passion for horses had not
diminished, and she still owned several, daily visiting the barn where
she stabled them. Often she would bring Holly along and give her pony
rides around the corral just as Patty's mother had done when she was
an infant. The stable owner, PAUL KLEMAN, thought the world of Patty,
who he claimed was always the first to tend to any injured animal on
the premises. Kleman considered her a compassionate person and a
great mother, very loving to both children and animals.

Regarding the Katrinak investigation, Patty was open and honest
with her friends, insisting the police had the wrong person, and they
believed her. Few of them could imagine her committing such a brutal
and horrific crime, especially against a baby. They had all witnessed how
loving and nurturing she was with Holly, and each would later describe
her as an excellent mother.

Law enforcement saw her in a far different light. The sheriff of
Davidson County called her a "brute of a woman" and told the press
that Patty taunted them throughout the investigation. He was quick to
recount an incident from the Davidson County annual barbeque in the
fall of 1996. The sheriff was selling autographed T-shirts to raise money
for his department when Patty approached the stand. "She took one look

at the shirts," the sheriff said, "and immediately bought one," then held it up and said with a laugh, "Go get the bad guys."

"What shirt and what barbecue?" Patty asked, sounding bewildered. "This is completely false. I never taunted the police, and this story *never* happened."

By the summer of 1997, Patty had quit her job at the car dealership and settled into a family routine. She spent the majority of her time with Seth, Holly, and her horses, blissfully unaware that life as she knew it was about to come to a sudden and abrupt end.

12

At 5:50 AM, on the morning of June 24, 1997, a group of law enforcement officers assembled outside the little house on Wilson Road and rang the bell. Patty answered, bleary-eyed and wearing a light blue nightgown, obviously still half asleep.

"Patricia Lynne Rorrer," Detective Tony Roberson said, "you're under arrest for the kidnapping and murder of Joann and Alex Katrinak." As Roberson began reading the Miranda warning, he noticed the color drain from Patty's face and her body begin to tremble.

"I was terrified," Patty remembered. "I couldn't believe this was happening. All I could think of was Holly and the fact that there was no one there to take care of her. Seth had already left for work, and we were alone in the house."

Pushing blindly past the officers, she rushed into the bedroom and scooped up her fifteen-month-old daughter. Patty was crying, and soon Holly was wailing as well.

Detective Chris Coble asked whom he could call to come get the baby, and Patty told him to call her mother. While Coble left to make the call, Sergeant Suzanne Pearson stayed in the bedroom with Patty as another officer positioned himself at the bedroom door. Both the officer at the door and Sergeant Pearson would remain at their posts throughout the entire ordeal.

Patty took a seat on the edge of the bed, rocking back and forth, and cradling her daughter. According to Sergeant Pearson, Patty was telling Holly that she was sorry, repeating it over and over again.

"I'm so sorry for doing this to you. I'm so sorry."

And then, in an electrifying moment, Pearson said she heard Patty say, "If I had known I would get caught, I never would have brought you into this world."

The detective stood stark still, knowing the statement was tantamount to a confession. Oddly, however, Pearson had no notepad to write on and so began frantically jotting down Patty's words on her hands. "I have big hands," she later said.

Patty continued apologizing to Holly and then turned to Pearson and sobbed, "I don't want to live like this. That man Egan has hated me from day one!" At that point, Detective Coble came into the room and heard Patty say to Holly, "I'm sorry I did this to you."

Coble told Patty that her mom was on the way and she could get dressed, but Patty just shook her head and looked at him in disbelief. "I'm not worried about my clothes!" she shouted, "I'm never going to see my daughter again! I'm going to the electric chair!"

Holly was sobbing, and Patty told Pearson she wanted a bottle. Pearson asked Coble to get the baby some milk, and he left to do so just as Detective Roberson came into the room. Patty turned to him and asked, "Why is this happening? Why is he doing this to me?"

Soon, Coble returned with the milk, and as Patty began feeding Holly, he heard her say, "I never hurt that baby. I would never hurt a baby." Then, starting to cry again, she said to her daughter, "I'm never going to see you again. I'm going to the electric chair."

Knowing they needed to move this along, Pearson interrupted to ask if she could hold the baby while Patty got dressed. Patty seemed angry at the suggestion and snapped back, "Why are you doing this to me? Why do you want to torment me and my child? My child doesn't want to go to you. She wants me, someone she knows, someone she knows cares about her. You don't care."

Pat and Ray Chambers finally arrived, and as soon as they did, Patty handed Holly to her "step-pop," who quickly took the baby outside. Pat

Chambers hugged her daughter and then told her not to say anything. Sitting on the bed, she asked Patty if they'd read her the warrant, and Patty said no. Turning to Pearson, Pat Chambers said, "She's not doing anything without seeing that warrant."

Presently, Detective Roberson came back into the room, read the warrant aloud, and then handed a copy to Patty, who in turn handed it over to her mother. After Patty had gotten dressed, Pearson heard Pat Chambers say to her, "I'll contact Bill [Fritts]. Don't say anything to them, and don't let them extradite you."

The police placed Patty in handcuffs, and Pearson and Coble escorted her out of the bedroom. Patty began to sob again. "I'm not going to live like this," she wailed. "How can they do this to me? I wasn't in Pennsylvania. I was in North Carolina."

The two officers walked Patty toward the waiting patrol car, and just as they were getting ready to help her inside, Pat Chambers came rushing over. "I'll tell you one thing," she shouted angrily, "if she goes down for this, Andy's going with her. He killed his wife and daughter [sic]."

Coble told her he didn't know anything about it. "I'm just serving the papers," he said, dismissing her. Pat Chambers shook her head and then spat back, "Detective Roberson and Pennsylvania have been on her ass for two years. I guess they think they're going to get an award."

After placing Patty in the front seat, Coble got behind the wheel, and Pearson took a seat in back. As the car pulled away from the curb, Patty, still sobbing, turned to Coble and cried plaintively, "How can they do this? I know they talked to Mike [Gaines] at the gas station. How could I be up there when I lost my keys down here?"

Coble didn't know what to say, so he said nothing, remaining silent as he drove his prisoner to the Davidson County Courthouse.

Because Patty faced two counts of first-degree murder and two counts of kidnapping, bail was immediately denied and she was ordered to appear in court the next day to face extradition back to Pennsylvania.

That same day, she called Paul Kleman at the stable where she boarded her horses and told him what had happened. She was worried about her daughter, she said, and the animals, since she wouldn't be there to care for them.

Kleman was shocked by Patty's arrest but not surprised that her primary concern was for others. That was the type of person Paul knew Patty to be: kind, considerate, and caring. She sounded so scared and forlorn on the phone that after hanging up, Paul Kleman sat down and wept.

Despite what her mother had told her, when Patty appeared in court the next day, dressed in an orange jumpsuit, her wrists and ankles shackled, she surprised everyone by immediately waiving extradition.

Appearing with her attorney, Bill Fritts, Patty stood before the judge looking weary and defeated but ready to return to Pennsylvania and face the music.

"She's very interested in appearing in court and being exonerated," Fritts said. "Patty wants to prove her innocence."

Her family knew she'd be taken back to Pennsylvania soon, and, afraid they'd miss her departure, they began arriving at the courthouse early the next morning. By 4:00 AM they had someone stationed at every door in the building, determined not to let the authorities sneak Patty out without them seeing.

They needn't have worried. Patty was allowed a brief visit with them, and as she made her way down the courthouse hall, shackled and in tears, reporters snapped pictures of her.

Disappearing behind closed doors where her family waited, Patty clung tightly to Holly, reluctant to let her go. When Pat Chambers realized she'd forgotten to bring a picture of the little girl, Patty became even more upset. One of her jailers, troubled by what was happening, walked over and knelt down beside her.

"Do you remember me?" the man asked gently.

Patty shook her head, no, and the jailer smiled. "We met before, at the stables you manage." Then, glancing away from her, he shook his head. "I cannot believe they are doing this to you," he said softly. "Is there anything I can do to help?"

Patty told the man that she didn't have a picture of her daughter, and the jailer immediately excused himself and left the room. He returned momentarily with a Polaroid camera and after snapping a photo of Holly, handed it over to a grateful Patty.

It was almost time to go, and Patty sobbed as she hugged her mother and step-pop, then broke down completely when she turned to Seth and Holly to say good-bye. Her family's words of encouragement helped to compose her, however, and when she finally left the room, she was no longer crying but still blinking back tears.

That same afternoon, Davidson County sheriff Gerald Hege informed the press that the death of Patty's first child, Charlie, was "being looked into."

All along, authorities had implied that Patty had killed Charlie, alluding to his death with dark connotations. For Patty, this was the absolute lowest the police and the press could sink, and the allegation ripped her heart out.

Charlie's body had undergone a complete autopsy, and there was no indication that his death was anything other than natural. Since his mother was a suspect in the murder of Alex Katrinak, Charlie's death was carefully investigated, and had the police found anything suspicious, there's no doubt they would have brought Patty up on charges. The authorities knew Patty had not killed her son, but they let the public believe she had anyway.

By the end, Charlie would fade from the story—but not from the public's mind. The notion that Patty had killed her first child would forever linger, an unfair and unfounded stigma she will live with for the rest of her life.*

---

* Sheriff Hege's word may have meant something at the time of Patty's arrest, but within a few short years, his credibility and reputation would be shredded. Always a controversial and eccentric sheriff, in 2003 he was charged with fifteen felonies, including embezzlement and obstruction of justice, and suspended from office. Eventually Hege accepted a plea agreement, but by then his career was in ruins.

As the public demanded, on June 25, 1997, Lehigh County district attorney Robert Steinberg announced that he would seek the death penalty against Patricia Rorrer.

That same day, Lehigh County detective Dennis Steckel, accompanied by Pennsylvania state troopers Joseph Kocevar and Linda Goecke, escorted Patty onto a crowded Boeing 737 jetliner in Charlotte, North Carolina. For much of the flight, Patty sat in the back of the plane, weeping softly and staring at the picture of Holly the kind jailer had taken.

Her plane was due in Pennsylvania at 8:30 PM, and, anxious to see the monster who could leave a baby to freeze to death on top of his dead mother, crowds began forming early. They stood across from Magistrate Edward Hartman's office, where the police would take Patty upon her arrival. Delays caused their flight to run behind schedule, however, and it wasn't until 10:30 PM that the plane finally touched down at the Lehigh Valley International Airport.

Patty looked dreadful, her face puffy and tear-streaked, her hair a mass of tangled knots. She wore a blue marines T-shirt, black pants that appeared a bit too short, and dark loafers. Whisked to the state police barracks in Bethlehem, Patty was fingerprinted and photographed before being driven to Magistrate Hartman's office for arraignment.

The crowds that had gathered earlier had shrunk in number, but there were still about sixty people milling around, and as soon as the police car slowed to a stop, they began to converge.

"Hang her!" they screamed as the police held Patty by the elbow and escorted her into the building. The shouts continued: "Baby killer!" "Murderer!" "Monster!"

Patty kept her eyes downcast, but she shook her head slightly, a silent protest.

"I wanted to respond," she said later. "I wanted to explain that I hadn't done this, that I could never do such a thing. But my lawyer told me not to say anything, and I listened to him. It was an incredibly surreal moment."

Inside the magistrate's office, Patty met with two attorneys hired by Telly Fiouris. Telly had made a promise to Bob Rorrer seventeen years earlier, and he intended to keep it. With his own money, he had retained James Burke from Bethlehem, and James Pfeiffer, an attorney licensed to practice in both Pennsylvania and New Jersey. Telly was there too, having rushed from his home to meet Patty when she arrived. He looked stunned and worried as she and her two attorneys took a few private moments inside a small office.

When the trio emerged, Telly went to Patty and put his arm around her. As they listened to Magistrate Hartman read the charges, he could feel her entire body trembling. He clung more tightly as Patty shook her head at the magistrate's words.

"Do you understand the charges against you?" Hartman finally asked.

"Yes," Patty whispered.

The magistrate scheduled a preliminary hearing for July 3 and ordered Patty held without bail in the Lehigh County Jail.

Afterward, Patty's attorneys stayed behind to face the waiting press. Jim Pfeiffer, appalled by the reaction of the crowd, said he'd ask for a change of venue or a jury to be brought in from another county, both later denied.

Pfeiffer insisted Patty was innocent and claimed she wasn't even in Pennsylvania at the time of the disappearances. He suggested the only physical evidence the police had against her was the DNA, which the defense intended to challenge.

That much was true. Without the DNA, the case was entirely circumstantial and a weak case at best. In essence, Patty was facing the death penalty on the strength of one hair, linked to her by a science few at the time had ever heard of. In fact, with regards to the mitochondrial DNA, Patty's case would be a test case, the first criminal proceeding in the state of Pennsylvania to use this new form of DNA evidence.

———————

Public sentiment toward Patty ran hot, and death threats on her life postponed her preliminary hearing until the first week of August. Ten witnesses were scheduled to testify for the prosecution, including four state troopers and two forensic scientists.

When Dr. Isadore Mihalakis took the stand, he admitted that he couldn't tell whether the shooting or the beating occurred first, but he believed Joann had been alive for at least part of both attacks.

The man who sold Patty the .22 Jennings testified, and so did Jill Sarney, the young girl who rode horses with her at the Silver Shadows Stable. The most anticipated witness, however, was Andy Katrinak, and the most interesting testimony came when he began describing Joann's jewelry. In addition to her watch, earrings, and wedding band, Andy also mentioned several other rings of which his wife was particularly fond.

At the defense table, Patty sat looking at the police report that inventoried the jewelry found with Joann. Noting that the only ring found was her wedding band, Patty leaned over to her lawyer and whispered, "There weren't that many rings."

Seated behind her, Joann's family heard the remark and felt their blood run cold. How could Patty know how many rings Joann had on if she had not seen her that day?

At their first opportunity, Joann's family told the prosecutor what they had heard, and he requested he be allowed to use it at trial, but Hartman ruled that the statement fell under the attorney/client privilege and denied the prosecutor's request.

Patty's family was also seated in the gallery, and she often turned to smile and wave at them. At other times she doodled or wrote furiously on a yellow legal pad, and occasionally she'd lean over to whisper to her attorneys.

After twelve hours of testimony, Hartman bound Patricia over for trial, setting a trial date for early 1998.

The police and prosecution were convinced that Patty Rorrer had killed Joann and Alex, but that didn't stop them from worrying. They knew their case was largely circumstantial, and juries were not always receptive to that. Laymen wanted tangible evidence—a confession, an eyewitness, fingerprints, footprints, a murder weapon—none of which the prosecution had.

The gun used to kill Joann had never been found, but they had witnesses who would testify that Patty owned a weapon of the same type and caliber. They had no outright confession, but they had Suzanne Pearson, who would testify to the incriminating statements Patty had made on the morning of her arrest. They had no fingerprints or footprints, but they had hair that they were convinced came from her. They had no eyewitness to the crime, but eyewitness testimony was often the least credible in a case.

The prosecutors hoped the jury would understand it and connect the dots, but they worried just the same.

Patty, on the other hand, remained extremely confident. "How can they convict me of something I didn't do?" she repeatedly asked.

13

On February 2, 1998, less than eight months after her arrest, Patricia Rorrer went on trial for capital murder at the Lehigh County Courthouse in Allentown, Pennsylvania.* Apparently anxious about his case and eager to win, Assistant District Attorney Michael McIntyre hired a local psychiatrist to work as a jury consultant.

McIntyre had a reputation as an aggressive prosecutor and a master showman in the courtroom. He was also, according to those who knew him, a man who hated to lose. Now, along with Troopers Robert Egan and Joseph Kocevar as co-prosecutors in the case, McIntyre stood to begin his opening before the jury and Judge Thomas A. Wallitsch.†

He began by admitting that his case was largely circumstantial but added, "It was a methodical investigation, ruling out one suspect after another until the only person left standing was Patricia Rorrer."

---

* Compared to many other high-profile crimes, eight months seems an unusually short amount of time. For instance, it took two years between the arrest and trial of Scott Peterson for the murder of his wife Laci, three years between the arrest and trial of Casey Anthony for the murder of her daughter, Caylee, and five years between the arrest and trial of Jodi Arias for the murder of her boyfriend, Travis Alexander. The Katrinak investigation spanned three states and was far more complex than any of these others. Additionally, in the cases of Anthony and Arias, the defendant was facing only one count of capital murder, whereas Patricia was charged with two.

† Being named co-prosecutors meant that both state troopers would be held to the same high standards and strict rules of law as that of the prosecutor.

He described Joann and Andy's marriage as "about as perfect as a marriage could be" and claimed the couple was still "basically on a honeymoon."

"And, I'm almost apologetic to say [this]," he added, "but Andy may end up being a suspect with the defense. However, you're going to see that there's absolutely no possibility that Andy had anything to do with the murder of his wife and child."

McIntyre acknowledged that both Katrinaks had "baggage" from their past. Joann had her ex-husband, Jhared Starr, and Andy had Patty.

"His past came back to obliterate his future," McIntyre said, because there was no one else "who had any animosity or reason to be angry with Joann, other than the defendant."

In describing the discovery of the tan Toyota, the prosecutor glossed over the possibility that Andy had contaminated evidence when he sat in it.

"He didn't sit entirely in the car," McIntyre said. "You'll see he just took his butt and sat sideways in the seat, about halfway in the car." He explained that Andy had wanted to see what position the seat was in and that both he and Joann's sister, Peggy, would testify that the seat was pulled as far forward as it could go. (This was different from what Andy and Peggy initially told the police, which was that the car seat was in the same position Joann always kept it in to drive.)

McIntyre went to great lengths to downplay Andy's feelings for Patty. "He might have called her once in a while or sent her an occasional card," he said, but that ended when Andy met Joann. It did not, however, end for Patty, he said. McIntyre claimed that Patty continued to call Andy and that when she called in April 1994 and found out Andy was married and about to become a father, Patty's demeanor suddenly changed.

"She got real quiet and basically hung up," McIntyre said, "and after that, Andy was done with her." The prosecutor claimed that Patty called Andy in October and November 1994 and again on December 7 but was unable to reach him. Then she called on December 12, and Joann answered. The two argued, McIntyre said, "And three days later, Joann and Alex disappeared." He paused for a moment, perhaps letting that thought sink in.

Andy remembered that argument, McIntyre continued, and during the early morning hours of December 16, he called Patty's mother to find out where Patty was. Pat Chambers told him that Patty was home, that she woke her, and she also said that Patty had jury duty that day. "And Andy's relieved to hear this," McIntyre said, shaking his head as if at the betrayal. "He's relieved."

The motive for Joann's murder was "the anger she felt over being hung up on," but the reason for Alex's death was anger at Andy for allowing it. "We're not going to show you that it was a reasonable reaction," McIntyre said, turning to point at Patty, "but it was her reaction."

The prosecution claimed that Patty's lifestyle enabled her to commit the crimes. "She had no steady job, which allowed her to slip away at any time." She was also familiar with Joann's house and the body site, and the jury would be hearing from someone who personally rode horses with Patty in that area. "And by area, I mean literally within inches of where the bodies were found."

McIntyre told the jury that Patty had no alibi for the day of the murder and, in fact, had been "shopping for an alibi." He described Cowboys Nitelife as "hard to get into" and insisted that if Patty's name wasn't on the sign-in sheet, "then she wasn't there."

In regards to the hair evidence, the prosecution stated that one of the hairs from Joann's car contained a root. "We can prove, through the DNA, that the killer was a woman, not a man—a woman who had some reason to be angry at Joann Katrinak."

McIntyre ended his closing with both a warning and a promise. "Don't expect us to answer all the questions in this case, because we can't. But we are going to prove our case beyond a reasonable doubt."

———

Jim Pfeiffer appeared confident as he rose to give the defense's opening. Urging the jury "to keep an open mind," he pleaded with them to use their common sense.

"Does it make sense for someone to drive from North Carolina to Pennsylvania—a nine-hour and forty-one-minute drive—to murder two people over a hang-up call? Motive does not exist in this case if you apply common sense."

He disagreed that Patty "basically hung up" when she learned Andy was married and expecting a child. "It was the first thing Andy told her, and the phone call lasted 20 minutes." Patty was not angry about Andy's news. She was happy for him.

He accused the Commonwealth of having "tunnel vision" and focusing on Patty to the exclusion of anyone else. "They dismissed any evidence that didn't tend to implicate her."

Pfeiffer told the jury that hair analysis was an exclusion tool and not an "exact science."

"They are not going to be able to tell you that that's Patty's hair," he stressed. He also mentioned Dr. Jensen's contamination and the fact that the DNA, when amplified, was "amplifying the contaminant as well."

In regards to mitochondrial DNA, he spoke of how the science was brand new and had never been used in a Pennsylvania criminal case before. "Are there problems with it?" he asked. "Is it as reliable as they say?"

Touching on Patty's alibi, he told the jury that Cowboys was not hard to get into and that Seth Alden and Jake Beamer would testify that Patty was there the night Joann and Alex disappeared. There were other suspects, Pfeiffer said, and the jury would soon see that the pieces of this puzzle "do not fit together."

"The Commonwealth has to prove their case beyond a reasonable doubt," Pfeiffer concluded, "and if they don't prove their case against Patricia Rorrer beyond a reasonable doubt, then you should find her not guilty."

The police had done little to pin down the events that occurred on the night of December 15, 1994, and that became abundantly clear with the State's first five witnesses. Andy and his parents and Joann's mother and sister would each tell contradictory stories about that night.

For instance, what time did Andy's parents arrive at his house? The elder Katrinaks testified that it was 7:30 PM and that the O'Connors were already there. Sally and Peggy each testified that they arrived at Joann's house a little after 1:00 AM, and Veronica and Andrew were not there. Andy said his folks showed up when the Catasauqua police were there responding to his first call, which would have been somewhere around 10:45 PM.

There were also discrepancies as to who was in McCarty's parking lot when the police arrived. Andy and Sally both said that Andy's parents were not there, while Andrew Sr. and Peggy each insisted that they were.

Sally testified that she didn't recall anyone searching for Joann before her husband found the car, but Andy, Peggy, and Andrew Sr. each claimed to have done so.

Veronica Katrinak now told the jury that when Joann invited her to go shopping, she told Joann she would need "thirty-five to forty minutes to get ready," and Joann agreed to wait. This scenario was different from what she initially told the police, which was that Joann said she would pick her up in "ten minutes." If Veronica's new version were accurate, then the abduction would not have occurred around 1:30, as the police surmised, but closer to 2:00 or 2:15, which could have opened up an entirely new avenue of suspects and witnesses the police never questioned.

Veronica also denied ever going back to the basement after speaking to Joann and claimed she never told the police that Joann might have left without her. "Joann would never do that," she now said. Nor did Andy's mother remember hearing Alex in the background during her and Joann's conversation, and she insisted she was "very worried" when Joann didn't show up and that she tried to call her "several times."

None of Veronica's testimony supported her earlier statements to the police. In fact, everything Veronica testified to at trial was contrary to what she initially reported, but for some unknown reason, the defense didn't question her about these discrepancies.

Nor did they point out that Peggy's recollections had changed as well. According to police reports, Peggy confirmed on December 16, 1994, that the driver's seat in the Toyota was consistent with where her sister always kept it, but now she told the jury the seat was "pulled too far forward for Joann to have driven the car." Peggy did confirm, however, that she knew Andy was sleeping in a different room, because "Andy was exhausted and needed to get some sleep."

Peggy also told the jury that when the Catasauqua police officers responded to McCarty's parking lot, they began pulling things out of Joann's car, which greatly upset the family. "We were screaming at them to stop because we were afraid they were destroying evidence," she said. However, neither Sally, Andy, nor the Catasauqua police officers seemed to recall this.

Sally denied ever telling anyone that her daughter was depressed about the baby, or that Andy had a problem with Alex's crying and he and Joann were no longer sleeping together because he couldn't stand the noise. Kim Malti's husband, however, had told Detective Barry Grube that Sally had said all three.

Many of those in the courtroom were anxious to see Andy's reaction to Patricia Rorrer. Although he had never said anything derogatory about her to the press, they wondered what he would do when he actually came face to face with her. Would he confront her? Scream at her? Attack her? They waited eagerly, but Andy's reaction was anticlimactic. Seated only a few feet away from his old girlfriend, Andy appeared neither angry nor upset. Often he was seen smiling and chatting with court spectators or laughing with friends in the courthouse halls. His blasé response toward the woman who had supposedly destroyed his life was so unemotional that it prompted one jailer to ask Patty, "Why isn't he jumping over the railing to strangle you?"

On the stand, McIntyre first led Andy through the events of December 15, 1994, and the finding of Joann's car. Then he began to question him about the Catasauqua authorities' decision to release the vehicle to him, and Jim Pfeiffer immediately objected.

At a sidebar, McIntyre fiercely argued that he be allowed to bring Andy's decision not to move the car before the jury.

"It's being offered to show that Andy's not a possible suspect in this case," he said. "The police told him to take the car home, and he said no, he wasn't going to touch it. It shows he's preserving evidence, Judge."

Despite the fact that Andy *did* get in the car and *did not* preserve evidence, Wallitsch sided with the prosecution and allowed it to come in.

"Why didn't you take the car home?" McIntyre asked softly.

"I just figured if she were abducted or something, there might be evidence in the car, and I didn't want to damage it," Andy replied. He admitted "backing into the car" and noticing Joann's Mace on the floor but denied placing his feet inside. He also recalled seeing the red low-fuel warning light and the gas gauge reading below empty.

The low-fuel light had caught his attention, Andy said, because "Joann always stopped for gas when the gauge was between a half and a quarter tank."

It's unfortunate that Patty's defense didn't examine this issue in more detail. Joann's vehicle was a stick shift, requiring the clutch to be depressed in order to turn the key. The low-fuel warning light would not have displayed if the key were not turned in the ignition. Unless the vehicle was left in neutral, Andy would not have been able to see this without placing his feet inside the car, and the evidence suggests that the car was *not* left in neutral. According to state trooper Kenneth Coia, when Joann's car was taken into custody, he himself had put it into neutral so the attendant could "pull it onto the flatbed."

In discussing his wife's phone call with Patty, Andy insisted that Joann had not used foul language, but he said her tone was "stern."

"Was that unusual?" McIntyre asked.

"Yes," Andy said, nodding emphatically. "Joann was about as sweet as you could get. It was probably one of the only times I had seen her in that frame of mind."

Andy was reluctant to say anything negative about Joann, and Judge Wallitsch had ruled that nothing detrimental to her character would be allowed. The ruling was made to prevent the defense from putting the victim on trial, which is completely understandable. However, the ruling also tied the hands of the defense in their attempt to give the jury an accurate picture of the victim. The prosecution's portrayal of Joann as sweet, shy, and timid did not fit with what those who knew her had to say. As a result, the jury would never hear about her temper or her tendency to speak her mind. Nor would they hear about the altercations she had with ex-boyfriends, her ex-husband, and others. The type of person Joann was, *was* relevant, and the jury should have been allowed to garner an accurate picture of her. The fact that the defense was barred from putting on this evidence was unfair to both Patricia and the jury.

Andy testified that the call from Patty occurred on December 12, between 9:00 and 9:30 PM, and he heard Joann say, "Just a minute." She turned toward him with the phone held out, but as he started to get up, Joann suddenly put the phone back to her ear and asked who was calling. After that, he heard her say, "Andy is married now. We have a baby, and we don't want you calling here anymore."

When she hung up, Andy said, Joann turned to him and smiled. "You really didn't want to talk to her, did you?" she asked.

Andy testified that he told her no, and Joann said, "I don't understand why she would call here."

When they found the Toyota in McCarty's parking lot, Andy said he "had a gut feeling" that Patty might be involved, so he called her mother to see where Patty was. Unfortunately, no one bothered to ask Andy why he didn't call Patty himself. If he had, and he reached her in North Carolina at 3:00 in the morning, *he* would have become Patty's alibi.

Pat Chambers said she'd call him back, and she did, about ten minutes later, to tell him that Patty was at home and she'd woken her up.

"Patty was . . . I don't know if [Pat Chambers] put it court duty or jury duty . . . something like that," Andy said.

The police had checked and learned that Patty had not been serving on a jury that day, proving in their mind that she was lying, but both Patty and her mother would always deny ever telling Andy that Patty had jury duty. What both insisted—and Andy admitted could be true—was that Patty said she had "court duty" on the day she allegedly argued with Joann. It's an odd expression but one that Patty continues to use even today when describing having to appear in court, and she had appeared in court on December 12, 1994, to answer to the animal abandonment charge.

In discussing his relationship with Patty, Andy went to great lengths to downplay the romance. He told the jury that the two had met in 1984 and had a "four- or five-year" relationship but denied they'd ever talked seriously about marriage or children.

"I didn't want kids with her," Andy said. He admitted, however, that he went down to North Carolina to see her "a half dozen times or more" and that at one point, the relationship resumed while he was there.

"Patty initiated it," he insisted, and it had lasted "for a very short period, about a week." When he broke it off, Patty took it with "a combination of anger and sadness."

He admitted the two remained friends and that he'd allowed her to stay at his Front Street house for "two or three days" after Frank Alonzo's assault but insisted it was he who asked her to leave.

He'd last spoken to Patty in April 1994 when he told her he was married and expecting a child. He described her as becoming "quiet and depressed" after hearing this but admitted that the two had continued chatting for quite some time afterward.

Andy had initially told the police that the intruder "may have used a cordless screwdriver" to loosen the screws on his basement door, and now he told the jury that he had seen a cordless screwdriver at Patty's house in North Carolina. However, the police had found none when they searched her house, and no one else recalled her owning one. When asked who originally replaced the window in the cellar door, Andy answered casually, "Me, with a cordless screwdriver."

On cross, Jim Pfeiffer got Andy to admit that his breakup with Patty was a mutual decision and that it was her choice to move out of the Bethlehem house. He denied ever saying that it was he who broke up with her or that Frank Alonzo had threatened him, although police reports prove that he had said both.

Andy said that within weeks of the disappearances, Pat Chambers had called him twice to see if there was any news, and he'd spoken to Patty both times yet he never once asked her about being on jury duty. It would seem that after making such a business of it, that would have been one of the first questions he asked.

Other than Joann, Andy claimed to have had only two serious relationships: one with Patty and the other with his old girlfriend, Sara. He had lived with Sara in California, he said, and continued his relationship with her long distance after he returned to Pennsylvania. When the two finally broke up, Sara had moved to—of all places—Colorado, and they continued to keep in touch while she was there. He thought they last spoke around 1984.

Pfeiffer asked Andy whom he dated after he and Patty split up, and Andy answered, "Maria."

"What about Donna Long?"

Appearing uncomfortable with the question, Andy said, "Donna is one of my best friends."

"Did you have a relationship with Donna?"

"A long time ago. We're more friends. We were each other's best friend."

Pfeiffer nodded. "When you say a long time ago, when was that relationship?"

Andy seemed to hedge on his answer. "It wasn't really . . . it's a friend type of relationship. It started in the early '80s, probably '83 or '84."

Pfeiffer tried again. "And did you have a romantic relationship with her?"

"For a very, very brief time," Andy said, claiming it was after he split up with Patty and before he met Joann.

Again Pfeiffer nodded. "So this would have been in '91? '92?"

"Somewhere in there, yeah," Andy said.

"How long did the romantic relationship last?"

"Very, very, *very* brief," Andy answered, glaring at the attorney.

Donna Long would turn out to be one of the more elusive characters in the Katrinak/Rorrer story. She was a pretty girl, tall, with long blond hair, and although the police had not investigated her in the Katrinak murders, they did speak to her regarding them.

The authorities first interviewed her at Andy's house on December 20, 1994, only five days after Joann and Alex disappeared. She told investigators that she had met Andy at a restaurant where she waitressed and that the two had had an "intimate relationship" at one time. She became friends with Joann after Andy began dating her, and the last time she saw her was when she stopped by the Front Street house to drop off a gift for Alex.

Patty had never met Donna, but she was aware of her. Years ago, as Patty and Andy's relationship began to deteriorate, Patty was certain that Andy was seeing Donna, although he denied it. It wasn't until they split up for good that Patty said Andy finally admitted he *had* been seeing Donna while they were still together.

Andy and Donna dated for a while after Patty left, but eventually Andy met Joann and fell head over heels in love. If Donna was upset by this, she gave no indication of it. In fact, she not only remained friends with Andy but also became friendly with his new wife as well.

While there is nothing to suggest that Donna was involved with the murders, she perfectly illustrates the tunnel vision the police seemed to develop in regards to Patricia Rorrer. Everything that first led them to suspect Patty was also true of Donna, yet the police never investigated her.

- Donna had blond hair, which was never compared to the hair found in Joann's car
- Donna had had an intimate relationship with Andy
- Donna knew the victims, which Patty did not
- Donna was far more familiar with the Katrinak house than Patty
- Donna lived only four miles from the body site, a fact Andy failed to mention when authorities asked him if he knew anyone who lived in that area

Additionally, Donna's family owned a landscaping nursery, and soil samples taken from the soles of Joann's shoes were found to contain particles of flower petals, which seemed a strange finding in the dead of winter in Pennsylvania. The authorities compared those samples to every known location associated with the crime but failed to compare them with soil from the Long nursery. To date, the police have been unable to determine where the flower petal particles came from.

Nor did the police seem to wonder why Joann was unconcerned that Andy had maintained his friendship with Donna but was so obviously upset by Andy's minimal contact with Patricia Rorrer. Patty lived more than five hundred miles away, and her relationship with Andy consisted of one or two phone calls a year, while Donna, another of her husband's ex-lovers, actually lived in the same town and remained in not only Andy's life but that of his wife and son as well.*

And despite Donna and Andy both insisting that they were just friends, courtroom watchers noticed that they seemed overly affectionate and acted like a couple, as apparently they were. For soon after the trial ended, Donna joined Andy in Colorado, where the two married and began a new life.

---

* While the police found Patty's habit of staying in touch with Andy incriminating, Andy appears to have done the same with his old girlfriends. It's not in dispute that he called Patty and sent her cards and letters after they broke up, and Patty remembers Sara occasionally calling their house when she lived with Andy. And obviously, Andy continued to keep in touch with Donna Long after their relationship ended, too.

14

On day two of the trial, the jury was loaded on a bus and taken to visit several locations that figured prominently in the crimes. Their first stop: 740 Front Street.

Andy's old house had been sold nearly two years earlier, but the new owner gave the court permission to view it and acknowledged that it had not been renovated in any significant way since the time of Joann and Alex's disappearance. The jury members were allowed to examine the basement door and the area where Andy discovered the cut phone line before walking the short distance to McCarty's parking lot where David O'Connor had found Joann's car on that cold December night so long ago.

Returning to the bus, the jurors sat quietly as they traveled twelve miles to the intersection of Friedens and Best Station Roads. This time, they remained on the bus as Trooper Egan pointed out the Silver Shadows Stable Patty once managed.

Two miles farther on, they crossed into Heidelberg Township, and the bus came to a stop at its final destination. From there, the jurors would have to walk. Following Trooper Kocevar, the entourage made its way down the old logging trail and into the woods. Reaching the railroad bed, they crossed over and continued along the path on the other side until they reached the campfire ring, and Trooper Kocevar stopped.

"These woods are pretty much the same as they were then," he said, glancing around before turning left and pointing toward a fluorescent orange stake, "And that's where we found the baby rattle." Continuing on, the jury moved cautiously. Although the weather was mild, the ground lay covered in dead leaves and dry, broken branches. The stillness of the location was eerie and the thought of what had happened here frightening. Farther ahead, they could see another orange stake, its brightness standing in stark contrast to the dull grays of winter. When Trooper Kocevar reached it and told them they were standing on the spot where the killer left the bodies of Joann and Alex, several of the jurors instinctively stepped away.

Patty showed little emotion while visiting the sights. Dressed in a skirt and low heels—hardly proper attire for a walk in the woods—she spent some time picking burrs from her clothing. On their return to the bus, the group of people walked in a jumbled mass. At times, jurors found themselves walking beside Patty or with members of the media or police officers. Sometimes Patty walked alone, appearing lost in thought; at other times she would hurry to catch up with her attorneys and whisper in their ears. When they finally reached their vehicles, everyone appeared relieved to be out of the dismal and depressing woods.

Back in the courtroom, jurors listened to Andy's 911 calls from December 15, and then Judge Wallitsch dismissed court for the day.

Although the authorities claimed that the Katrinak investigation was "some of the finest police work done in the history of the Commonwealth," they had little to be proud of in regards to the evidence handling. There had been some major mistakes made, as Patty's attorney would bring out with several of the prosecution's next witnesses.

Jim Kovack, the farmer who discovered the bodies, revealed that the crime scene might not have been as secure as it should have been. Watching from his house, Kovack had seen numerous unofficial people enter the scene, including his own son and several members of the Germansville Fire Company.

Trooper Thomas Mase, who was in charge of the entry log, admitted he had logged in only those people who came inside the yellow tape, which initially encompassed only the bodies, not the entire scene. Eventually, the tape was moved seventy-five to one hundred feet beyond the bodies, but still, Mase logged in only those who came within the tape. If people approached the scene from a different route, such as the old logging trail or through the woods, he did not include them in the entry log, which meant that it was possible there could have been a breach in the yellow tape.

Trooper Coia of the records and identification unit, told the jury of using Post-it Notes to collect evidence, at the instruction of Dr. Thomas Jensen. Why was Jensen instructing the PSP on evidence collecting? He was not a police officer but a civilian working for the PSP and probably had no experience or training in investigating crimes. The use of Post-it Notes was a nonstandard procedure, never before used, and one that may have come with hidden risks of contamination.

There were other mistakes as well, such as the authorities' habit of hand-delivering evidence and keeping evidence in unsealed envelopes as they had with Patty's hair exemplars and Alex's diaper bag. The diaper bag had been taken to the Montgomery County Sheriff's Office, where a laser was used to examine it, but when it was returned to the PSP evidence locker, no one bothered to seal the evidence bag in which it sat.

There was also the "exciting discovery" of the "Windmere" tag found among the victim's apparel. The fact that the tag had not come from either victim's clothing convinced the police that it had come from the killer's. For weeks, they worked at tracking down the lead, only to discover that the tag was not a clothing tag at all but a tag from a Windmere electric heater the PSP used to dry the victim's clothes.

Dr. Mihalakis, who performed the autopsies, testified that the bullet that entered Joann's face had nicked her carotid artery and that she would have been "bleeding profusely," not only from that but also from the head wounds and her broken nose. However, he could give no logical explanation for why there was not enough blood on her leather coat to DNA test. Nor could he give a time of death for the two victims, admitting that Joann and Alex could have been alive as late as mid-January.

Kurt Tempinski, the PSP firearms and tool mark examiner, could not say if the bullet that killed Joann had come from a rifle or a handgun, nor could he tell the jury what make and model gun had fired the fatal shot. He knew of at least seven different weapons capable of being used.*

Tempinski also admitted that he had examined seventy-five spent .22 bullets and fragments collected from areas where Patty was known to target practice with the gun, but none of those slugs matched the bullet recovered from Joann's face. Nor did Tempinski bother to compare any of Andy's tools to the pry marks left on the basement door, despite the fact that Andy was a carpenter.

Over and over again, the police took the stand and told of blunders and mistakes made in the investigation, but of all the "expert" witnesses to testify, it was Dr. Thomas Jensen of the PSP crime lab who came off as the least credible.

Jensen was not an expert in hair analysis, nor was he certified in it, nor had he ever taken a proficiency test on the subject. In fact, the last course Jensen had taken in hair analysis lasted "for the better part of one day" and occurred more than twenty years earlier, in the 1970s. He did not work in the hair analysis unit of the PSP crime lab at the time of the murders but in their serology department. Once involved in this case, Jensen was also allowed to instruct the police on how to gather evidence.

Despite his lack of credentials, Patty's lawyers did not object to the court qualifying Jensen as an expert witness in hair analysis, nor did they have any qualms with referring to him as such while he was on the stand. On at least one occasion, Patty's attorneys began an objection by saying, "Your Honor, if the expert witness…" It was a tactical error on their part, conveying to the jury that even Patty's own attorneys considered Jensen an "expert" in the field and worthy of belief.

Dr. Jensen began by admitting that he had not examined most of the evidence sent to him from the Katrinak house: neither the

---

* Interestingly, neither Tim Sellers nor the man who sold Patty the gun was sure of what make and model her gun was. Though they thought it was a .22 Jennings, neither man was certain, leaving one to wonder whether Patty even owned a gun capable of firing the fatal shot.

bloody toilet paper nor the tissues containing an unknown substance. He didn't bother to examine any hairs from any of the scenes that he thought "could have come from Joann, Alex, or Andy." If he "thought" they could have come from the Katrinaks, he simply discarded them.

Jensen's forensic reports stated that the fingernail found on Joann's chest "differed in size from the victim in width and grooming," but he told the jury that "all the fingernails found at the crime scene came from Joann." Patty's attorneys didn't bother to challenge him on this, which they certainly should have.

Throughout his testimony, Dr. Jensen would continue to lose credibility, but it was when he began discussing the six hairs found in Joann's car that his bungling of the evidence became clear.

Jensen testified that he received six hairs recovered from Joann's car on ten Post-it Notes and that he sent three of those six hairs unmounted to the FBI. The other three hairs he had permanently mounted on glass slides and retained in his lab.

Although Jensen had never noted any roots on the six hairs, he now said he sent the three unmounted hairs to the FBI "because one of the hairs appeared to have a much better root tag capable of DNA testing." He also claimed he photographed only one of the three unmounted hairs, but not the one with "the better root tag." As for the other five hairs, well, he didn't bother to photograph them at all—not until December 1997, less than two months before Patty went on trial.

Over and over and over again, Jensen made reference to "a lot of hairs" being found in Joann's car, but he claimed the six from the driver's side seat back were the only ones inconsistent with the Katrinak family. For that reason, he didn't bother to analyze or test any of the others.

Midway through his testimony, the court called a brief recess, and afterward, McIntyre again led Jensen back to the six hairs found in Joann's car. "I think the last thing that we had testimony on was the report in which you found and examined the six hairs that had been taken from the Katrinak vehicle?"

"Yes, that's correct," Jensen replied.

McIntyre first showed the jury photographs of the three car hairs Jensen had mounted and retained in his lab. Then, holding up exhibit 17-B—a photograph of a hair—he asked the doctor if it was a picture of the unmounted car hairs that he had sent to the FBI.

"Yes," Jensen said. Then, pointing at the picture, he added that in the corner you could see another small section of the hair.

"Is that a picture of one hair or three different hairs?" McIntyre asked.

"It's three pictures of one hair," Jensen explained.

"All right," McIntyre said, beginning to move on to something else. But Jensen interrupted him.

"That hair was mounted on a microscope slide and looped around to keep it within the confines of the slide," Jensen said. "That's the hair that we call hair number three of the *remounted* slides."

Hair number three of the remounted slides? What remounted slides? Jensen was testifying about the three hairs that he had never mounted. There were only six hairs in question—the three unmounted hairs and the three that Jensen mounted. What hairs were *remounted* and why?

McIntyre looked confused as he approached the witness holding the exhibit in his hand. "Let's see," the prosecutor said, "as I look at this, I wanted to determine whether or not we have made a mistake in the labeling. Do you see a label?"

"I can't read it," Jensen replied.

McIntyre read the label for him. "Microscopic view, apparent dried blood on three car hairs sent to the FBI crime lab in July 1995. Photo taken prior to sending."

"That's mislabeled," Jensen said quickly.

"Right," McIntyre answered.

"We'll have to relabel that one," Jensen said, reaching for it. McIntyre handed the exhibit to the doctor, at which point Jensen *relabeled the exhibit right there on the witness stand.* Incredibly, there was no objection from Patty's lawyers.

In a case in which no hair roots are reported for almost three entire years and then a root is magically discovered—*but only after the suspect in the case provided hair samples with roots attached*—this highly suspicious testimony simply cries out for an explanation. Jensen's use of the word *remount* indicates that the hair was once mounted, removed from the mount, and then mounted again, but Jensen never mounted these hairs. If anything, they were mounted for the first time by the FBI after Dr. Dizinno tested them, and the available evidence indicates that only one of them—the one Dr. Deadman cracked open to perform nuclear DNA testing—might have needed to be remounted. Yet Jensen clearly testified that multiple slides were remounted: "That's the hair that we call hair number three of the remounted *slides*." So how many hairs were mounted repeatedly, and for what reason? Additionally, the purpose of affixing a label to an item is to correctly identify that item, and Dr. Jensen's relabeling of an exhibit in open court is unusual to say the least. It also raises a number of unanswered questions that Patty's appellate attorney would bring up on appeal:

- What did the existing label say that was wrong?
- What was the label changed to?
- Who affixed the inaccurate label?
- Under what circumstances was the inaccurate label affixed?

No explanation was ever offered for any of these questions. Instead, McIntyre quickly moved on to the three hairs from Joann's car that Jensen had mounted. "Let's make this clear to the jury," the prosecutor said. "The three hairs that you testified about—that were mounted on a microscopic slide and maintained by you—did you eventually send them to the FBI?"

"Yes," Jensen replied.

"When were those sent to the FBI?"

"Those went much later, on the 24th of June 1996. Trooper Kocevar picked those up to take to the FBI. That was approximately a year later."*

"Now, in the meantime," McIntyre continued, "what did you do with those three hairs that you mounted on the microscope slides? Why did you retain them for yourself?"

---

* Curiously, the three mounted hair slides don't appear on an FBI report until September 16, 1997, more than a year after they supposedly received them.

"I used those for comparison purposes in comparing to hairs that were brought to me later."

"All right, did you eventually get hairs that were taken from the defendant, Patricia Rorrer?"

"Yes, I did," Jensen answered.

"And after you made the comparison, was it at that time that you sent those hairs [the three mounted car hairs] on to the FBI?" McIntyre asked.

"That's correct."

"All right, I just wanted to clear that up."

Despite the attempt at clarification, Jensen's testimony still seems odd. After all, the FBI returned the three unmounted car hairs to the PSP in October 1995, and there is no documented evidence that those three hairs were ever sent back to the FBI. The PSP obtained Patty's hair samples one month later, in November 1995, and Jensen sent three of Patty's unmounted samples to the FBI that same month. If he never sent the three contaminated car hairs back to the FBI, and didn't send the three mounted car hairs to the FBI until late June 1996, what hair was the FBI comparing Patty's samples to during that seven-month gap?

McIntyre next asked Dr. Jensen if he had measured the six hairs from Joann's car, and Jensen gave another strange response.

"Yes and no," he answered. He had measured only one of the three unmounted hairs, but, "the three [hairs] I mounted, I determined their length after mounting." Concerning the one unmounted hair, "I grasped the hair in the center with my thumbs and index fingers and slid my fingers along the hair to pull it taut," then simply placed the hair next to a ruler to get its measurement. For the mounted hairs, Jensen said he first made an "enlarged Xerox copy" of both the hair slides and a ruler. Then, using a pencil, he traced out the overlapping and missing portions of the hair on the Xerox copy. Afterward, with a "wheel division," (commonly used to measure mileage on maps) he ran the instrument along the Xerox copy of the hairs, up and down the strands and over and under the loops and curves, then "ran the wheel division along the Xerox copy of the ruler to get the hairs' length."

Why this intricate process to measure the mounted hairs? He measured the first hair by stretching it out and placing it next to a ruler, a simple and precise procedure. Though it's true that he contaminated the hair by doing this, *he didn't know he was contaminating it.* The way he measured the hair was not the problem; the problem was that he failed to wear gloves when he did so.

Jensen went on to tell the jury that the three mounted hairs from Joann's car were "forcibly pulled out" and that two of the hairs had roots, one of which contained "traces of blood and a fair amount of tissue attached."

Blood and tissue clinging to the hair root? If true, then why had no scientist—including Dr. Jensen—noted a root on any of these hairs during the two and a half years they studied and examined them?

Jensen told the jury that the optical glue he used to mount these hairs made it "very difficult to get at the hair once it is mounted in this way. It's not intended that a hair I mounted that way would be de-mounted. That is not a temporary mount."

Why would a scientist permanently mount hairs with perfect roots to test? Jensen had already testified that he "kept the hair with the best root tag unmounted for the FBI." Was it possible to have a better specimen than a root tag with "blood and tissue attached"? If all these perfect roots existed, why did it take the FBI years to find something to test? With all these perfect roots, why were they forced to use mitochondrial and PCR testing? If Jensen's testimony is true, then they obviously had more than enough material to perform nuclear DNA testing very early in the investigation.

Having just told the jury that the three mounted car hairs were encased "in a permanent mount," Jensen again contradicted himself by saying that after the FBI had returned the hair slides, one of the mounts was cracked and, "sections of one of the hairs was missing. So the FBI did get into one of the slides."

FBI analyst Dr. Harold Deadman's report on the three hairs mounted by the PSP, however, does not support Jensen's testimony. Deadman noted that he "attempted to get into the slide but was unsuccessful," and in a letter to prosecutor McIntyre dated December 10, 1997, Deadman wrote:

In this case, three head hairs were submitted to the FBI Labora-
tory after having been examined by the Pennsylvania State Police
Laboratory and were assigned specimen numbers Q4, Q5, and Q6.*
The hairs had been mounted in a mounting medium identified as
Norland Optical Adhesive.

It is extremely difficult to remove mounted substances from this
medium which precluded standard body fluid identification and
DNA testing procedures from being used.

Well, which one was it? Jensen was testifying that the FBI did get
into one of the three mounted hair slides and removed a section of the
hair. Deadman was saying the FBI couldn't get into the slides so didn't
conduct DNA testing. If the FBI never DNA tested the three previously
unmounted car hairs—which they admitted they did not when they
returned them to the PSP because of the contamination—and the three
mounted car hairs *could not* be tested, then what hair was tested against
Patty Rorrer's blood and "matched" to her?

Jensen was not a good witness. The longer he testified, the more bizarre
his story became. In discussing Patty's hair samples, Jensen said he
mounted fourteen of them on slides "in the same way I mounted the
ones from Joann's car," and then selected two more to test with a methylene blue solution to determine if there was bleaching action on the hair.
Afterward, he washed and dried the two hairs and mounted them on
slides as well.

Incredibly, while Jensen was testifying about this, McIntyre found
another mislabeled slide. "There are two number fifteen slides here,"
he said.

Unperturbed, Jensen casually replied, "Yes, that should be number
sixteen," but offered no indication of how he could know which one
should be number fifteen and which number sixteen.

---

* The three unmounted car hairs were labeled Q1, Q2, and Q3.

When McIntyre then handed the doctor an envelope that was marked, "2 hairs found with Alex Katrinak," the envelope actually contained three hairs.

Again, Jensen seemed unconcerned. "That's not unusual," he said.

Not unusual to be mixing up evidence and having no idea where that evidence was found or recovered? How could anyone now determine which two hairs in that envelope were actually the two found with Alex?

If Jensen didn't find the mixing up of evidence unusual, some people might have found the way he determined the length of Patty's hair back in 1994 to be downright bizarre. Jensen had devised his own method to do this, with something he called "pupillary distance." Jensen took the picture of Patty and her two team penning mates from Oklahoma, measured the distance between the eyes of each person in the picture and then divided that number by three—the number of people in the photograph. Somehow, this supposedly allowed him to come up with a ballpark figure for Patty's hair length: eight and one-half inches long, the same approximate length as the hairs found in Joann's car.

McIntyre spent a lot of time questioning Jensen about the six hairs found in the victim's car but touched only briefly on the best evidence in the case: the hair found in Joann's right hand.

Jensen testified that the hair in Joann's hand was of human origin, narrow, and had a very irregular pigment distribution. He also said it was markedly different from Joann and Andy's hair but could not say if it was "markedly different" from Patty's *because he never bothered to compare it to Patty's hair.* Nor did he bother to photograph it or note its color. This was incredible testimony. How could a forensic scientist not compare a hair found in the victim's hand to the hairs of the prime suspect in the case?

By all rights, Patty's attorneys should have crucified Jensen on the stand. They had more than enough ammunition to do so, but unfortunately, they did not.

Jim Burke brought out that for a "reliable hair comparison," it is recommended to have at least one hundred hair samples, but no one in the case had provided anywhere near that number. Andy provided twenty hairs, Lauren Brenner fourteen, and Debbie Marchek only four.

He also got the doctor to admit that hairs shed naturally and can stay around for years.

"What about animal hair?" Burke asked.

"Yes," Jensen replied, anyone who owned a pet would know how proficiently they shed.

"Did you find any horse hair in Joann's car?"

"No."

"Any horse hair at the body site?"

"No," Jensen admitted, shaking his head.

Burke waited until just before the end of Jensen's cross-examination to finally ask him the million dollar question: "Dr. Jensen, I assume you didn't see any roots?"

Jensen hesitated for a moment and then launched into a long and detailed explanation—not of hair roots, nor his lack of seeing any, but of the type of microscopes used to compare them and the process used to examine them. On and on the doctor droned, using technical language that could have easily put a listener to sleep. His answer was so long and tedious that by the time he finished, Burke may have forgotten what he initially asked, because Jensen never answered the question and Burke didn't repeat it. Instead, he moved on to something else.

"Doctor," Burke asked, "did you ever compare the hair in Joann's hand with Patty's hair?"

Jensen admitted that he hadn't but did admit that in looking at his notes, "I would very strongly suspect that it *would not match.*"

Burke then asked about two other hairs recovered from the body site—one found on Alex's diaper bag and one on his baby blanket. "Did you compare those two hairs with Patty's?"

"Yes," Jensen said, and he had seen both similarities and dissimilarities. "Therefore, I could not form an opinion as to whether Patricia Rorrer was a possible source for those two hairs." However, he could not exclude her as a potential source for two other hairs: a different one discovered on Alex's diaper bag and one recovered from the forest litter.

Between Joann's car and the crime scene, the police had collected more than two hundred hairs, but they focused on only eight, the six from the car and the two from the body site. These were the only hairs for which he could not exclude Patty as a source. Though it's likely that many of those two hundred hairs belonged to Joann, Alex, and Andy, there were also numerous foreign ones. To whom did all *those* hairs belong?

Hair analysis is hardly a precise science, as even Dr. Jensen admitted. "There's a lot of subjective opinion that goes into making hair comparisons," he said.

15

In a bizarre twist, on the fourth day of trial, the prosecution called Patty's mother to the stand. Approaching the bench, McIntyre asked permission to treat Pat Chambers as a hostile witness, and Wallitsch agreed to give him some latitude.

McIntyre started out by asking the witness a rhetorical question. "I take it there's no way in the world you would ever believe Patty is capable of doing what she's charged with?"

Pat admitted that was true. "She couldn't have killed them," she said, "because I spoke to her on December 15, and Patty was at home."

McIntyre asked if there was any way Pat could prove that, since the phone call was a local one and would not appear on her bill.

"No," Pat said. "You just have my word."

"Did you see Patty that day or just talk to her?"

"Just talked with her."

McIntyre frowned. Hadn't she told the FBI that she had also *seen* her daughter on the fifteenth of December? he asked.

"I never told them that," Pat said, shaking her head.

McIntyre moved on. "Didn't you call the owner of a tanning salon and try to get her to say Patty was there on December 15?"

Again, Pat shook her head. She had called the salon, she admitted, but only because "I wanted to find out if she had any records that would show Patty was there that day."

Well, McIntyre continued, didn't she also call IAN MURPHY and attempt to get him to give Patty an alibi? Didn't she want him to say he did work for Patty on the day the Katrinaks went missing?

No, Pat said, she had called Murphy to ask about the return of some auto parts from Patty's truck. Her daughter was supposed to return the parts for a refund, and with Patty now in custody, Pat figured they were going to need all the money they could get.

"Have you been asked to contact any witnesses in regards to an alibi?" McIntyre asked, clearly implying that Patty had requested her mother to "shop for an alibi."

Pat Chambers shook her head. "I just did that myself," she insisted.

Patty's mother also denied ever saying Patty didn't own a gun but did admit she had told the FBI Andy might be sterile.

"I thought he was," Pat shrugged, based on the fact that Patty had never gotten pregnant when she was with him.

Referring to Andy's 3:00 AM phone call on December 16, McIntyre asked, "Why did you have to call Patty to find out if she was in North Carolina?"

"Because Andy asked me to," Pat replied.

"But you know how far Lehigh County is from there, don't you?"

"Not necessarily."

"Doesn't your brother live in Phillipsburg, New Jersey?"

Pat looked confused. "I have no brother."

Now it was the prosecutor's turn to look confused. "Well, who is Telly Fiouris?"

"He's been a friend of mine for twenty-seven years," Pat answered, "but he is not my brother."

McIntyre quickly moved on. Was it true that sometime in 1995 she had taken a gun to another daughter's house and asked her to hide it?

"Now what's this?" Pat asked, sounding wary. She had never given anyone a gun to hide, she said, but she had given her daughter, Sandy, a gun to hold for her. Going on to explain, Pat told the jury that she worked as a school bus driver and also had a permit to carry a gun. One day, on her way to pick up the school bus, she realized she forgot to remove the gun from her purse. She could not take the gun onto school property, and Sandy's house was on the way to the school. Rather than drive all the way back home, she stopped at her daughter's house and asked her to hold the weapon for her.

McIntyre nodded, as if to say, 'that makes sense,' then turned and thundered at her, "Well, then why would your daughter have buried that gun?"

Unfazed by the prosecutor's theatrics, Pat replied calmly, "I have no idea." She had returned to her daughter's house the next day to retrieve the gun and was stunned to learn that Sandy's husband had buried it in their backyard. The gun in question was right now sitting on her television set, and she'd be happy to bring it into court so he could show it to Sandy, Pat said.

"I think we'll do that," McIntyre snapped.

But he never did.

After a long three-day weekend, the prosecution called FBI agents William Bradbury and Dwight Ayers to the stand. Bradbury had interviewed Pat Chambers on December 22, 1994, while Ayers had questioned Patty at the same time.

Bradbury corroborated Patty's story about Cowboys Nitelife but said he didn't recall Pat Chambers telling him that she had spoken to Patty on December 15.

When Ayers took the stand, he, too, confirmed the Cowboys conversation and admitted that he had not checked out Patty's alibi because the PSP didn't ask him to. They had made it abundantly clear that she was not a suspect in the case.

Ayers described Patty during the interview as "obviously concerned about Andy and the welfare of his wife and child" and agreed that she appeared "willing to cooperate in any way requested of her." He also testified that Patty wore short sleeves during the questioning, and he had noticed no injuries to her hands, arms, or face.

Patty's old boyfriend, Tim Sellers, took the stand to say that he had no idea what make and model Patty's gun was. He described it as being tiny, missing one of its wooden grips, and having the serial number scratched off. The last time he had seen the gun, he said, was when he and Patty broke up and she was pointing it at his head. Regarding Andy, Sellers spoke about Patty taking out his picture and looking at it "when we was drinking, and we'd fight about it."

"Do you consider yourself an honest man?" McIntyre finally asked.

Sellers nodded. "I don't use—I had a drug problem—I don't use drugs and alcohol. I'm an honest person."

On cross, Jim Burke brought out just how honest Tim Sellers actually was. Sellers admitted he'd been convicted of crimes "fifteen or more times," and "a bunch of times" for gun-related thefts. He also acknowledged that as a convicted felon he was not allowed to purchase, own, or have a gun in his possession.

"Mr. Sellers," Burke asked, "how many times were you arrested or convicted of a crime while you were dating Patricia Rorrer?"

"None," Sellers admitted, other than the theft charge in which Patty was cooperating with the police.

"How's your criminal record since you and Patty split up?" Burke asked.

Patty's old boyfriend glared at the attorney but reluctantly admitted that it wasn't very good. Since he and Patty separated—less than four years earlier—Tim Sellers had been convicted on five more occasions and currently had new charges pending against him.

That afternoon, McIntyre began calling witnesses to cast doubt on Patty's alibi. Several employees of Cowboys Nitelife took the stand to testify that Patty's name was not on the sign-in sheets on December 15, nor did they recall her being in the club that night.

Of course, that could have been due to the police waiting so long to try and verify Patty's alibi, which created other problems as well.

There were one hundred and nine people signed in at Cowboys on December 15, 1994, but there was no way to determine if that number tallied with the "clicker" count because, by the time the police inquired about it, the records no longer existed.

Also brought out was the fact that no one was required to sign in for dance class on Thursdays, nor were the sign-in sheets available to sign during that time.

McIntyre's next witness, ABBY BOGAN, gave Patty an icy stare as she took her seat in the witness chair. Abby was the daughter of Jerry Bogan, the dance instructor at Cowboys, and it was clear from her demeanor that she did not care for Patricia Rorrer.

Bogan testified that "about a week before Christmas 1994," Patty called her house on a Thursday night "between 7:00 and 7:30 PM," and asked for her father. Abby told Patty that Jerry was not at home, and according to her, Patty then said, "This is Pat. I'm calling from Pennsylvania, and it's important. Tell him I'll call him back later."

Though Bogan couldn't give a precise date for the call, both she and McIntyre strongly implied that it had occurred on Thursday, December 15.

Patty would adamantly deny this at trial and later go on to make a logical point. "Why would I call him between 7:00 and 7:30 on a Thursday night?" She asked, shaking her head. "I knew he taught dance class at that time, so I'd have known he wouldn't be home. Besides, I'm not stupid. Do you honestly think that after carefully planning the murders of two people, I'd be dumb enough to call anyone and say 'I'm calling from Pennsylvania'? Come on."

There were other troubling things about Abby Bogan's testimony. She insisted she had told her father about the call, but Jerry Bogan would testify that he had no recollection of it. Abby also claimed she first met Patty at Cowboys in March 1994, during her eighteenth birthday party, but again, her father would testify that he didn't remember Patty being there. In fact, Patty didn't start going to Cowboys until later that summer, when she purchased her membership in August 1994.

Abby had also been present on at least three separate occasions while the police questioned her father, but she hadn't mentioned this incriminating phone call until January 18, 1996, more than a year after it allegedly occurred. When the defense asked her why she waited so long, Abby said the police never questioned her.

"But you were present on at least three occasions when they questioned [your father], weren't you?" Pfeiffer asked.

"No," Abby replied, "not before that date."

Not before that date. It was an interesting answer. The police had interviewed Jerry Bogan in May, July, August, and September 1995. Abby Bogan now appeared to be saying that he was also interviewed, in her presence, at least three more times *after* January 18, 1996. Jerry Bogan initially corroborated Patty's alibi of being at dance class on December 15. It was only after repeated questioning that he changed his story and told the police, "I can't say she was there, and I can't say she wasn't there."

A recorded phone call between Patty and Jerry suggests that the police were putting heavy pressure on the dance instructor and insisting that he provide specific dates, which he could not do. During the call, Patty's voice sounds desperate and Jerry's sounds scared.

"Did I miss any other dance classes in December 1994 besides when I went to Oklahoma?" Patty asked.

"As far as I can remember, no," Jerry answered.

"That's all [the police] need to know, and do you remember the conversation that Friday saying my ex-boyfriend's wife had disappeared the day before?"

"Like I said, as far as I do remember the conversation now."

"Well if you tell them that, you don't have to give them a date."

"But they're asking for specific dates, and you know I cannot give them a date for anything."

Patty, near tears, explained that if he simply told them that he remembered the conversation about her ex-boyfriend's wife disappearing, and didn't recall her missing any other dance classes other than when she was in Oklahoma, the police could figure out the dates themselves.

"They're trying to put me in the electric chair!" Patty cried.

"They can't do that unless you done it!" Bogan answered back.

"Jer, they're trying to pin it on me!"

The repeated visits by the police, and the fact that Jerry Bogan eventually changed his story, leads one to wonder: When does "questioning" become harassment or intimidation?

Patty apparently *had* called Jerry Bogan's house at one time, because a friend of Abby's told investigators that Abby had mentioned the call and wasn't happy about it. According to the friend, Abby thought Patty was calling to stir up trouble between her father and his girlfriend. Obviously, Patty would not have called from Pennsylvania after murdering two people, just to cause trouble between Jerry and his girl, but there could be a logical explanation for the description Abby Bogan gave of where Patty was calling from.

During the trial, Patty testified that when she lived in Pennsylvania, "people always told me I sounded like a southerner, and in North Carolina they would say I sounded like a Yankee. So sometimes, to distinguish me from other Pattys at the club, people would refer to me as 'Pat from Pennsylvania.'"

Later, Patty would wonder if that is what happened. "It is possible that I did call for Jerry sometime—although definitely not on December 15, 1994—and told his daughter it was Pat from Pennsylvania, just so he'd know which Pat I was."

———————

On February 17, McIntyre began calling Davidson County, North Carolina, investigators to testify about Patty's arrest.

Some of the investigators involved that morning remembered hearing Patty tell Holly she was sorry, but only Detective Suzanne Pearson allegedly heard her make the statement, "If I'd known I would get caught, I never would have brought you into this world."

When Pfeiffer got Pearson on cross, he brought out that she had never made an arrest in a murder case or taken a statement from a murder suspect. He also got her to admit that it was "standard practice for officers to carry a notebook," but she had no explanation for why she didn't have one that morning.

Pearson gave the impression that Patty was having a complete breakdown and was so hysterical that she didn't realize what she was saying when she blurted out her quasi-confession. Pfeiffer, however, brought out that neither Patty nor Holly was crying the majority of the time, and that no one else heard Patty utter those words.

Patty's attorney suggested that with the chaos of the morning, perhaps Detective Pearson didn't hear what she thought she had. When Pearson denied it, he asked about a conversation between Detective Chris Coble and Patty that occurred right next to her.

"Were they whispering?" Pfeiffer asked.

"No," Pearson answered, but she admitted she didn't hear what either of them said.

Pfeiffer asked about a promotion she received after helping to secure Patty's hair samples. Pearson acknowledged that she'd been promoted to sergeant, a position that came with more prestige and better pay and also that if she were to receive another promotion, her rank would rise to that of lieutenant.

"Wouldn't making a significant contribution in this highly publicized case be good for your career?" Pfeiffer asked.

"I wouldn't think so," Pearson answered.

All along, McIntyre had insisted that Patty had "shopped for an alibi," and now he brought in witnesses he believed could prove it.

The first was Ian Murphy, a blacksmith and auto mechanic who had met Patty in the spring of 1994. Murphy testified that Patty called him from jail on the day of her arrest and asked him to look through his old receipts and see if he had done any work on her horses in December 1994. At some point during the conversation, Murphy said Patty began referring to the receipt as a "package."

Later that same day, Murphy said he received a call from Patty's mother, who also mentioned the "package." Murphy had asked Pat Chambers what date she was looking for, and Pat told him December 15, 1994.

Four days later, Patty called Murphy again, and again asked him about the "package." By this time, Murphy had realized he hadn't begun doing work for Patty until sometime in 1995, but that didn't stop her from calling again on July 7, from the Lehigh County Jail. Murphy said it was his impression that Patty wanted him to provide her with a false receipt.

"Did she ask you to give her a false receipt?" Patty's attorney asked.

"No," Murphy admitted; nor did she or her mother ever ask him to lie.

It was the same with TERI OWENS, Patty's hairdresser and the owner of a tanning salon. Patty had never asked her to lie, but . . . her mother had called the shop in the summer of 1995 and asked Teri to check and see if Patty was tanning on December 14 or 15, 1994. Owens immediately knew that Patty could not have been there on the fourteenth because she had closed the shop that day. When she pulled Patty's tanning card, it looked like she might have been there on the fifteenth, but it was hard to tell because the date appeared to have been scratched out and written over.

McIntyre insinuated that Patty had altered the card in an attempt to provide herself with an alibi, but there were other dates on the card that were scratched out and written over as well.

When asked about this later, Patty explained that "it was an honor system at the shop. You would pay for ten tanning sessions, and then when you came in to tan, you'd pull your card and write the date. There were a lot of times when I'd write a date and Teri would tell me it was wrong. She'd say, 'Pat, it's not the tenth, it's the eleventh,' or whatever date it was, so I'd scratch it out and write in the correct date."

Owens also testified that she started new cards for her customers every January and removed the old cards from the shop when she did.

If Patty had forged the card, she would have had only a short opportunity to do so, before she even realized she was a suspect in the case.

Despite the witnesses testifying that they believed Patty was attempting to coerce them into providing her with an alibi, none was willing to say that Patty asked them to give her a false alibi or lie for her.

When later asked about this, Patty claimed it was not her intention to get anyone to lie. "We're talking about six to eight months after the date in question. I didn't know where I might have been that day. I was calling anyplace I could think of: my dentist, my doctor, my friends, my relatives, the tanning salon, the horse farrier, the vet, the bank, *every-body.*"

It hurt Patty to see all these people she once considered her friends testifying against her, but the next witness to take the stand left her heartbroken: her own sister, Sandy.

Patty and Sandy had had a strained relationship from the start. Though the two shared the same mother, Pat Chambers had not raised Sandy but had left her in the custody of her father when the two divorced. As a result, Pat Chambers was not close to Sandy, and, in fact, the two had only recently reconnected when Sandy and her husband, Steve, came to North Carolina in early 1995.

At that time, although Sandy and Patty were virtual strangers, Patty allowed Sandy and Steve to move in with her. It was a trying time for everyone, and the new relationship between the two girls and their mother caused tension in the household. When the situation became too difficult, Patty asked Sandy and Steve to move out. By the time Sandy walked stiffly to the witness stand and took her seat, she and Patty were no longer speaking.

Sandy testified that her mother had brought a gun to her house in May 1995 and asked her to hold it for her—not hide it, hold it. Her mother had said she didn't want the gun in her "possession" and then mentioned something about "the police doing something down at the lake by her house." Her mother was only at her house about ten minutes, Sandy continued, "because she was on her way to work."

The police had, in fact, searched the lake at Pat Chambers's house, and McIntyre was quick to imply that the gun Pat Chambers brought to Sandy's house was the murder weapon. According to him, Pat Chambers was trying to hide the gun because she feared that once the police were done searching the lake, they would also search her house.

Sandy said that later that night, when her husband came home, she had shown him the gun, but he didn't want it in the house and had taken it outside and buried it in their backyard. The next day, Sandy's mother came back to reclaim the weapon and got very upset when she learned that Steve had buried it. According to Sandy, Pat Chambers told her, "Just give me the fucking gun," which surprised her, Sandy said, because her mother didn't "typically use the F-word."

McIntyre showed Sandy a blown-up picture of a .22 Jennings, which made the gun look big and sinister, and then asked, "Is that the gun your mother asked you to hold?"

Sandy couldn't be sure but said, "It looks very, very, close."

When Sandy's husband, Steve, took the stand, he couldn't say it was the same gun either. He recalled Pat's gun as having light-colored square grips, which a .22 Jennings does not have. Nor did Steve's description of the gun match that of Tim Sellers. Sellers remembered Patty's gun as having wooden grips, one of which was missing, and the serial number scratched off, but neither Sandy nor Steve recalled anything about a missing grip or serial number.

Steve also claimed that Sandy told him her mother gave her the gun because she was afraid the police would find it, which tallied perfectly with McIntyre's theory that the police were searching the lake at Pat's house and she was fearful that they would also search her home. The only problem was, the police didn't search the lake at Pat Chambers's house until October 1995—*five months after Pat asked Sandy to hold the gun.*

In truth, Sandy's testimony corroborated that of her mother. Pat Chambers testified she dropped the gun off on her way to the school bus because she could not have the weapon on school property. Sandy testified her mother was on her way to work and didn't want the gun "in her possession."

The most suspicious thing about Sandy and Steve's story, however, was the fact that neither of them told the police about it until one week before they testified. *One week.*

Unlike many other witnesses, when Frank Alonzo took the stand, he appeared to have no desire to embellish his testimony in order to make Patty look worse.

Frank admitted that when he and Patty fought, she sometimes threw Andy up in his face, but as for pictures she kept of him, he knew of only one, a picture of Andy on a horse that she kept in a photo album.

McIntyre tried very hard to get Frank to say Patty was "fixated" on Andy, but Alonzo wouldn't take the bait.

Finally, the prosecutor asked, "When would she look at this album and his picture?"

Alonzo shrugged. "I guess anytime, really."

"OK, no particular time?" McIntyre asked.

"No," Alonzo replied shaking his head.

Frank wouldn't say Patty was fixated on Andy, but he had seen the "love letters" Andy had sent to her. In them, Alonzo said, Andy was attempting to get Patty back.

He acknowledged that he and Patty remained friends after they broke up and continued to call each other occasionally "just to chat." When Patty told him about making the finals in Oklahoma, she asked if he'd sponsor her and put up five hundred dollars so she could go.* Frank declined, but Patty made it to the finals anyway and called him on December 7, 1994, to tell him of her win. She sounded really excited and happy about it, Frank added.

Frank's mother, Rose, who loathed Patty Rorrer, also took the stand to tell of finding the love letters Andy had sent her. In them, Andy had written to Patty, "'One day we'll be together and move to . . .' Wyoming, Montana . . . different places," Rose said with a wave of her hand.

It seemed like strange behavior on Andy's part if he had no feelings for Patty, and even more unusual that Patty didn't jump at his offer if she were so "fixated" on him.

Clyde Liddick, another forensic scientist with the PSP, took the stand and testified that the forest litter collected at the body site contained a number of brown and black hairs. However, he said he failed to note any of the hairs' characteristics because "It's not my job. It's Dr. Jensen's."

---

* An indication of how desperate Patty was to raise funds for the trip to Oklahoma.

Although Liddick's report contained an extensive list of all the items contained in the forest litter, including leaves, grass, stems, leaf fragments, stem fragments, grass fragments, seeds, pieces of fiberglass and red, black, and clear synthetic fibers, nowhere in his report did he mention hairs.

It seemed strange, especially since Dr. Jensen matched one of the hairs found in the forest litter to Patty, and Jim Burke asked him about it. "In that finding, Doctor, that result, you don't list at any time finding hairs, is that correct?"

"Yes. Yes, sir, that's true," Liddick answered.

"Why wouldn't you have listed hairs when you seem to make a relatively exhaustive analysis of other items?" Burke asked.

The witness frowned, shrugged and answered, "I'm not sure."

Moving on, Liddick stated that he had matched the soil from Joann's shoes to that found in the plowed field near the body site, but he could find no match to the flower petals recovered from the soles of her shoes. The soil from the top of Joann's boots matched the soil in the erosion ditch between her body and Alex's rattle, indicating that she had probably fallen there.

Liddick also stated that the soil samples taken from Joann's tan Toyota matched only samples taken from McCarty's parking lot. There was no dirt on the car from the body site.

How was it possible that Joann's vehicle, a small, compact car, low to the ground, could have been driven into those woods and not retained some soil from the area? McIntyre tried to explain it by saying fallen leaves at the site prevented the soil from adhering to the car, but Joann's shoes showed evidence of that soil, and she would have been walking on those same fallen leaves. Joann weighed only 140 pounds. Wouldn't a 2,300-pound vehicle tend to collect even more of this debris?

––––––––––––

Everyone was anxious for the prosecution to complete its case, but McIntyre still needed to present his DNA evidence. The first scientist called was Dr. Harold Deadman of the FBI, who gave the jury a mini-course on the differences between PCR and RFLP DNA testing.

"The RFLP test is much more convincing [than PCR]," Deadman said. "RFLP shows rare and uncommon markers in the DNA, whereas the polymarker DQ alpha tests [used in PCR testing] are not rare markers and are relatively common." For instance, everyone has two eyes, two arms, two legs, two ears, etc., and these are the "common" markers that PCR testing—the testing used on the hairs from Joann's car—reveal. Also, Deadman continued, "the PCR process can be affected by contamination more than the RFLP process."

Of course, Dr. Jensen had contaminated the hairs that Deadman tested, and although the FBI would have preferred to use RFLP testing on them, they didn't have a large enough sample to test that way. Instead, they'd had to use the PCR method to amplify the DNA, and in the process, they amplified the contamination as well.

Dr. Deadman told the jury that Dr. Dizinno performed mitochondrial DNA testing on one of those three contaminated hairs and then mounted the three hairs on glass slides. After Dizinno returned the hairs to Deadman, he immediately saw a "forcibly removed" hair root on one. Extracting a small sample of DNA from the root, Deadman used PCR to amplify the sample and, through nuclear DNA, matched it to Patty Rorrer with the odds of one in thirty-seven thousand.

Deadman, however, could not say the hair found in Joann's car was Patty's hair. "I cannot say Patricia Rorrer is the source of the DNA. I can only say that she is consistent with being that source. It could be her DNA, but it could also be the DNA of someone else who has the same test results."

On cross, Deadman told Patty's attorney that the DNA comparison was made using Patty's blood rather than her hair. He admitted he never compared her hair sample to the hair found in the car because "I was relying on the fact that a match had been made by Mr. Jensen."

Why did Dr. Deadman rely on Dr. Jensen's testing when he had seen firsthand the errors Jensen had made in handling the hair evidence? Regardless, Deadman did rely on it and again explained why the odds were so low for his match to Patricia Rorrer. "The RFLP test shows rare and uncommon markers in the DNA, which is why, with that test, you can see odds of one in a billion or even one in several billion. But with PCR testing, the markers are not rare but relatively common," and the hair had been tested and matched to Patty using PCR, not RFLP.

When Dr. Dizinno took the stand, he too, could not say the DNA was Patty's, only that she was a possible source for it. Dizinno told the jury that he had entered Patty's DNA sequence into the FBI's database and found the agency had never seen that particular sequence before, a result he implied was highly incriminating.

At the time of Patty's trial, however, the FBI database contained only 1,043 individuals, and although these were random, anonymous people, unrelated to each other, the FBI had already found instances in the database of two people sharing the same mitochondrial DNA sequence. In fact, Dizinno admitted, "eighty-nine of [those in the database] have sequences common to more than one person, and 30 percent of the entire database have shared sequences," testimony that indicated the "match" to Patty Rorrer was hardly incriminating or convincing.

"Doctor," Patty's attorney asked, "do you agree or disagree with the following statement: 'The most critical potential source of error in mitochondrial DNA sequencing is in contamination?'"

"Yes," Dizinno answered.

"In fact, did you write that?"

"I think possibly so," Dizinno said.

Yet, Dizinno had conducted his mitochondrial DNA testing on contaminated hair, and the Commonwealth of Pennsylvania was asking a jury to sentence Patricia Rorrer to death on the basis of this evidence.

In addition to the unconvincing DNA results and the lack of an established chain of custody on the hair evidence, Patty's defense also questioned the PSP's unusual habit of hand-delivering evidence in the case. According to the FBI, most agencies customarily send evidence via FedEx because it not only establishes a valid chain of custody but also makes it highly unlikely that anyone would tamper with it. However, between Troopers Robert Egan, Joseph Kocevar, and Joseph Vasquez, there were nine separate instances where evidence was transported and hand-delivered in Patty's case:

- Five times in 1995: April 10, April 18, July 12, November 10 and November 16
- Four times in 1996: June 10, June 24, August 6, and December 11

One of the most critical dates was November 10, 1995, when the police transported Patty's hair samples from North Carolina to the PSP lab and hand-delivered them to Dr. Jensen. North Carolina detective Tony Roberson admitted that he had handed Patty's hair samples over to Trooper Egan in an unsealed evidence envelope.

On the stand, Egan acknowledged that was true but insisted, "We sealed them and then took them back to the North Carolina evidence room."

In questioning Egan about the potential for evidence tampering, Jim Pfeiffer uncovered a mistake made by Trooper Joseph Kocevar. According to Egan, the evidence recovered from Joann's vehicle was not taken directly to the crime lab as was customary but instead was first brought back to the general evidence locker at PSP headquarters by Trooper Kocevar before it was subsequently delivered to Dr. Jensen at the crime lab.

"And in terms of that evidence locker, there's not a log or a list of people that are in and out of that locker?" Pfeiffer asked.

"People in and out of that locker every day. No, sir," Egan answered.

Unfortunately, Pfeiffer didn't have the witness clarify his answer. Was Egan saying that there was no record kept of people entering the evidence locker or simply that people were not in and out of the locker every day?

No one had asked Andy about the screws on his basement door, but now Pfeiffer asked Egan if his investigation revealed that the screws, in fact, *had not* been tampered with.

"No sir, it did not," Egan said.

In questioning him about the search at Patty's house, Egan reiterated that while in Detective Roberson's car, he did not hear Patty say she never owned a gun, but he did believe he heard her say it when they first arrived to conduct the search.

The last witnesses for the prosecution were Lauren and Jim Brenner and Debbie Marchek. Both Brenners testified about Andy working late at their house on December 13 and discussing Patty's phone call to Joann from "the night before." Debbie Marchek recalled for the jury her lunch date with Joann when they went to Pizza Hut on December 5, 1994.

After Debbie stepped off the stand, McIntyre turned to the judge. "Your Honor, Commonwealth rests."

16

Court watchers had mixed feelings about the prosecution's case. Many believed the evidence was overwhelming, thanks in part to McIntyre's creativity and skill in questioning witnesses, as well as Pfeiffer and Burke's inexperience in doing the same. Others, however—those who listened strictly to the evidence—were not so impressed. To them, the case appeared weak, faulty, and almost entirely circumstantial. Despite that, most people in the courtroom believed Patty would be convicted, simply because the state of Pennsylvania, and in particular Lehigh County, demanded it.

Patty continued to remain confident—apparently even more so than the prosecution, who had offered her a deal before the defense began. They would take the death penalty off the table if she agreed to plead guilty.

When Burke and Pfeiffer approached their client with the offer, Patty shook her head adamantly. "No way," she said fiercely. "Absolutely not. I didn't do this, and I'd rather die than plead guilty to something I didn't do."

———————————

The first witness for the defense was Patty and Seth's friend from Cowboys, Jake Beamer. A nice-looking young man, Beamer had traveled to

Pennsylvania at his own expense to provide Patty with an alibi for the night of the crime.

Although the prosecution strongly implied that Beamer was lying because of his friendship with Seth, in truth, Seth and Jake had met only in October 1994, barely two months before the disappearances. Beamer had nothing to gain by testifying and much to lose, as perjury was a criminal offense punishable with jail time.

Beamer described Patty as a nice girl, outgoing and sociable. "She liked to have fun," he said. "She liked to dance." After the first week of December 1994, Patty was "ecstatic" about her win in Oklahoma. "That's all she wanted to talk about."

Pfeiffer handed Jake the December 15, 1994, sign-in sheets for Cowboys, and asked him if Patty's name was on it.

"No," Beamer said, but he had been at the club every Thursday, Friday, and Saturday in December 1994, and his name was not on some of the sign-in sheets either. He knew that signing in was "never a big issue," because he used to work at Cowboys. In fact, most of the time he didn't sign in at the club himself; he just let Seth sign in for both of them.

Pfeiffer handed his witness a ream of sign-in sheets and asked that he point out whenever Seth had signed in for him. Beamer glanced through the pages and identified several instances.

When asked about what occurred in the parking lot after he, Seth, and Patty left the club on December 15, 1994, Beamer's recollections matched those of Patty. He remembered that the heater's blower wasn't working and the smell of the grain in the back of the van made him sick.

On cross, McIntyre first asked Beamer a number of questions concerning dates and times. After eliciting several "I don't remember" and "I don't recall" answers, McIntyre shook his head and frowned.

"How, then," he asked, his voice skeptical, "can you be so sure of what happened three years ago on December 15, 1994?"

"At first, I couldn't be," Jake admitted, but after thinking about it, he had realized that Seth's drill was the weekend of December 9 and his employee Christmas party was the weekend of December 22, so he knew it had to be the weekend in between: December 15.

There was another reason Jake remembered that particular date. While in the club that night, he was called to the front desk because his brother, PAUL, who was not a member, had come to the club, and Jake had to sign him in as a guest. Glancing through the sign-in sheet to find his name, Jake said he discovered that Seth had not signed either of them in, so Jake signed his and Seth's names at the bottom of the sheet, then added his brother's name as a guest next to his.

McIntyre quickly moved on. He asked his witness if he remembered that before Patty's arrest, he (McIntyre), along with Trooper Robert Egan and Detective Tony Roberson, had gone to Beamer's home in North Carolina in an attempt to question him.

Yes, Jake answered, he remembered that.

Upon finding that Jake wasn't home, Detective Roberson had left his card with Beamer's father, and McIntyre now asked why Jake didn't call the detective back.

"I did," Jake insisted. "I left several messages for him, but he never called me back."

"Well, why didn't you call me or Trooper Egan?"

"Because I didn't know who you were. My father told me a Detective Roberson and two men from Pennsylvania came by, but neither you nor Trooper Egan left your card."

Perhaps unable to challenge that, McIntyre let the witness go.

Seth Alden testified in a quiet voice as he recalled first meeting Patty at Cowboys in the fall of 1994 when he asked her to dance. He described her as a very pleasant person who liked to have fun. "We were there to have a good time, and everyone was happy and in a good mood."

Seth said he never heard Patty talk about Andy or Tim or Frank, either, and he never knew her to own a gun. He was at Cowboys every weekend in December except the weekend of his drill, which was December 9 and 10. After Patty had returned from Oklahoma, she was "thrilled and excited" about her win and was "in an extremely good mood the whole month."

Seth recalled that he arrived at Cowboys around 8:00 PM on December 15 and found Patty already there. He went on to describe the events in the parking lot when they left that night—Patty's broken heater and the smell of the grain—exactly as Patty and Jake Beamer had described them.

Seth recalled Patty owning three vehicles at the time of the disappearances: the Dodge van, a Chevy Blazer, and a Ford Thunderbird. Neither the Blazer nor the Thunderbird was running, and in his opinion, the van was not capable of making the one-thousand-mile round trip to Pennsylvania.

McIntyre wasted no time as he rose to begin his cross.

"You love the defendant?" he asked.

Seth nodded. "That's correct."

"You would like this jury to find the defendant not guilty?"

"I would like for that to happen, yes."

"How's your memory, Mr. Alden?"

"Fairly good," Seth replied.

"Well let's test your memory. You were living with Miss Rorrer the day she was arrested. What date was that?"

"June 26, 1997."

"Wrong," McIntyre said, suppressing a grin. "It was June 24, 1997."

The prosecutor then asked Seth why he never told the police he was an alibi for Patty, and Seth said the police never questioned him.

"The only thing I ever got was a letter from you," Seth said, indicating McIntyre.

"You didn't respond to my letter, did you?" McIntyre asked.

"No," Seth admitted, because by then he was advised not to.

When asked why he didn't contact the police himself, Seth said he was reluctant to, for fear of them twisting around anything he said.

"Do you know why Miss Rorrer never mentioned your name as an alibi?" McIntyre asked.

"No, I don't," Seth said.

Of course, Patty insists that she did mention Seth as an alibi but admits it may not have been by name, so McIntyre's question may have been based on the police mistakenly believing that "my boyfriend, Jake, and the dance instructor," were two people rather than three.

Sherry Storm took the stand to tell of the pretty young woman who spent a hundred dollars in a Whitehall convenience store, still insistent that the lady she saw that day was Joann Katrinak.

Ben Stan felt the same way about the girl he saw being led down the railroad tracks behind the Katrinak house on December 15. Despite McIntyre's attempts to get Stan to agree that the woman he saw was not Joann Katrinak, the witness would not budge. It was her, Stan insisted, "or she has a twin sister out there."

Others took the stand as well. Dave Wilson, the Katrinaks' neighbor, testified about the gunshots he heard coming from Front Street in the early morning hours of December 15, gunshots that sounded like they came from a small weapon, possibly a .22. He did not, however, testify about the young woman he saw leaving the Katrinak house in the summer of 1992 when Andy and Joann were already in a relationship, the woman who looked as if she'd been beaten and sat crying in her car for nearly thirty minutes before driving off.

Several other witnesses took the stand as well—including a relative of Frank Alonzo—to testify about a strange vehicle seen parked near the body site around December 15, 1994.

On Wednesday, February 25, the defense called its first expert witness: Doctor Ke Chung Kim, a professor of entomology at Pennsylvania State University. Kim told the jury that insect development in a body can often tell precisely when a person died and that he would explain the process as simply as possible but added, "This is going to take some time."

The comment brought an audible groan from jurors and spectators alike. Much of the DNA evidence had been technical and tedious, but Kim's testimony turned out to be fascinating.

The doctor began by telling the jury that "flies and beetles will lay their eggs in a corpse, but at what point they do depends a lot on the weather conditions." Flies could move only at temperatures above fifty degrees, which provided only a small window of opportunity for insect activity in winter months. After analyzing weather conditions for the area at the time of the crime, as well as a "massive collection of insects" from Joann's body, Dr. Kim came up with only three "windows of opportunity" for insect activity: December 23, 1994; January 14 through 17, 1995; and February 18 through 22. These were the only dates when weather conditions would have allowed for flies to lay their eggs at the body site.

When the doctor determined the age and development of the insects found on Joann, however, he realized there was a problem. The December and January time frames would not have allowed the insects to reach the specific age and development of the insects he found. Apparently, all of the insects were of an age of five days or older. Due to this fact, Kim felt the earliest date the insects could have gotten on the body was February 18, 1995.

"I cannot say the bodies were not there before February 18," Kim said, "but from the insect activity I saw, in my opinion, this was the first opportunity for them to have activity."

McIntyre admired Dr. Kim and had been so impressed when he saw him testify at an earlier trial that he initially contacted him to give evidence as a prosecution witness in the Rorrer case. When Kim's testing did not support McIntyre's theory of the crime, however, the doctor was told his services would not be needed. Still, McIntyre's respect for the scientist was clearly evident in his cross-examination.

"Doctor," McIntyre began, "could the bodies have been there before February 18?"

"I really can't say," Kim answered.

"Can you tell the court when Joann Katrinak died?"

"No, I can only tell you the time when insect activity occurred."

"Doctor," McIntyre concluded, "is it possible the victims were killed and left at the scene on December 15, 1994?"

"It is possible," Kim conceded, "but I have no scientific evidence to support or negate that."

The defense should have explored this testimony in greater detail. If insect activity was occurring in Heidelberg Township on December 23, 1994, and again on January 14, 15, 16, and 17, 1995, then surely the bodies of Joann and Alex would have attracted them. Why did Dr. Kim see no evidence of insect activity for these dates? What was it about the insects' age and development that led him to believe the bodies might not have been there before February 18, 1995?

When Patty's stepfather, Ray Chambers, took the stand, he corroborated his wife's testimony by telling the jury that Andy had called at 3:00 AM and his wife had called Patty immediately after. He knew Patty was home because he had listened as the two talked. Ray also testified about Patty's van, claiming she could not have driven it to Pennsylvania because of the mechanical problems. She had purchased a new universal joint at the local AutoZone on December 10, 1994, and he replaced it for her on December 17. He still had the AutoZone receipt, because the part had come with a lifetime guarantee.

If nothing else, Ray Chambers's testimony tended to prove that Patty was telling the truth about needing to replace the universal joint in her van. The prosecution was alleging that Patty had left for Pennsylvania on December 12, which would have given her only one day—December 11—to replace the part. Perhaps because that seemed unlikely, the prosecution preferred to imply that Patty was lying about the bad U-joint and spent a significant amount of time trying to discredit Ray Chambers's AutoZone receipt.

Patty's old friend Kathy Barber flew in from Washington State to testify on Patty's behalf. Barber told the court that in 1988, she moved from Allentown to Washington, and Patty accompanied her on the trip. At the time, Kathy said, Patty and Andy's relationship was coming to an end, and Patty was considering moving across the country with her.

"Patty wasn't happy in her relationship with Andy," Kathy said, but by 1994, Patty appeared extremely happy. "Everything seemed to be going good in her life. She rarely mentioned Andy, although she did tell me about him getting married."

McIntyre had few questions for the witness, but he did ask her if she would agree that people change.

"Somewhat," Kathy answered.

When she finally stepped down from the witness stand, both Kathy and Patty were in tears.

The defense's DNA expert, Dr. William Shields, was a professor of biology at the State University of New York and the operator of a genetics laboratory. Although McIntyre had had no objection when Dr. Kim was qualified as an expert witness, he strongly opposed Dr. Shields being classified as one.

Under questioning, McIntyre brought out that Shields had a lucrative side job testifying in court and was paid dearly for that testimony.

"Yes," Shields said, "that's true." In fact, he added, he sometimes made double his professor's salary doing so.

Judge Wallitsch overruled McIntyre's objection, saying it was up to the jury to decide whether Shields was an expert in his field or not.

Dr. Shields attacked the FBI's DNA analysis of the hairs, especially the mitochondrial testing, and told the jury that the DNA in Patty's hair was not as rare as the prosecution would like them to believe. Challenging the FBI's odds of one in thirty-seven thousand, Dr. Shields testified that he had come up with his own figure: one in thirteen thousand.

On cross, McIntyre brought out that Shields had never tested the hairs from Joann's car and asked how he could then say there was contamination in the mitochondrial DNA?

Shields didn't feel his failure to test the hair was a problem, since the hair was already known to be contaminated. "Contamination results in wrong answers," he said with a shrug. "Even the FBI states that."

The next day, court spectators got a chance to see the prosecutor in rare form. Having just learned that the defense intended to call three alibi witnesses: Joyce Reagan, Audrey Brussels and Leroy Rouse, McIntyre was furious. At sidebar, the irate prosecutor asked Judge Wallitsch to disallow their testimony.

"We would never have presented our case the way we did if we thought these people were named alibis," McIntyre argued. "If you remember, we sloughed over them. We had officers testify that they interviewed these people, and the defendant couldn't be excluded. Now we think it will look bad for us to have these people brought in, and we believe we had the right to rely on the fact that they were not named as alibis."

After listening to thirty minutes of argument, Judge Wallitsch decided to allow McIntyre to examine the witnesses "in camera"* to determine what they planned to say.

Without the jury being present, Patty's neighbor, Joyce Reagan, testi-fied that Patty had called her between 5:30 and 6:00 AM on the morning of December 16, and Audrey Brussels, the woman from the Exxon sta-tion recalled the problem that occurred with the kerosene pump. Patty's grain dealer, Leroy Rouse, however, was nowhere to be found. He had assured the defense that he would be there, but he was not present in the courtroom.

"I think he had a death in the family and supposedly is going to be driving up here," Pfeiffer told Judge Wallitsch. "We've had no contact with him. He hasn't arrived yet."

When the in camera concluded, Wallitsch ruled to allow Reagan and Brussels to testify in front of the jury, much to McIntyre's displeasure.

"Your Honor," the prosecutor shouted, "we strenuously object to both of them."

Reagan and Brussels were not the only witnesses McIntyre objected to that day. MIKE SENSER, a former Pennsylvania state trooper, had been hired by the defense to go through Patty's phone records and determine how many days reflected no long-distance calls.

From June 1, 1994, through February 1, 1995, Senser found a total of eighty-six days when Patty had made no long-distance calls. There

---

* A hearing conducted in private, often held in the judge's chambers.

were two five-day gaps, four four-day gaps, two three-day gaps, and nine two-day gaps.

McIntyre objected to Senser testifying to this, telling the judge, "The records are in evidence, Your Honor, and the jury can figure that out for themselves."

Judge Wallitsch, however, shook his head. He would let the witness testify, he told McIntyre, because "there was some inference [from the prosecution] that maybe that [four-day gap on Patty's phone bill in December 1994] was one of the only times."

———————————

When court adjourned for lunch, most of the gallery stayed put. The courtroom was packed beyond capacity in anticipation of Patty testifying, and few spectators were willing to risk losing their seats. When court reconvened, those who had waited were rewarded for their patience.

"Defense calls Patricia Lynne Rorrer," Pfeiffer boomed.

Patty, dressed in a black suit and white blouse, looked very ladylike as she walked calmly to the witness stand, took her seat and shifted to a more comfortable position. She would testify in a low, soft voice, often turning to talk directly to the jury.

Patty began with a brief history of her life: her birth in Phillipsburg, New Jersey, in 1964, the family's move to North Carolina, and the death of her father when she was fifteen. She quit school at sixteen, she said, to get a job and help pay bills. She told the jury of the many places she had lived, the numerous jobs she had held, and the men she had loved.

She described her relationship with Andy and the eventual deterioration of it. "He's a nice guy," she said, "but we just weren't making it as a couple." She said they remained friends after the breakup and tried to keep in touch with calls and letters.

She spoke of the phone call in the spring of 1994 when Andy told her he was married and expecting a child. She had not been upset by the news; she was happy for him. She had a new man in her life, and she was glad Andy had found someone special, too.

She reminisced about her involvement with horses and how they became her entire life. She admitted renting the barn near Heidelberg Township but denied she was familiar with the nearby trails or regularly rode them.

The phone call with Joann had occurred on December 7, Patty said, and no, she was not angry when Joann hung up on her. In fact, she kind of laughed about it, assuming Joann was uptight because of the new baby.

Patty said she had "court duty" on December 12, then met a friend for lunch before driving to her mother's house. She believed she stayed at home on December 13, but on December 14 she bought kerosene at the Exxon station and stopped at Mike Gaines's for gas. She bought grain on December 15, and having realized her key ring with the van's gas cap key was missing, went back to the gas station to see if anyone had found it. When she returned home, she saw Joyce Reagan in the yard getting her mail and waved to her. That night she went to dance class at Cowboys and then met Seth and Jake inside the club. Her recollection of what transpired in the parking lot afterward tallied perfectly with theirs.

When Pfeiffer asked her about the day the police drove her to the hospital to take blood and hair samples, Patty began to cry softly.

"I was seven and a half months pregnant," she said, "and I was upset by what was happening." It didn't help matters that the nurses at the hospital could not find a vein to draw blood. "I'm scared to death of needles," she said.

Patty often broke down and cried during the proceedings, but court watchers noticed that she always regained her composure quickly. When later asked about this, Patty shook her head.

"That was my lawyer's fault," she said. "They told me not to show emotion because the jury might interpret it as remorse. I remember one time—the prosecution put up a picture of Alex's rattle, and I started to cry because Holly had the same one, and Jim actually kicked me under the table to stop."

Perhaps her attorneys thought they were doing the right thing with these instructions, but it turned out to be a huge mistake. At times,

Patty appeared hard, even cold, and both the jury and the public rarely saw her human side. Her voice betrayed it, however. On the stand, Patty testified in such a soft and quiet manner that spectators found themselves leaning forward just to hear her. And as Pfeiffer brought her direct examination to a close, the entire gallery was sitting on the edge of their seats.

"Patricia, did you kidnap and murder Joann Katrinak?"

"No, sir," Patty replied firmly, shaking her head.

"Did you kidnap and murder Alex Katrinak?"

"No, sir."

"Would you lie to us today?"

"No, sir."

As Pfeiffer sat down, those in the courtroom settled back in their seats. Patty had done remarkably well on the stand, but she had been answering questions posed by her own counsel. They were eager to see how she'd hold up under the wrath of Michael McIntyre.

McIntyre rose and got right to the point.

"Do you have any explanation for how your hairs ended up in Joann Katrinak's vehicle?" he began.

"I don't believe it is my hair, sir."

Wasn't it clear that Andy suspected her of having something to do with the disappearance of his wife and son when he called her mother at 3:00 AM on December 15? the prosecutor asked.

No, Patty said. Andy had used the words "grasping at straws," and she didn't think he was accusing her. She thought he was wondering if she were the reason Joann had left. She had not realized she was a suspect in Andy's eyes until Trooper Egan interviewed her on May 4, 1995.

Ignoring her answer, McIntyre continued. If she knew Andy suspected her, why didn't she establish an alibi after she talked to him?

Again, Patty denied knowing Andy suspected her. She wasn't aware of that until after May 1995, at which point she did begin trying to establish an alibi. She called different people and places in an attempt to find out if she had been there on December 15.

"But you never went to Cowboys to look at the sign-in sheets, did you?" McIntyre asked. She never contacted people who might have seen her at the club that night, never mentioned being at Cowboys or seeing Seth Alden and Jake Beamer. She had done none of that, had she?

Patty insisted that was not true. She had mentioned Cowboys in her first interview and Seth and Jake in every one after that. She didn't check the sign-in sheets because she didn't think she needed to establish an alibi; she hadn't committed the crimes. She had no explanation for why her early interview reports didn't mention Cowboys, Seth, or Jake, because she had mentioned all three.

In fairness, McIntyre knew the police didn't include everything said at an interview in their reports. Ayers had already testified that the Cowboys conversation did occur but he'd made no mention of it in his report, and Trooper Egan testified he didn't note Jake Beamer's name on his May 4 report, although he admitted that Patty had mentioned him.

McIntyre made much of Patty's remark that she was "going to the electric chair" and accused her of having actually researched the punishment for murder in the state of Pennsylvania. Pennsylvania, however, didn't even use the electric chair in 1994; they used lethal injection. Patty knew she was going to be charged with capital murder and "going to the chair" is a common euphemism for the death penalty, regardless of the method actually used.

McIntyre accused Patty of lying about buying grain on December 15 because she couldn't produce a grain receipt. "You were ordered to keep grain receipts, weren't you?" he asked.

"Yes," Patty replied calmly, "and to produce them upon demand." Twice, she had produced them when asked and afterward was no longer required to retain them. An SPCA officer had come in December 1994 and February 1995, so the December 15 receipt would have been discarded after one of those dates, long before the police came looking for it.

Patty's phone call to Joann had always been troublesome for the prosecution. Although Andy continued to maintain that Patty had called on December 12, all the evidence pointed to the call occurring on December 7, just as Patty said. Perhaps because he could not produce evidence to the contrary, McIntyre suddenly turned to his witness and asked, "Were you in Pennsylvania on December 12, 1994, and did you call Andy from up here?"

It was a telling moment; a literal admission that the prosecution had doubts about their theory of the crime. Throughout the trial, McIntyre had maintained that the phone call was the trigger for the murders and that Patty, intent on killing Joann, had hidden her trip to Pennsylvania. If she was already in Pennsylvania at the time of the phone call, why would she have hidden the fact that she was traveling north? She would have had no way of knowing that an argument with Joann would lead to her murder.

Patty appeared dumbfounded by the suggestion and adamantly denied it.

Reminding her of her taped phone call with Andy in which she told him she had numerous people who could verify she was at Cowboys the night Joann and Alex disappeared, McIntyre asked, "Were all those people who didn't provide you with an alibi lying?"

No, Patty replied, she would not say they were lying, but she did believe some of them were either "mistaken or interpreted things differently."

Hadn't she told the police she never owned a gun? Wasn't that a lie?

"I never said that," Patty insisted. What she had said was "I don't own a gun" (because at the time she didn't) and "I no longer own that gun anymore."

Well, what about her claim that she hadn't been in Pennsylvania at all during 1994? Wasn't that a lie, McIntyre asked?

No, Patty said, "That was an honest mistake." She had been thinking about when she had last been in the Bethlehem/Catasauqua area and had simply forgotten about the horse auction in Quakertown.

McIntyre was an aggressive interrogator, and he had a habit of cutting Patty off in mid-sentence and refusing to let her finish when she tried to explain her answers. Often, Patty kept right on talking anyway, an action that infuriated the prosecutor. At one point, a frustrated McIntyre turned to the bench and demanded that Judge Wallitsch admonish her.

Wallitsch leaned over and patiently told Patty to answer the questions "yes or no."

"I'm trying to," Patty said pleadingly.

Wallitsch smiled at her. "Just answer the questions yes or no, and then go ahead and explain if you feel the need to."

It was hardly the admonishment McIntyre wanted, and his annoyance with the judge was clearly evident.

Moving on to her June 24 arrest, Patty began to cry as she insisted she never made the incriminating statements Detective Suzanne Pearson testified to. Yes, she admitted, she did tell her daughter that she was sorry, but only because Holly was so upset and Patty felt responsible. Her words were meant to soothe and comfort her daughter, not apologize for murdering Joann and Alex, and she vehemently denied saying anything about being "caught" or wishing she had never brought her daughter into the world. "I would never say that," Patty said, "because there is nothing that could ever make me wish Holly was not born. Nothing."

Again, McIntyre reminded her of her taped conversation with Andy and the many witnesses she had claimed would come to court with her.

"Where are those witnesses?" he asked sarcastically.

Patty blamed the lack of alibi witnesses on the police. They waited so long to talk to them that by the time they got around to it, the people were no longer sure of dates. She insisted she never tried to get anyone to lie for her.

The prosecutor suddenly switched tracks. "Do you get angry very easily, ma'am?"

"No, sir," she answered.

Had she gotten angry when Joann Katrinak hung up on her?

"No. I laughed about it."

"Well, why didn't you ever call Andy again?"

"Because I was respecting his wife's wishes."

"Do you like to get the last word in, ma'am?"

"No, sir," Patty replied.

"Haven't you been trying to get the last word with me, with every question I've asked you?"

"I took an oath to tell the whole truth, not just part of it."

"If you didn't get the last word, would that irritate you at all?" McIntyre continued.

"No, sir. You made me cry; you didn't get me irritated."

"Joann Katrinak didn't give you a chance to get the last word in on December 12, 1994, did she?"

"No, sir, but it wasn't December 12. It was December 7."

"But you got the last word on December 15, 1994, didn't you, ma'am?"

"No, sir," Patty insisted. "I've never talked to her after that date."

McIntyre stared at her for a moment and then lowered his voice. "Here's what I want to know. After you killed Joann Katrinak, did you kill that baby or just leave him there to die?"

Patty began to cry at the question. "Sir, I would not kill somebody, and I definitely would not kill somebody I never met. I did not know the woman."

McIntyre stared at her, then slowly shook his head back and forth. "I have nothing further for this witness," he said with disgust.

———————

Patty had spent four days on the witness stand, and despite McIntyre's grueling cross-examination, she had done quite well. At no time had she come across as the tough, mean, brute of a woman McIntyre so desperately tried to portray.

The defense rested after Patty stepped down, and McIntyre called only one rebuttal witness: Dr. Mark Stoneking, a professor of anthropology at Penn State.

Stoneking had been working with mitochondrial DNA since 1989, but this would be his first experience as an expert witness and the first time he was testifying about this new science.

Stoneking stated that the validation tests for DNA showed that you could introduce any contaminant to it, and it would not alter the original DNA. In other words, you could put blood, saliva, semen, or any other bodily fluid on a strand of hair, and it would not change the hair owner's DNA.

Stoneking had not personally tested the hair from Joann's car, and McIntyre inquired about this.

"Do you know of a better way to verify whether or not Dr. Dizinno made any mistakes in the mitochondrial DNA testing of those three hairs, other than to retest the hairs?" he asked.

"No, that would be the best way to do it."

"From Dr. Dizinno's notes and reports, did you find any evidence of contamination on those three hairs?"

"Based on the information that was given, no, I didn't."

That seemed strange, since the three unmounted hairs found in Joann's car were proven to be contaminated by Dr. Jensen.

Asked about using mitochondrial DNA as evidence, Stoneking took great pains to emphasize that it should be used only as an exclusion tool.

"We certainly would never say that [just] because a mitochondrial DNA sequence matches the known [suspect in a crime], that the known [suspect] must have contributed the sample. Mitochondrial DNA is a test for exclusion and can be compared with the old ABO blood typing. A known blood sample [from a suspect] could be the same type as [a sample] left at a crime scene, but there's no way to say [the crime scene sample] is the known [suspect's] blood. If, however, the known [suspect's] blood type is different [from that at the crime scene], you can exclude them."

So in other words, Stoneking was asked, mitochondrial DNA is not exclusive to its owner?

That was true, Stoneking agreed. "We would never say everyone has a unique mitochondrial DNA sequence."

17

Closing arguments in the case of *Commonwealth vs. Patricia Rorrer* began on the morning of March 5, 1998, when a visibly shaken Jim Burke rose and turned toward the jury. Perhaps he felt what many others did, that despite any amount of reasonable doubt, in the end, it was not going to matter. Lehigh County expected a conviction, and there was little doubt they were about to get one.

"There's a lot of pressure here," Burke began. "Family and friends of the victim, police officers, people who believe they arrested the right person. I understand there's a tremendous pull for citizens who want to help those people out. But remember, nobody saw Patty's van in Pennsylvania."

The prosecution had made a big deal over nobody seeing Patty at Cowboys Nitelife—with the exception of Jake and Seth—but Burke reminded the jury that nobody saw her in Pennsylvania either, and no one took the stand to say she was not in North Carolina.

He touched on Joann's Toyota, asking if they believed it was possible the car was driven up the railroad bed three hundred and twenty-three feet into the woods. He reminded them that Joann had defensive injuries and was bleeding profusely. Why was there no blood in the car? Why no soil from the body site in or on the car? Why were no fingerprints found in it? No horse hair, no goat hair, no nothing.

If this was a "fatal attraction," he asked, why didn't Patty make a move for Andy after the murders? "Why didn't she call him? Why didn't she come up here?"

The prosecution wanted to say they had proof Patty committed these murders because there were no long-distance phone calls on her telephone bill and she didn't write a check during that time. They said she was guilty because her only alibi witnesses were friends and family. But, all of that was true of Andy as well.

The lack of long-distance phone calls meant nothing, Burke said, reminding the jurors that there were 86 days out of 245 when Patty made no long-distance calls from her phone.

The prosecution claimed the police "systematically eliminated all other suspects until only Patty was left standing." Was that true, Burke asked?

"Jhared Starr, was he systematically eliminated? He said he worked until 2:00 PM that day, then went to a bar and home to his mother's house. But the police didn't question any of the bar patrons. They didn't question his mother."

The prosecution claimed there was no sexual assault involved in Joann's death, but how did they know? Her clothing was in disarray, and Dr. Mihalakis admitted that any biological evidence from a sexual assault would have disappeared or disintegrated before the police found the bodies. They claimed there was no robbery either, but Joann's purse was missing.

He reminded the jurors that the prosecution admitted that whoever cut the phone line had to be familiar with the Katrinak house. But Patty was not familiar with the house. She had only stayed there for one or two nights, back in February 1991, and at that time there was no phone wire in the house. Andy did not install a phone until the following August.

He touched on Tim Sellers's lack of credibility and mentioned Patty's sister and brother-in-law, Sandy and Steve. "They didn't remember the serial number being scratched off the gun or the missing grip, and they claimed the police were searching the lake at Pat Chambers's house five months before it ever happened."

Burke appeared saddened when he spoke of Patty's mother. "[The prosecution] treated her like an unindicted co-conspirator," he said, shaking his head. "They didn't have enough evidence against Patty, so let's put her mom on trial too."

The defense, however, reserved their harshest criticism for the PSP evidence men.

Dr. Thomas Jensen: He didn't reference size, shape, or character-istics of any of the hairs in his reports. He never talked about the size of diameter or the medulla—whether it's consistent or not, absent or present—and he didn't use gloves when doing his analysis.

He used his own method to determine Patty's hair length in 1994, and he mounted the car hairs before measuring them. Burke then detailed the complexity of this task, telling the jury about Jensen making copies, tracing out missing portions of the hair, and using a wheel division to measure them.

"He had all the time in the world to do all of this but didn't have time to test a hair found in the victim's hand?" Burke shouted. "A hair that was not consistent with either Patty or Joann."

Shaking his head, he moved on to Trooper Coia of the R&I unit. Coia never labeled where he found the hairs in Joann's car, and he deemed any hairs that looked like they came from the Katrinaks as insignificant. "Why didn't he deem those six seat-back hairs insignifi-cant? He initially thought they came from Andy."

He reminded the jury that right up until December 1997—two months before Patty went on trial—police were still taking hair samples from people to test. "If they still weren't sure then [that it was Patty's hair in Joann's car], how can they be sure now?"

When Jim Burke finally concluded his closing and sat down, Patty felt confident. As long as the jury members used their common sense, she didn't believe they could possibly convict her.

McIntyre didn't see it that way. "Those hairs had roots," the pros-ecutor insisted, "roots that were healthy."

He told the jury that the baby's death was a result of anger at Andy because Patty heard Andy tell Joann, "I don't want to talk to her." Andy, however, had never said any such thing. In fact, he had testified he had never said a word during the call.

Again, McIntyre praised Andy for refusing to move Joann's car, saying if he had, "those hairs probably would have been destroyed."

As for Patty's alibi witnesses, Seth Alden and Jake Beamer: well, McIntyre didn't think Seth was a bad guy, just "young and naive and someone Patty could manipulate." Apparently, the prosecutor thought it very telling that all of Patty's boyfriends before Seth were older. As for Jake Beamer, his motivation was easy to determine. He was Seth's best friend.

McIntyre told the jury that they would not see the police and scientific reports, because "the law believes you'll put more reliance on the reports than on the people who testified."

Well, shouldn't they? The reports were taken within hours and days of the events when memories were fresh and intact. For those testifying, it was years later. Perhaps McIntyre might have been reminded of that old Chinese proverb, "The palest ink is better than the best memory."

Those listening carefully to McIntyre's closing soon realized that the prosecutor often contradicted himself or even changed his theory for the crime. For instance, McIntyre had argued all along that Patty's call to Joann occurred on December 12, but, unable to prove that, he now told the jury that "the date of the call really didn't matter." Nor, apparently, did the location from where Patty placed the call. The authorities always maintained that Patty called Andy from North Carolina, but now McIntyre told them that Patty was "up here" when she made the call. In the very next breath, however, the prosecutor contradicted himself again. Patty, McIntyre said, "had tried to reach Andy in October and November, and again on December 7, without success. By December 12, she was desperate to speak to him, and when Joann wouldn't let her, Patty hopped in her van and sped to Pennsylvania."

Well, which is it? Was Patty "up here," when she called Andy's house, or was she in North Carolina? Apparently, Mr. McIntyre didn't know.

Motive seemed to be a stickler for the prosecution as well. Throughout the trial, their contention had been that the motive for the murders was Patty's anger over Joann's hang-up. Now, however, McIntyre told the jury that Patty, filled with anger and jealousy toward Joann, killed her not because of the hang-up call but because "Patty was thirty years old at the time, single, and not even in a relationship. Joann had everything Patty didn't have: a husband and a baby."

It seemed no one knew what happened to Joann and Alex on December 15, 1994. Like a child with a sticky ball, the prosecutor threw out one scenario after another, hoping something would stick. The entire case appeared to be based on speculation, yet they were asking a jury to sentence Patty to death on such.

After arguing that Patty killed Joann because her biological clock was running out, McIntyre went on to enumerate the other reasons they should find her guilty. Patty knew where Joann lived (as did Andy). She knew the Heidelberg Township area (as did Andy). She had only friends and family to alibi her (as did Andy). She had a lifestyle that enabled her "to just get up and go that day" (as did Andy).

Pacing before the jury, the prosecutor suddenly paused and turned to them. "She doesn't have the gun," he said. "Think of how powerful that is. That's almost as good as having the weapon! She had it; she doesn't have it." Then, spinning on his heels to face the defendant, the prosecutor suddenly shouted, "Where's the gun, Patty?"

McIntyre was a master showman in the courtroom and adept at keeping a jury hanging on his every word. Now they watched as he set up a huge poster board and smiled. "I don't know if you ever watch David Letterman," he said, unveiling his prop, "but he sometimes goes into the top ten list." Placing the poster on an easel, the jurors read the heading: "TOP TEN LIES PATTY TOLD." Beginning to read, McIntyre reminded the jury that each of the entries represented "consciousness of guilt" on Patty's part.

1. I don't have dirty blonde hair.
2. I haven't been to Pennsylvania since 1991.
3. The FBI hasn't investigated my alibi.
4. I can give you the number of the club and the people if you want to check them yourself.
5. I have twenty to thirty people who will testify for me.

6. I never heard of Heidelberg Township.
7. I never rode my horses on the road or the trails.
8. I never owned a handgun.
9. Tim Sellers bought the gun.
10. Me and Tim bought the gun.

"Either she's guilty," McIntyre said, "or she's the most unlucky person who ever walked this earth. She has the same hair color, and length of hair, *the same DNA*, and the same type of gun as the killer."

Astoundingly, Patty's attorneys did not object to this portion of the prosecution's closing. McIntyre was clearly arguing facts not in evidence and was unable to prove any of those allegations, but Patty's counsel remained silent at the defense table.

McIntyre ended his closing with the following statement: "If you can find Patricia Rorrer untruthful in one thing, then you can find her untruthful in all things. If you can find any witness was untruthful in one thing, then you can find that they were untruthful in everything they said."

It was a strange statement that, if taken literally, should have rendered the entire trial void. There were very few people who had not contradicted themselves, changed their story, or testified to something that was known to be untrue. And, although not a witness and not under oath, that included prosecutor McIntyre as well.

All that remained was for the judge to charge the jury and deliberations to begin. For the first time since the trial opened, the jurors had been instructed to bring their suitcases to court, the decision having been made to sequester them during deliberations. No one was willing to render a guess as to how long that might be. The trial had lasted an entire month, and the jury had heard more than one hundred witnesses and seen more than two hundred exhibits.

Patty tried to remain calm, but her nerves were frazzled and she had little reason to hope. Her attorneys were aware of the public's sentiment toward their client, and they were desperately trying to prepare her for the worst.

After deliberating for less than two hours, the jury buzzed in, summoning the bailiff. No one got excited, assuming they either had a question or wanted to see an exhibit, but it turned out to be neither. Incredibly, the jury had reached a verdict.

It took some time to gather the main players. No one had expected the jury to return so quickly. Patty arrived in the courtroom in tears and took her seat next to her attorneys, her left leg jittering uncontrollably beneath the table. Joann's family was present, holding hands in the gallery, a row of solidarity. Soon, Judge Wallitsch arrived and, perhaps seeing Patty's distress, did not order her to stand.

"The foreman will read the verdict."

"We the jury, in the above-entitled action, find the defendant, Patricia Lynne Rorrer, guilty of the crime of murder in the first degree."

For a moment, Patricia's breath caught, and she was unable to breathe. Her mind reeled, incapable of comprehending what she had just heard. Breaking into sobs, she turned toward the gallery in search of her family but instead, locked eyes with a woman named Margaret Sneary. Margaret was a journalist for a local newspaper who had sat through the entire trial, listening as each witness testified and becoming more and more troubled by what she heard. By the time Patricia Rorrer turned and locked eyes with her, Margaret Sneary had no doubt that she had just witnessed the wrongful conviction of an innocent woman.

Patty had no idea who Margaret was, but finding her eyes glued to her, she instinctively mouthed the words, "I didn't do this."

Much to her surprise, the journalist immediately answered back, "I know."

The moment passed, and soon Patricia spotted her mother, whose face bore a look of absolute agony. She sat clinging to Seth Alden, who appeared dazed and confused himself. Only little Holly seemed oblivious to what had just happened. Seeing her mother looking, the little girl waved excitedly and blew her a kiss.

Now a convicted double murderer, Patty had no doubt the State of Pennsylvania was about to put her to death. It was so hard to grasp.

So utterly unbelievable. The jury's words kept reverberating through her head: "Guilty, Guilty, Guilty." As she sat there weeping, all she could think about was her precious Holly, the child she would never see grow up.

―――――――

Having been convicted, it was now time for stage two of the trial, the penalty phase. Patty was morose and told her attorneys she would not testify again. She didn't care if the state killed her; she'd rather die anyway.

Although Pfeiffer and Burke understood her feelings—that keen sense of hopelessness—they were terrified by her attitude. If the jury caught a glimpse of it, they were certain they would have no problem sentencing her to death.

Everyone tried to talk to her—her mother and step-pop, her uncle Telly, Seth, even the jail's chaplain—but Patty was not listening. When one of her attorneys mentioned Holly, Patty glared at him.

"Don't you do that, Jim," Patty shouted. "Don't you dare bring Holly into this."

That, however, is just what her attorneys did. When they brought Holly into the room, and Patty saw the little girl's face light up, she folded. Scooping her daughter into her arms, she realized she had to fight, "if only for Holly's sake."

Patty's attorneys were praying for just one juror to vote life. In Pennsylvania, a unanimous verdict was needed to sentence someone to death, so in order to spare Patty's life, they needed at least one juror to refuse to vote death. According to Patty, Jim Pfeiffer was especially scared.

"He kept telling me that all we needed was one, but he also tried to prepare me for the worst by reminding me several times that Lehigh County was a "hanging county."

The sentencing phase was brief. Patty took the stand in tears and immediately disregarded her attorney's advice. Maintaining her innocence, she told the jury that she understood they believed they had done the right thing, "but all you did was create more victims," she said sadly.

Others took the stand as well, including Andy's father, who asked the jury to spare Patty's life. McIntyre didn't press hard for the death penalty and neither did Joann's family, but Patty and her attorneys were still surprised when the jury came back with a unanimous verdict of life without parole rather than death.

"I asked Jim why he thought they didn't give me death if they believed I committed this awful crime, and he told me he thought it was because I looked each of them in the eye and told them they were wrong. 'They might be having doubts,' Jim said, 'but they'll let the next jury figure that out.'"

"You mean on appeal?" Patty had asked.

"Yes," Pfeiffer answered.

"How long will that take?"

"At least five years."

"I was devastated," Patty recalled, "Because I didn't think I'd be able to do one year in prison, let alone five."

18

Within days of her conviction, Patty was sent to SCI Muncy in central Pennsylvania and assigned inmate number 0E2170. Opened in 1920 as a training school for incarcerated girls, Muncy was one of only two female prisons in the state, housing both the youthful offender program and the women's death row. Muncy's gothic stone structures were built on fertile farmland and stood amid towering trees and lush shrubbery. Had it not been for the razor wire fence surrounding it, the prison might have resembled a small college campus.

Patty's first two years at Muncy were tough. The nature of her crime left her vulnerable to abuse from other inmates, and with her remaining family and friends living in North Carolina, she had little local support. In the blink of an eye, her once-normal life had turned into a living nightmare. Although her parents tried to visit when they could, Seth rarely did. He'd been stunned by Patty's conviction and left to raise a toddler daughter on his own. He relied heavily on Pat and Ray Chambers for help, leaving Holly to stay with her grandparents while he worked. Once a month Pat and Ray brought the little girl to Pennsylvania to visit her mother, but Seth, at twenty-six years old, quickly moved on with his life.

Pat Chambers occasionally received a call from Margaret Sneary, the journalist who had locked eyes with Patty in the courtroom. Margaret had not been able to forget the scared young woman she watched stand trial, and she felt compelled to keep tabs on her. Whenever she called, she always asked after Patty's welfare, and Pat always relayed the messages to her daughter. After a while, Patty told her mother that she'd like to meet this journalist, and Margaret made the trip to Muncy. Soon a close relationship developed between the two women.

Patty could not have asked for a better champion than Margaret Sneary, for Margaret was nothing if not tenacious. She pored over thousands of documents relating to the case and, upon discovering the myriad problems that plagued it, became even more convinced of Patty's innocence. In no time at all, Margaret had become obsessed with the case. She began making phone calls, interviewing witnesses, and traveling down to North Carolina. She sent requests for information through the Freedom of Information Act, and eventually quit her job to devote all her time to the case. Patty had high hopes of overturning her conviction with Margaret in the picture, but her first round of appeals ended in failure.

As depressing at that was, back in North Carolina, Seth had met a woman he wanted to marry and decided he no longer wanted Pat and Ray Chambers to have contact with his daughter. Holly had practically lived with her grandparents since Patty's arrest, and they were worried and upset by Seth's decision. Seth wouldn't budge, however, and Pat Chambers had no choice but to go into court and enforce her grandparental rights. The judge granted her one weekend a month with Holly, and she and Ray continued to take the little girl to Pennsylvania to visit with her mother.

The stress of Patty's arrest and conviction had taken its toll on Pat Chambers's health, and on March 9, 2001, at only age fifty-nine, she died suddenly of a massive heart attack. Her mother's death devastated Patty and sent her into a downward spiral of depression, but for Seth, things could not have worked out better. Ray Chambers was not Patty's biological father and thus had no grandparental rights where Holly was concerned. Seizing the opportunity, Seth cut Ray off from all contact with Holly, and although Patty fought to retain her parental rights, Seth eventually took her to court and had her rights severed. Holly was only five years old at the time, and after that, neither Patty nor Ray ever had contact with her again.

It was a terrible time for Patty, who was mourning both the loss of her mother and her daughter, but Margaret was still looking into her case and slowly making progress. She persuaded a local attorney, Craig Neely, to help, and together, they had uncovered a PSP report that had never been handed over to the defense. The report was vague, listing the witness' name and age—Walter Troutman, fifty-five—but no contact information. The report, written by Trooper Robert Egan and dated November 27, 1995, described Joann and Andy arguing violently on the day Joann disappeared.

It was an important discovery, because Andy had always maintained that he never saw Joann again after leaving for work that morning, but it took Craig and Margaret some time to locate Walter Troutman. Trooper Egan had not only failed to include any contact information for the man, but he had also provided an incorrect name and age for him as well. Eventually, Margaret and Craig learned that the witness' actual name was Traupman, not Troutman, and his correct age sixty-eight rather than fifty-five. Even more alarming, they also discovered that Egan had not only misidentified this important witness but had completely ignored the crucial information Traupman was trying to reveal.

On the afternoon of December 15, 1994, Walter Traupman had witnessed a heated argument between a man and a woman that concerned the paternity of a baby. The incident occurred around 1:00 PM on Lloyd Street in the city of Bethlehem, and as the terrified woman, who wore a black fuzzy jacket, sat in her car, the man pounded on the windshield screaming for her to open the door. At one point, Traupman heard the man yell, "What do you mean it's not my kid?"

Traupman, concerned because he had never seen anyone in such a fit of rage, immediately called the Allentown police. They told him the incident was not in their jurisdiction, and he would need to call the State Police, which Traupman did, reporting what he had seen.

Traupman didn't hear anything else about the matter, but only days later, when local newspapers ran a picture of Joann Katrinak, he recognized her as the woman he'd seen sitting in the car. So, once again

Traupman called the PSP, this time giving his information to Trooper Robert Egan.

Months later, while watching coverage of Joann and Alex's funeral on television, Traupman saw a familiar face flash across the screen: Andy Katrinak. Instantly, he felt the hair on the back of his neck stand on end. He was sure Andy was the same man he had seen arguing with Joann back in December. Once again, Traupman contacted Trooper Egan, only this time, Egan didn't seem interested in what he had to say. Of course, Walter Traupman had no way of knowing that the PSP was already focusing on Patricia Rorrer.

Time passed, and Traupman heard nothing. Nobody came to question him, and no one called. Undeterred, he sat down and wrote out a statement about the incident, which he handed over to Trooper Robert Egan. Egan, deciding that Traupman's story was not important, *threw the statement away.*

Again months passed, and Walter Traupman heard nothing. Finally, on October 31, 1995—more than six months after the discovery of the bodies and ten months after he first reported the incident—Traupman drove to PSP headquarters and confronted Trooper Egan.

Traupman recalled for Craig and Margaret what transpired that day. "Egan came charging out of his office yelling, 'I'm sick and tired of you coming in here. If you come in here again, I'm going to arrest you!'" Egan then "spun me around and started slamming his hands in the middle of my back, causing my head to snap back. He shoved me towards the exit door and kept violently shoving me. I hit my head on the exit door and nearly flew down the steps. I had constant pain in my neck after that."

In fact, Egan's manhandling of the witness would result in Traupman making two separate trips to the emergency room.

Walter Traupman was not some crackpot. He was a credible witness, sixty-eight years old, a World War II veteran, a college graduate, and a man who spent much of his life working in security. Shocked and angered by the treatment he received, Traupman contacted an attorney and reported Egan's assault. In turn, the attorney wrote a letter to Captain Robert Werts of the PSP.

It was at this point, November 27, 1995, that Trooper Egan sat down and wrote his first and only report concerning Walter Traupman. In addition to misidentifying the witness and failing to include his contact information, Egan also wrote that "Troutman" had previously appeared at the PSP barracks approximately fifteen times. His visits had become "disruptive and harassing," and he had thrown away "Troutman's" statement because he felt it was "irrelevant." Egan, however, gave no explanation for why he never made any reports of "Troutman's" prior visits or his "disruptive and harassing" behavior.

For Craig Neely, the fact that Walter Traupman, a material witness, had been kept from the defense was clearly a Brady violation, based on a 1963 US Supreme Court ruling that required the prosecution to disclose all evidence that might tend to exonerate a defendant. On the basis of this, Craig filed a Post Conviction Relief Act (PCRA) appeal on Patty's behalf and also asked that the evidence found on Joann's body be released for DNA testing.

The appeal landed before Judge William E. Ford, who grew concerned upon learning of Walter Traupman and Egan's dismissal of him. Ford ordered that Traupman be immediately deposed and also instructed the PSP to verify that the physical evidence found with Joann was still intact and available for testing. After checking on the evidence and assuring the court that everything was intact and preserved, Judge Ford issued the following order: "The Commonwealth shall preserve and not permit tainting of the following items: the fingernail with material attached found on the body of Joann Katrinak, the six hairs found in the victim's car, the hair found in Joann Katrinak's right hand, and the cigarette butt."

Patty was thrilled when, in 2007, Ford granted her the right to have the fingernail tested. The nail had been found with skin still attached, making it a perfect specimen to test. Combined with Walter Traupman's testimony and the Brady violation, she and Craig had high hopes that they would finally overturn her conviction.

Patty was responsible for the cost of the testing, and once again, Telly Fiouris provided the funds. Patty had the fingernail sent to Orchid Cellmark laboratories in Texas, where, incredibly, it was found to be completely devoid of material. Somehow, a violation of Judge Ford's order to "preserve and not taint with" the evidence had occurred, and there was no longer anything on the nail to DNA test.

Patty was stunned and despondent by the news. "I couldn't believe it," she said. "I absolutely could not believe it. Judge Ford had the nail checked on and determined that it was still intact and preserved. He even referred to it as "the fingernail with material attached." How, between that time and the time it got to Cellmark, could it have accidentally been cleaned? Someone obviously tampered with that nail because they knew it wasn't going to match me. They did it so I couldn't test it and so that I would never get out of jail."

With no nail to test, Craig petitioned the court to have the hair found in Joann's hand tested. That too was denied, due to something called "law of the case," a ruling that precluded the relitigation of issues once they have been decided. Judge Wallitsch may have put this ruling into place after the prosecution stipulated that the hair in Joann's hand "does not belong to Patricia Rorrer." This was something the jury never heard at trial, as the prosecution had always maintained that the hair in Joann's hand had never been DNA tested. It's curious to wonder how they could now say with certainty that the hair did not belong to Patricia Rorrer. Is it possible that they had tested the hair at some point, developed a DNA profile and then compared it to Patricia Rorrer without a match?

Despite the unanswered questions, without the fingernail or the hair from Joann's hand, Patty was left with only two options: to test the cigarette butt or test the other hairs found in Joann's car. Neither Patty nor Margaret trusted the hair evidence, and Craig agreed, as it concerned the unmounted hairs from Joann's car. However, he felt comfortable testing one of the three mounted hairs, believing they had been immediately mounted right after they were found, leaving no time for tampering. Patty was hesitant—she'd prefer to test the cigarette butt—but reluctantly agreed with her attorney.

The three hairs from Joann's car initially mounted by the PSP—those the FBI had labeled Q4, Q5 and Q6—were sent to Orchid Cellmark in Texas, where lab personnel discovered a root on one of them capable of DNA testing. This time, however, the results were beyond devastating. According to Cellmark, the mounted hair from Joann's car was a perfect match to Patty.

For Patty, the results were unbelievable and unexplainable. The hair was tested in the same manner—using mitochondrial and PCR testing—as the unmounted one the FBI had tested back in 1997. How could it have gone from one in thirty-seven thousand to a perfect match? DNA doesn't get better over time; it degrades. Even more suspicious was the fact that Dr. Jensen's DNA was not found on the hair, nor was Joann's. This lack of contamination was important. Dr. Jensen had initially left his DNA on the hairs when he touched them with his bare hands. Likewise, if Joann and Patty struggled, and Joann ripped out a portion of Patty's hair, her DNA should have appeared on the hair as well. In addition to these problems, Patty also made a logical argument: "If I killed Joann and Alex and I knew that hair in the car was mine, do you really believe I would have given permission to have them tested? I'm not stupid. I had a choice. I could have insisted that Craig have the cigarette butt tested instead. They couldn't have used that to frame me, because I've never smoked. And think about this," she added, "if I were guilty, testing the cigarette butt would have provided a foreign DNA, which would have cast suspicion away from me. Those hairs were switched. That's why they cleaned the fingernail, and that's why they won't let me test the hair in Joann's hand because the only evidence they could frame me with was the hair evidence. They won't let me test anything else because they know nothing else will match me, and then they'd have to explain."

That much is true. The police would have to explain, as well as admit that even if Patty were involved in the crimes, she did not act alone and they willingly allowed a brutal killer to walk free. In fact, years later, prosecutor McIntyre would admit as much.

Regardless of Patty's suspicions, that perfect DNA match obtained by Orchid Cellmark effectively destroyed any chance she had of overturning her conviction. From that point on, anything brought up on appeal would be routinely denied because of the DNA match.

For instance, the Brady violation concerning Walter Traupman no longer mattered because, with the DNA match, Traupman's testimony would not have been enough to prove Patty's innocence. When she later brought up the PSP tampering of the fingernail—a direct violation of Ford's order—she was again denied. This time, Judge Douglas Reichley—who replaced Judge Ford after his retirement—wrote in his denial, "Even if arguendo [for argument's sake] the state police did tamper with DNA evidence, it is irrelevant." To the courts, the DNA match proved Patty was the killer, and no other evidence would negate that.

For Patty, who had been so hopeful and excited, all hope was suddenly gone. The thought of all she had lost over the years left her despondent and unable to focus. She no longer had her home, her job, her horses, or her friends, but that was nothing compared to the fact that her mother was dead, her child lost to her forever, and the chances of overturning her conviction now practically nil. Patty had been depressed before, but this time she found herself sinking into the blackest void she had ever faced. She could no longer eat or sleep; her body broke out in angry red welts that she scratched and tore at until her skin bled. The darkness enveloped her, weighed her down, and smothered her. It was a despair so bleak that it would take nearly two entire years for her to emerge.

Patty was not a quitter, however, and as she watched her supporters rally around her, she realized that she could not give up. Holly was out there, and Patty was determined to prove to her daughter that she was not a monster and had not committed these crimes. The thought of Holly kept Patty going, but she also had Margaret and her step-pop, Ray, as well as her Uncle Telly and his new wife, Mary.

In 2011, Patty suffered another devastation when word reached her that Margaret Sneary had passed away. By that time, Margaret had become Patty's most trusted friend and confidant as well as her strongest supporter. Patty was distraught by the news and frightened of what would become of her now. Although she refused to resign herself to a fate of dying in prison for a crime she had not committed, she couldn't help but wonder if anything good would ever again happen in her life.

She had no idea that that there was someone on the outside who was just beginning to take an interest in her case.

19

I, of course, was that someone on the outside, and once I had made contact with Patty and realized that she was eager to cooperate with me, things moved quickly between us: from letters to phone calls to visits at SCI Muncy. I had come into this project convinced of Patty's guilt, but what she was not only telling me but also *proving* to me with actual police and FBI reports, left me dumbfounded. The problems in her case were so numerous and so serious that they shook my faith in our justice system almost to the core. I knew then that this book was going to go beyond anything I had initially planned.

As soon as I began earnestly looking into the case, I realized that I owed a tremendous debt to Margaret Sneary. Margaret had been tenacious in her investigating and had managed to get her hands on a plethora of documents, making it that much easier for me to piece the case back together. And once I had done so, I was left to wonder how the jury ever convicted Patricia Rorrer of these crimes.

It seemed several things had combined to work against her, perhaps the first being her choice of defense attorneys. Jim Burke and Jim Pfeiffer were undoubtedly competent and capable lawyers, but it seemed clear that they were in way over their heads in this case. Neither had experience with the death penalty; Pfeiffer had never tried a capital case, and Burke had only participated in one other, sitting second chair. I soon discovered that if Patty's case were to come to trial today, neither attorney would be allowed to represent her. Today, an attorney trying a capital case must be "death penalty qualified."

Pfeiffer and Burke's first mistake was allowing their client to come to trial so quickly—less than eight months after her arrest. The Katrinak case was huge and complex, spanning a three-year investigation across three different states. It's doubtful that any attorney could have prepared to try it in such a short amount of time. According to Patty, she rarely met with her legal team, and, in fact, had done so only four times before trial, once to discuss nothing more than finances.

"I kept telling them they didn't know me well enough to defend me," Patty said, "but they just kept telling me, 'we don't need to know you.'"

Not only did Burke and Pfeiffer fail to call witnesses who were vital to the case, they didn't seem to have a good handle on the evidence, either. At times they appeared unprepared and unable to cross-examine witnesses properly and effectively. They erred in their decision not to examine Andy as a viable suspect in the murders of his wife and son. Even the prosecution expected them to do that, as Michael McIntyre told the jury in his opening that Andy might be a suspect with the defense.

Patty claimed that neither Burke nor Pfeiffer wanted to "hit too hard" on Andy for fear of alienating the jury, which would be sound logic if there were nothing to hit Andy with. But Andy had been the primary suspect for a reason, and his actions needed to be explored and explained. Why was he so unconcerned when he found his house broken into and his wife and son missing? Why did he repair the basement door before the police arrived? Why did he splice together the cut phone line? How did he describe what Joann was wearing on the day she disappeared if he last saw her undressed and in bed? Why did he make such a fuss about not destroying evidence in Joann's car and then immediately sit in it after the police left?

Pfeiffer and Burke should have delved into each of those issues when they had Joann's husband on the stand, and in not doing so, they failed Patricia Rorrer.

Andy, however, was not the only one who might have been further investigated. There were other people and other tales that should have raised red flags, including Joann's good friend, Josh Bloom.

Bloom had supposedly told Joann that he would set up the December 13 luncheon with their former coworkers, but the police learned that Bloom had never contacted anyone about getting together for lunch. The fact that three others joined them that day was merely a coincidence. They had gone to the restaurant to eat, spotted their old friends there, and decided to join them.

Bloom also appeared to downplay his relationship with Joann for the police. While everyone at Six Flags described the two as "extremely close," Bloom told the authorities that his friendship with Joann was a "casual one."

After Josh and Joann had stopped working at Six Flags, Josh had continued to keep their former coworkers updated on Joann's life. He called to let them know when she started a new job and when she got married. He called again to tell them of her pregnancy, the birth of her baby, and her plans to move out west. But when something as serious as Joann's disappearance occurred, no one at Six Flags heard from him.

Joann's worried friends told the police that they tried calling Josh for information, but he never returned their calls, nor did he answer his pager when they repeatedly beeped him and left messages. Josh Bloom had kept Six Flags employees apprised of every occurrence in Joann Katrinak's life, but when she and her son became the possible victims of a kidnapping and murder, Bloom failed to call anyone.

Bloom also had no one to verify his alibi for the day Joann and Alex went missing. He told the police that he worked the night shift on December 14, arrived home around 7:00 AM on December 15, went straight to bed and didn't wake until 5:00 PM. Though there is nothing to connect Bloom to Joann and Alex's disappearance, the fact that the police never checked his story further reveals a pattern repeated throughout the investigation. As soon as they began focusing on Patricia Rorrer, they seemed to ignore anything that didn't tend to incriminate her.

They did the same thing with Billy Opel, the police officer Joann met and began dating before Andy. When the authorities first contacted Opel, he denied knowing Joann. "You got the wrong person," Opel said. "It wasn't me who dated her."

When Joann's friends continued to insist that it *was* Opel who dated her, the police tried to question him again, but Opel made it a point to avoid them. Each time the police called, Opel had an excuse not to see them. Finally, after weeks of playing cat and mouse, the police caught up with Billy Opel and confronted him. It was only then that Opel reluctantly admitted he had dated Joann, but he insisted their relationship was brief and casual. "I hardly even knew her."

Opel had not worked on the day Joann and Alex disappeared, but his wife gave him an alibi; according to her, the two had gone Christmas shopping that day. When the police asked Opel why he lied about knowing Joann, he cited "unwanted publicity" as the reason. His excuse was repugnant. Billy Opel was a police officer who certainly knew the importance of being honest in a case of this magnitude. Hindering an investigation is a criminal offense, and the authorities should have charged Opel with it.

Josh Bloom and Billy Opel were both policemen, so perhaps law enforcement can be forgiven for accepting the word of two fellow officers; however, there is absolutely no excuse for their decision not to investigate further the story of thirteen-year-old JESSICA MASON.

Jessica and her siblings lived with their mother and their mother's boyfriend, who was both violently abusive and a drug addict. Not long before Christmas 1994, Jessica overheard her mother's boyfriend talking with an associate about a missing lady and her little baby.

Only days later, Jessica's mother found rope, bloody blue jeans, and some women's jewelry hidden in the basement of their home. Although Jessica didn't know what became of the rope or the jewelry, she did know that her mother had helped her boyfriend burn the bloody jeans in their backyard.

When police questioned Jessica's mother, she confirmed her daughter's story. Around Christmas 1994, she had found rope and jewelry hidden in her basement, and her boyfriend's bloody blue jeans tucked away in a bedroom closet. Her boyfriend was "very abusive," the woman said, and a "heavy drug user." She added that she, too, had used "a lot of meth in December" and couldn't remember what she had done with the jewelry or the rope, but she denied helping her boyfriend burn his bloody jeans. Her boyfriend had later "gotten rid of them himself," she said.

However, according to another witness, Jessica's mother had been telling people that one night her boyfriend had come home "full of blood" and told her that "something went wrong and it involved a Catasauqua woman and her baby." Jessica's mother also told them that she "helped her boyfriend burn his clothing."

Patty's jury never heard about Josh Bloom, Billy Opel, Jessica Mason, or Jessica's mother, nor did they learn about the credit card receipt discovered in Joann's backyard where she normally parked her car. The receipt was in the name of CARL WESLER, and bore a Whitehall, Pennsylvania, address. Running a check on Wesler's name, the police learned that he had no criminal record, but his brother, who resided with him, had done time in the past for rape. What was a credit card receipt from either of these men doing behind the Katrinak house in the same spot where Joann's abduction allegedly took place?

———————

The more I dug, the more unanswered questions I uncovered. It wasn't hard to understand why Margaret had become so obsessed with the case; so much of the story had never been made public. Margaret had been a godsend to Patty, and she became a godsend to me too. One of the most incredible things Margaret had discovered was that *Patty had been under surveillance in North Carolina during the critical time of the murders*, a fact her jury never heard.

In 2002, Margaret had tracked down and taken a statement from Darlie Peters, the SPCA officer who had once charged Patty with animal cruelty and abandonment. Peters told Margaret that in late 1994, area residents suspected Patty of stealing horses and selling them in Virginia, so Peters and several horse owners decided to pool their money and hire a private investigator to watch her. Running surveillance was expensive, however, and so the group decided to do the detective work themselves.

Beginning on December 12, 1994, the same day the police claim Patty called Joann and headed out for Pennsylvania, the group began watching her. The surveillance lasted until December 16 and was documented by Darlie Peters. Although Peters claimed, "Patty wasn't around much during those days," she never indicated that Patty or her van were missing the entire time, nor did anyone else who participated in the surveillance.

Peters told Margaret that she had handed over her surveillance notes to Pennsylvania state troopers Robert Egan and Joseph Vasquez, but neither Patty nor her defense team ever saw those notes, and what became of them is unknown.

There were other vital witnesses that Burke and Pfeiffer failed to call, such as KYLE and SHAUNA STEINER, who each saw Joann's vehicle in McCarty's parking lot twice on December 15, 1994.

The first time they saw the tan Toyota was between 12:30 and 12:45 when they stopped for lunch at the Front Street Tavern. The car was sitting all alone, backed into the second space on the south side of the lot, with its tires turned toward Front Street. The couple said they noticed the car because it was the only vehicle parked on that side of the lot.

Later that evening, the Steiners returned to the Front Street Tavern around 10:00 PM and noticed Joann's car still parked in the same space and same manner as it was earlier. To them, the car didn't appear to have moved all day.

Two other witnesses also saw Joann and her vehicle just before the Steiners's first sighting of the car. Around noon on December 15, 1994, the Katrinaks' neighbor, MARLO MADDIN, saw Joann dressed in jeans and a black fuzzy jacket, putting things into her car. When Marlo looked out again around 12:30, both Joann and her car were gone. There was also another neighbor who noticed Joann that afternoon, this time putting Alex into the car. This witness saw no other people in the vicinity and certainly no one brandishing a gun and forcing Joann into the car.

The timing of these witnesses coincides with the Steiners' first sighting of the Toyota in McCarty's parking lot, and the description of what Joann was wearing ties in with yet another witness, Walter Traupman, the man who saw Joann and Andy arguing in Bethlehem that same afternoon.

Both Traupman and Maddin described Joann as wearing a black fuzzy jacket, and interestingly, that description also matches evidence found at the crime scene. During Joann's autopsy, several dark fibers were recovered from the band of her wristwatch and from beneath her fingernail. Dr. Mihalakis said Joann would have been bleeding profusely from her wounds, yet there was not enough blood on her jacket to test. Is it possible that Joann was re-dressed before the killer dumped the bodies? The location of those black fibers in her watchband and beneath her fingernail could be consistent with the removal of a black fuzzy jacket.

In 2014, I received a box of documents from an elderly couple whom Patty lovingly refers to as Pastor Paul and Grandma Joan. The box had formerly belonged to Margaret Sneary and contained hundreds of police and FBI reports. Among this cache of documents, I discovered a report taken by Trooper Paul Romanic from a woman named Maureen McKenna. McKenna had also witnessed a couple arguing over a child on the afternoon of December 15, 1994, a couple she identified as Joann and Andy Katrinak. The report was almost identical to Walter Traupman's, but the jury never heard about McKenna either. In fact, the incident appears to have been entirely ignored by the PSP. Trooper Paul Romanic made a single notation on the bottom of the report that reads, "This trooper is aware that Mr. Andy Katrinak can account for his whereabouts on 12/15/94 and could not have been in Bethlehem."

That, however, is not true. Andy had only his father to provide him with an alibi for the time, and Andrew Sr. was an interested party in the case. Walter Traupman and Maureen McKenna were not. They had no connection to each other, nothing invested in the case, and nothing to gain by coming forward. Though the police and prosecution considered it highly suspicious that Patty had only family and friends to alibi her for the date in question, they apparently felt no such qualms about Andy having only his father as an alibi for himself.

The jury had a right to hear what both Traupman and McKenna had to say, and perhaps the only reason they didn't was because their statements cast suspicion away from Patty and onto Andy.

It's possible the authorities had dismissed Traupman and McKenna simply because of Andy's paternity test. When I interviewed Michael

McIntyre in 2016, one of the first questions I asked was how the police had finally cleared Andy, and McIntyre told me it was through the paternity test. He claimed that once it was proven that Andy was Alex's biological father, he was no longer considered a suspect because he no longer had a motive to commit the crime. The only problem with that reasoning is that Andy couldn't have known he was Alex's father until after the murders. What did he believe before the testing?

No matter how unlikely a tip, a lead, or a suspect, the authorities have a duty to investigate it, not ignore it. Traupman's and McKenna's statements should have been checked further.

Another troubling witness never called to testify was Patty's grain dealer, Leroy Rouse. Someone—although it's unclear who—told Patty's attorneys that Rouse was unable to attend the trial due to a death in his family. When Margaret and a private investigator tracked Rouse down in 2002, however, he adamantly denied this.

Rouse claimed he had no idea why he wasn't called to testify. He wanted to testify, he said, and was prepared to do so until Detective Tony Roberson of the Davidson County Sheriff's Office showed up at his front door and asked him to sign a paper releasing him from doing so. Rouse said he refused to sign, but he never heard from the defense after Roberson's visit. There had been no death in his family, nor had he told anyone that there had been.

Who told Patty's attorneys that Leroy Rouse had a death in his family? And why were the police interfering with a defense witness?

The more I delved into the case, the more I realized that when applying common sense to the evidence, the prosecution's theory didn't hold up. For instance, McIntyre had offered two motives for the murders: anger and jealousy. His argument had been that when Joann hung up on Patty, it unleashed in her a violent rage that had begun to simmer the moment she learned that Andy had married Joann. The prosecution's implication was that this was a fatal attraction case, that Patty was obsessed with Andy and wanted him back, and everyone else seemed to believe this too.

Patty's jurors believed it, and so did the North Carolina investigators. Davidson County sheriff Gerald Hege told the press, "It was a case of fatal attraction. Some people just don't know how to let go."

The O'Connors certainly believed it. When Joann's sister, Peggy, was asked why she thought Patty had killed Joann, she answered without hesitation, "Jealousy. I think [Patty] saw that Andy was happy with another woman and had a beautiful baby. I think maybe she still held out hope that at one point they would get back together, and once she realized that that was never going to happen, I think her jealousy just took over and she got enraged."

Even Jim Burke had asked the jury in his closing; "If this was a case of 'fatal attraction,' why didn't Patty make a move for Andy after the murders?"

Was Patty obsessed with Andy, and did she want him back? There is absolutely nothing to suggest that. Andy had testified that his and Patty's parting was a mutual decision and that the breakup was amicable. He also admitted that they had remained friends afterward and that Patty's calls were never an attempt to rekindle the romance. A close look at the evidence supports this. If Patty were obsessed with Andy:

- Would she have been seeing Frank Alonzo when she was still living with Andy?
- Would she have left him to move in with Frank?
- Would she have moved to North Carolina and left Andy living in a house that she solely owned?
- Would she have left Pennsylvania at all, or stayed to be close to him?
- Would she be calling him only once or twice a year?

There was no evidence to suggest that Patty was obsessed with Andy, but I realized that no one had ever put much thought into how Andy might have felt about *her*. Consider these points:

- It was always Patty who left the relationship and always Andy who persuaded her to come back

- Andy traveled to North Carolina on several occasions to try and reconcile the relationship
- Andy sent Patty cards and love letters in an attempt to cultivate her back into his life
- Andy had his telephone listed in Patty's name
- Andy continued to receive mail addressed to Patty at his house
- Andy was still accepting Patty's phone calls

There was one other document that revealed how Andy may have felt about his old girlfriend. Andy had told the authorities that he had no feelings for Patty and that he had gotten rid of her pictures long ago, but that is not what Joann's friend Debbie Marchek told them.

In a police report dated June 5, 1996, Marchek told Trooper Robert Egan that Joann hated Patty and referred to her as "the bitch." This may have stemmed from something else Marchek told the trooper: that Joann had found pictures of Patty that Andy kept in their bedroom closet. Pictures that Joann subsequently destroyed.

I had long wondered about that last phone call between Joann and Patty. Why was Joann so angry over that last call? The two had never met, and Patty and Andy spoke only once or twice a year. Joann had answered the phone when Patty called in the past, and had always been friendly and pleasant. So why all the anger now? Thinking about everything I had learned, I had to wonder whether Joann's anger was actually directed toward Patty, or her husband. Andy and Joann had been married for only eighteen months and had just had a child together, yet their phone was still listed in her husband's ex-girlfriend's name. Mail addressed to his ex-girlfriend was still being delivered to their house. Her husband was still accepting his ex-girlfriend's phone calls, and Joann had found pictures of this ex-girlfriend in her husband's closet. It wasn't hard to imagine how all of that must have made Joann feel. When Patty called this last time, did Joann just decide that if Andy wasn't going to banish her from their lives, then she would?

I realized that no one had ever taken the time to look at this case every angle and piece it together in a concise and comprehensive manner. Mentioning this to Patty one day, I said wistfully, "I wish I had done your closing."

"Then do it," Patty replied.

"I wish I had," I laughed.

"No, I mean it," Patty said. "You're a writer, write the closing you would have made if you were my attorney."

I realized she was serious, and after thinking about it for a while, I began to wonder if it might not be the perfect way to draw the case together for my readers. Although I wasn't a lawyer, I couldn't help but wonder what would have happened if Patty's jury had heard all the facts in the case? Would it have made a difference? You decide.

20

Ladies and gentlemen of the jury, over the past month, you've heard a lot of testimony from that witness chair, a lot of testimony. And I'm sure you're wondering what it all means. How it all fits together. This was a terrible case—tragic—and we all grieve for Joann and Alex and their families. Their deaths were a tragedy beyond comparison, and whoever killed them deserves to be punished to the fullest extent of the law. But that person is not Patricia Rorrer.

Don't compound this tragedy with another. Don't convict an innocent person. Patty is not guilty of these crimes, and the evidence you heard from that witness stand proves it.

The first thing you have to ask yourselves is this: Why would Patricia Rorrer want to murder Joann and Alex Katrinak? What was the motive for these crimes?

The prosecution would like you to believe it was a combination of anger and jealousy. Anger over the hang-up call and jealousy that Joann had "snagged" Andy Katrinak and had a child with him. Two emotions that produced such a fit of rage that Patty jumped in her van, drove five hundred miles, stalked an unknown woman and her baby for three entire days, and then cold-bloodedly murdered both. Two people she had never met.

It's ridiculous, ladies and gentlemen. The whole notion is ridiculous. People had done far worse to Patricia Rorrer than hanging up a phone on her. Men had beaten her, stolen from her. People lied about her. My God, look at Darlie Peters, her own relative, who hauled her into court on charges of animal cruelty and abandonment. Charges, by the way, that were unfounded. Did Patty ever react to any of these people with violence? No. Never. In fact, Patty has no real history of violence. Are we to truly believe that one day she just woke up as a monster capable of murdering two innocent people she'd never even met? One of them a three-month-old baby? Come on; it doesn't happen that way. It just doesn't, and you know it. Someone capable of that type of viciousness is going to have indications of it in his or her past.

Did Patty want Andy back? There's not one shred of evidence to suggest that she did. Not one. This was not a fatal attraction–type crime, and Patty was not jealous of Joann and Andy's relationship. Andy got up on that stand and told you that his and Patty's parting was a mutual decision. That the break up was amicable and the two remained friends. They called each other a couple of times a year, normal calls between two friends living hundreds of miles apart. Those calls weren't an attempt on Patty's part to rekindle the romance. Andy told you that himself.

There is nothing to suggest that Patty was obsessed with Andy or that she wanted him back. Absolutely nothing. By the time these murders occurred, Patty had long moved on with her life. She'd already met Seth Alden, the man with whom she would become engaged and have a child. Seth was every bit as good a catch as Andy, maybe even better. He was young, good-looking, a marine reservist with a bright future.

Now, you might be asking yourself, 'Well, what about the testimony that Patty threw Andy up to her other boyfriends and cried over his picture?' The first thing you have to remember is who it was that testified to those things: Tim Sellers, probably the least credible witness to take that stand. A known thief, a known liar, and a man who has an ax to grind with Patricia Rorrer. Don't forget, she was instrumental in having Sellers arrested.

Frank Alonzo didn't seem to put much importance on the picture gazing. In fact, he said Patty had only one picture of Andy, and it was in a photo album. Do you remember when Mr. McIntyre asked him when

Patty would look at this picture? Frank Alonzo shrugged his shoulders. "I guess anytime, really," he said. Does that sound like an obsession?

Even Sellers admitted that Patty would look at Andy's picture only when she'd been drinking and they were fighting. Does that prove an obsession or simply that Patty, angry with her lover, liked to push his buttons?

Did Patty throw Andy up to both these men? I'm sure she did. Let's face it, if Patty is guilty of anything, it's her lousy taste in men. Most of the men she dated were abusive, and most were ex-cons, but not Andy. He was the exception.

Remember Tim Sellers's testimony? "Patty said Andy treated her good, and she wanted Tim to treat her like that as well." Is that so unreasonable? Doesn't everyone want to be treated well? Does that show an obsession on Patty's part? I don't think so.

You know, Andy did treat Patty well, and despite that, she left him. And make no bones about it, *she left him*. Left him in her own house when she moved in with Frank Alonzo. Left him when she moved five hundred miles away to North Carolina. Left him when he wrote her love letters asking to try again. *She left him*. Yet the prosecution wants you to believe that she was so jealous of Joann's relationship with Andy that she drove all the way up here and killed her and her baby.

Well, let's talk about Patty's ability to do just that.

The prosecution claims that since Patty didn't have a job, she could easily leave North Carolina whenever she wanted to. We contend just the opposite. The fact that Patty wasn't working means she couldn't have committed these murders. We're talking about a four-day trip here, a four-day trip taken on the spur of the moment.

Ask yourself this question: Could you just up and take off on a four-day trip without any planning? Do you have the ready cash at home to just jump in the car and go? How did Patty finance this trip? She'd just returned from Oklahoma. She was broke. She didn't have any money, and she wasn't working, so there was no money coming in. She still had to eat on this trip, still had to buy gas, sleep somewhere. Remember, it was December and bitterly cold. She didn't just pull her van to the side of the road and sleep in it. She would have had to use the bathroom, take a shower, brush her teeth. Where did she do all of these things, and why didn't anyone see her?

You know, this was just before Christmas, a busy time. Is it plausible that she could be missing from home for so long and no one would notice? Who took care of her horses and her other animals? Don't you think the prosecution would have found someone—anyone—to get up on that stand and say Patty wasn't in North Carolina at that time? Someone to say, "Hey, I was looking all over for her during that time. I was calling her house and knocking on her door, and she wasn't there." Of course they would have. Yet they found no one.

And what about Patty's vehicles? The only vehicle she could have used to come up here was her van, the van with the bad U-joint. Remember the description of Patty's vehicles, that they were all run down with expired tags and couldn't pass inspection. Is it logical to think that anyone would risk using such an unreliable vehicle to drive five hundred miles and commit murder? It's ridiculous. Patty's van is a high-top custom van, three-tone in color, with chrome all over it and a bug shield across the front that reads "Riverwood Stables." It's got North Carolina plates on it, yet nobody in Pennsylvania saw this van. Come on; this thing would have stuck out like a sore thumb. Someone would have noticed it. But no one did.

What about Darlie Peters, who got up on that stand and told you that Patty was under surveillance during those same four days down in North Carolina? They were watching her down there, and no one ever said Patty's van was gone for those four days.

The fact of the matter is, no one missed Patty in North Carolina because Patty was there. And no one saw her, or her van, in Pennsylvania because they weren't here. It's that plain and simple. *They weren't here.*

Isn't it strange that there were no sightings of Patty in Pennsylvania during that time? When Joann vanished, there were dozens of sightings of her, but not one of Patty. Patty's a distinctive person, nearly six feet tall, with long hair reminiscent of Farrah Fawcett and a southern accent. No one saw her, ladies and gentlemen, because she wasn't here.

Patty had no motive to kill Joann. None.

The truth is, no one really knows what happened to Joann and Alex that day. The police don't know. The prosecution doesn't know. All they have is a theory. Maybe the real killer is someone the police never bothered to investigate. There were plenty of those, you know. It could have been someone from Joann's past. You heard the descriptions of her. She could have made enemies, could have offended the wrong person. Or it could have been someone from her present. She was a beautiful woman. Is it possible someone was infatuated with her? Is it possible Joann was simply in the wrong place at the wrong time, that this was a random thing? That some nutjob saw her, wanted her, and decided to take her? It could have been any of those, because nobody really knows what happened. And that's reasonable doubt, ladies and gentlemen.

When you really start looking at the Commonwealth's case, you'll see that it doesn't add up. Take Veronica's phone call to Joann on the afternoon of December 15. Is it possible that Andy's mother was mistaken about that call? I ask that because Veronica's story just doesn't make sense.

She supposedly made a definite plan to go shopping with Joann. Such a definite plan that she sat around in her winter coat for nearly two hours waiting for her daughter-in-law to show up. You heard the testimony of how overprotective she was with Alex. How Joann complained that if the baby so much as sneezed, Veronica thought she should rush him to the doctor. Yet when Joann doesn't show up for their planned shopping excursion, Veronica isn't even worried.

She testified that she was worried, but that's not what she first told the police. Nor do her actions indicate that she was worried. She didn't call Andy's house over and over again. She didn't find someone to drive the route to her son's house. What if they'd been in an accident? What if Joann's car had broken down and they were stranded on the side of the road? It was freezing out that day. Veronica didn't even bother to call Andy's house when she knew her son would be coming home from work. Is it possible that this wasn't a definite plan? Could Joann have said, 'I might stop by,' or 'Maybe I'll be over?' If Joann had said that, Veronica would have had no reason to be worried when she never showed up. Remember when Andy told the police that the screws on his basement door may have been tampered with? Why did he tell them that? Because he wanted them to take the disappearances more seriously. Could Veronica have done the same thing? Could she have said the shopping trip was a definite plan because she, too, wanted the police to take the disappearances more seriously?

You know, the police based their entire scenario of this crime on Veronica's recollections of that phone call. But Veronica told a different story when she took the stand. Now she says Joann agreed to wait thirty-five or forty minutes for her. That throws the time of the abduction completely off and opens up a whole new avenue of potential witnesses and suspects whom the police never questioned.

According to the prosecution, when Patty heard Veronica and Joann hang up, that's when she cut the phone line. But why cut it then? That makes no sense at all. Isn't it more logical that she would have cut the line when she first entered the house rather than when she was leaving?

And what was Patty doing in that basement anyway? She supposedly broke in right after Andy left for work, so she was in there for more than seven hours. Why? What was her original plan? How long did she intend to wait around in that basement? She couldn't have known Joann was going to leave the house that day, so why not confront her as soon as she entered? None of it makes sense.

The prosecution wants you to believe that once Patty heard Joann hang up, she immediately moved into action—and let me tell you, ladies and gentlemen, she really had to move. Supposedly, in the time it took Joann to put on her shoes, Patty had to cut the phone line, smooth out her footprints, gather up her cordless screwdriver, her wire cutters, and the crowbar she used to pop the hasp on the door and then get the gun out and ready. Isn't it amazing that Patty knew just what tools she'd need to bring with her when she raced out to her van and sped off for Pennsylvania?

She had to have the tools with her because none of them were found in the Katrinak basement. Does the prosecution want you to believe that Patty risked being seen running back and forth to her van to retrieve— and then return—the tools as she needed them?

Now, after Patty cuts the phone line, wipes out her footprints, and gathers up her tools, she has to get the gun ready and then get out of the basement unseen and unheard.

Remember, it's broad daylight outside; it's near the lunchtime hour, and here's Patty juggling a gun, a cordless screwdriver, a pair of wire cutters, and a crowbar while at the same time contending with a terrified woman holding a diaper bag, a purse, and a baby.

Why didn't Gary Anders, who was working only yards away, see or hear this? Why didn't Joann run, or holler, or fight? Even with a gun pointed at her, she had to know help was just a scream away. Don't forget, according to Debbie Marchek, Joann had seen pictures of Patty, so she would have known this was Patty Rorrer pointing a gun at her. Do you honestly believe Joann would ever have gotten into a car with Patty Rorrer? No way, absolutely not.

You heard the descriptions of Joann. She wasn't a meek and mild individual. In fact, she sounds like one tough cookie. In a life-or-death situation, especially involving her child, don't you think she would have fought rather than just follow along? But there was no indication that she did. No scream, no cry for help, no signs of a struggle, nothing. Don't you know that there would have been? I think it's obvious that Joann wasn't abducted from her house. If she left with the killer from her house, then the killer was someone Joann knew and trusted, and she went with that person willingly.

But the prosecution just wants you to believe that Patty forced Joann into the front seat at gunpoint, then took a seat in back and ordered her to drive. Joann's neighbor saw Joann putting Alex in her car that day, but she didn't see Patty coming up behind her brandishing a gun. Gary Anders was working within sight of the Katrinak backyard, but he didn't see Joann's car drive around from the house. And think about this; Joann always kept a canister of Mace in the console of her car. It would have been there when she first got inside. Why didn't she use it? Why didn't she crash the car? We're talking about a narrow, one-way street, lined on both sides with parked cars. Joann could have swerved into one of those cars at ten miles per hour without fear of injury. I mean, my God, her life and that of her baby were at stake. Wouldn't she have at least tried? Tried something?

But the prosecution wants you to believe she didn't. Instead, she just let Patty Rorrer lead her to that lonely patch of woods. I want you to really think about where those bodies were found. You all saw it. It's rugged terrain out there. There's heavy vegetation, sticks, tree limbs, rocks, and ruts. Do you honestly believe Joann's car could have been driven into those woods? Wouldn't there be some evidence on it if it had? Especially on the undercarriage? Of course there would. There'd be dents, scratches, vegetation clinging underneath. But you heard Trooper Coia's description of that car. "It was immaculate," he said, "both inside and out and even underneath."

We contend that Joann's car was never used in these crimes. That her car was never in that area. Now, if that's possible, then that's reasonable doubt, and by law, you must acquit Patricia Rorrer.

You know, there's no evidence to suggest that Joann and Alex were killed in those woods either. There are no signs of a struggle, no heavy concentrations of blood, nothing to say that's where they were murdered.

Dr. Kim, the "bug expert," believes the bodies weren't placed in those woods until sometime in mid-February. Even the prosecution's own expert witnesses all said they could have been placed there as late as mid-January. No one can say if Joann and Alex were killed on the day they disappeared. Maybe they were held somewhere first. If so, then Patty could not be the killer.

This case is just riddled with reasonable doubt, ladies and gentlemen. It's just saturated with it. How can the prosecution ask you to send this woman to her death when no one can even tell you what really happened here?

Their theory for this crime is just that, a theory. It's mere speculation on their part because they don't know what happened. But I'll tell you something: their theory doesn't make sense.

According to that theory, once Joann drives to that isolated spot, Patty forces her to take her baby and walk into those woods. Patty's behind Joann, pointing that little .22 Jennings at her back. Joann didn't fight in a populated area, but here, she finally stops and faces her abductor. A struggle breaks out. Joann grabs Patty and rips out some of her hair. Patty fights back, breaking Joann's nose, kicking her in the shin, and shattering Joann's finger. It's a violent struggle until Patty finally raises the gun and fires, only to be confronted with a dilemma. The gun jams.

Now I want you to think about that. Tim Sellers testified that the .22 was "a piece of junk." That it had a tendency to jam after it was fired and you'd have to clear the chamber before you could fire it again. Patty would have known that. Why would she have brought that particular gun to use in a double murder? She certainly had access to other weapons, better and more reliable guns. Why didn't she bring one of those?

OK, so maybe it was the only gun available when she scurried out to her van and began her nine-hour drive to Pennsylvania. That still doesn't explain why she resorted to beating Joann after the gun jammed if all she had to do was clear the chamber and fire again. Is the prosecution suggesting that Joann was still fighting after being shot in the face?

But hey, whatever. That's been the prosecution's attitude throughout this entire trial, hasn't it? It's pretty much been them telling you, "Don't worry if it doesn't make sense. Just believe us. Trust us."

Well, you don't have to "just believe them." You can insist that they prove their case, because that's their duty.

Now, after Joann was shot, her killer beat her about the head nineteen times. Vicious, violent blows delivered with such force that they fractured her skull. Her blood loss would have been massive. You heard the testimony: shot in the face, the bullet nicking her carotid artery, her nose broken, nineteen brutal head wounds. Each of those injuries would have been bleeding profusely, yet there's no evidence of this at the crime scene. There's not even enough blood on Joann's jacket to DNA test. I'm sorry, but that's impossible. It's simply impossible.

Whoever was beating Joann had to be saturated with blood. Had to be. If Joann were beaten with a .22 Jennings, then her killer had to be right on top of her, wielding the blows. That gun is tiny; it fits in the palm of your hand. If Patty were the killer, how could she have delivered these vicious blows with that little gun and not received injuries to her hands and forearms? It's impossible. But we know Patty had no injuries, because exactly one week later, the FBI interviewed her, and Patty was wearing short sleeves. There were no cuts to her hands or forearms, no bruising, no scratching, no nothing. Even more incredible is the fact that not one drop of blood was found in Joann's car. Not a drop, not a speck, not a trace, not a smear. None. That's impossible if these crimes occurred the way the prosecution is contending. If Patty were the killer, she had to be dripping with blood. How did she clean up before she got back into Joann's car? Did she kill the victims in the nude or take a swim in a nearby pond? Not likely. Not in mid-December in Pennsylvania.

Think about this too; what killer would risk returning a victim's car back to her house? Especially if that killer knew that by then, people would probably be searching for that victim. No one would be that bold or that stupid. No one. Joann's car would have been dumped somewhere else, even if only a block or two away from her house.

Look at the aerial view of where that car was parked and how it's parked. That car came from around the back of the Katrinak house and then backed into that spot. If it pulled in off of Front Street and then backed in, the wheels would be facing in the opposite direction.

The evidence literally screams out that Joann's car was never used in these crimes. Ask yourself this: Is it possible that Joann drove that car from around the back of her house and into McCarty's parking lot, intending to pull out onto Front Street? Is it possible that before she could do that, something happened? Could Joann have seen someone she knew in the lot? Could she have been flagged down or met someone just pulling into the lot off Front Street? Someone she knew and trusted? Could Joann have been the one to back the car into that space to either talk to this person or leave with this person?

Remember the Steiners' testimony? They saw Joann's car in that lot on the day she disappeared, at 12:30 in the afternoon and again at 10:00 PM that night. Both times the car was parked in the same spot and the same position. They didn't think Joann's car had moved all day. Remember, too, why they noticed it: because it was the only car parked on that side of the lot. We heard a lot about Joann's phobia of backing up a car, but if there were no other cars around, then that phobia would not have applied.

If it's possible that Joann's car wasn't used in these crimes, then that's reasonable doubt, ladies and gentlemen, and you must acquit Patricia Rorrer.

So, if the car wasn't used in the crime, why is the prosecution so adamant that it was? Well, think about it. They have to tie the car to the crime because it's from the car that they got the only piece of physical evidence linking Patty to the murders: the hair.

They did the same thing with the phone call, you know. All the evidence points to the call taking place on December 7, but the prosecution insists it happened on December 12. Why? Because they have to place the call closer to the time of the disappearances. They know no one is ever going to believe that Patty was still so angry *eight days* after a stupid, petty hang-up call that she'd drive five hundred miles to kill two people she had never met.

It's the same thing with the car. All the evidence points to the fact that the car was not used in the crimes, but if they don't tie the car to the crime, they can't tie Patty to the murders.

The only piece of physical evidence they have against Patty—that one hair—came out of that car. But I'll tell you something. That one hair isn't worthy of your consideration. It just isn't. The hair evidence, in this case, is deplorable. It's not credible, it's not reliable, and it most certainly is not trustworthy.

For two and a half years, three of the most reputable scientists in the country looked at those hairs. They placed them under microscopes. They studied them, they examined them, and then they looked at them some more. And in all that time, not one of those three scientists ever reported seeing a hair root. Not one.

Well, at least not until the police took samples of Patty's hair, and then what happens? Lo and behold, a root magically appears on a hair that had no root before. Of course, Patty's hair samples all had forcibly removed roots, and all of a sudden we have a forcibly removed root on one of the hairs from Joann's car. It wasn't there for two and a half years, but after they get samples of Patty's hair, Wow! A miracle! A forcibly removed hair with a root.

Is that just coincidence? I don't think so. I honestly don't, and you shouldn't either.

Doctor Jensen contaminated those hairs. Doctor Jensen had those hairs in his lab at the same time he had Patty's forcibly removed hair samples. The state police were hand-delivering those hairs. The FBI returned those hairs to the PSP without DNA testing them. There's no valid chain of custody, no evidence that they were ever sent back to the FBI. And yet somehow, the FBI allegedly finds this newly grown hair root on one of them.

It's the shoddiest scientific work I've ever seen in my life. Ask yourself if it's possible that Patty's own hair sample was mislabeled as one of the hairs found in Joann Katrinak's car. You all saw the evidence of mislabeling by Dr. Jensen. At least twice, prosecutor McIntyre brought out this evidence. You saw envelopes that were supposed to contain two hairs that actually contained three, and you saw Jensen relabel an exhibit right on the witness stand without giving any explanation for what was wrong with the label or how he relabeled it. You know, if it weren't for Joann and Alex, Jensen's inept handling of the hair evidence might be comical.

Is it possible that one of Patty's hairs was mislabeled as a hair found in Joann's car? You bet it is. And that, ladies and gentlemen, is reasonable doubt.

Are you honestly willing to send this woman to her death or condemn her to a life behind bars on such shoddy and untrustworthy evidence?

Scientists are not God, ladies and gentlemen. Testing is not infallible. The testing on a piece of evidence is only as good as the person testing it. People and laboratories make mistakes. You need to remember that.

Without a documented count on Patty's hair samples—which we do not have—there's no way to tell if one of her hairs was mislabeled as a hair found in Joann's car. And that, ladies and gentlemen, is reasonable doubt.

Despite all these problems, the police and the prosecution made a conscious decision to test this untrustworthy hair, and guess what? They can't exclude Patty as a source for the hair. Now, that's a big surprise, isn't it? And repeatedly, you heard prosecutor McIntyre tell you that the hair "matched" Patty Rorrer, but that is not a true statement. The hair did not "match" Patty. All the testing showed was that Patty couldn't be excluded as a *potential* source for the hair. Just like thousands of other people. Maybe even one or two of you. In fact, every scientist who took that stand told you that the hair could have come from someone other than Patty Rorrer. If that isn't reasonable doubt, ladies and gentlemen, then what is?

Contamination. No reliable chain of custody. Thousands of other people who could have left the hair. The hair is unconvincing evidence. My God, you cannot convict a person on evidence like that. You just can't. You need to be extremely careful of the weight you give this hair evidence when you go into that jury room to decide Patricia Rorrer's fate. Extremely careful.

I want to talk a little more about that phone call between Joann and Patty. All through trial the prosecution argued that the phone call with Joann occurred on December 12, but the only thing they have to prove that is Andy Katrinak. All the evidence points to the call being made on December 7. They also argued that the call was placed from North Carolina, but do you remember what prosecutor McIntyre asked Patty when he had her on the stand? He asked her if she was "up here" on December 12, when she made that phone call to Joann. He was throwing out another scenario, because he has no evidence that the call was made on December 12.

What's most interesting about this is, the prosecution has maintained all along that the phone call was the trigger for the murders. If Patty placed the call from Pennsylvania on December 12, why did she hide the fact that she was coming here? If she was already here, then murder wasn't her reason for the trip. And if that were the case, then she would have told people she was coming. She would have told her mother, her friends, even Frank Alonzo, who she spoke with on December 7. That call isn't in dispute. Frank testified that she called him on December 7. If Patty had been planning to come up here, she would have told Frank. She would have made arrangements with Joyce Reagan to care for her animals because *Patty could not have known that she was going to get into an argument with Joann Katrinak that would lead to murder.* She couldn't have known that. The prosecution's new scenario that she was here when she made that call makes no sense whatsoever. The call was placed from North Carolina on December 7, just as Patty said, and she was not still so angry eight days later that she drove to Pennsylvania and killed Joann and Alex.

How can the prosecution be changing their theory of the crime in the middle of the trial? The only explanation is that they have no idea what actually happened to Joann and Alex Katrinak. That's absolutely astonishing, but it doesn't surprise me that they'd do it. That's been the prosecution's attitude throughout the entire trial: "Don't worry if it doesn't make sense. Just trust us."

Well you know, you can't just trust them. The prosecution has the burden of proving guilt, and that burden never shifts to the defendant. Patty doesn't have to prove her innocence, but that's what the prosecution is demanding that she do. They're insisting she reasonably explain everything that doesn't make sense, and she has. Apparently, they don't believe they have to play by the same rules. Nothing they are touting before you makes sense. "Just trust us," they say. "Believe us."

Well, don't you let them get away with that. If they want you to take on the responsibility of sending this woman to her death or to a life behind bars, demand that they show you evidence that is strong and airtight. They haven't done that here, ladies and gentlemen. They just haven't.

Patricia Rorrer had no motive to kill Joann and Alex Katrinak. None. Zippo. Nada.

They want you to believe that just because Patty didn't make a long-distance phone call during that four-day period, she's guilty of killing Joann and Alex? What about the eighty-six days out of the prior 245 when Patty didn't make a long-distance call either? Was she out murdering people then too? Let me ask you: Do you make a long-distance phone call every day of your life? Because long-distance calls are the only ones that show up on your phone bill. Local calls don't. Patty could have made dozens of local calls over that four-day period.

Does Patty have a reasonable explanation for that four-day gap in long-distance phone calls? You bet she does. She'd just called everyone she knew to tell them about her team penning win in Oklahoma. Why would she need to call those same people again so soon? Common sense, ladies, and gentlemen, common sense.

Now, you heard prosecutor McIntyre use the phrase, "consciousness of guilt." That, of course, is when a person does something that tends to make him or her look guilty. If someone uses an alias or lies to the police, tampers with evidence, or flees after a crime is committed. All of those things can be referred to as consciousness of guilt. But I want to talk to you about something called "consciousness of innocence." Because over and over again, Patty exhibited behavior that showed a consciousness of innocence.

She cooperated with the police. She admitted the argument with Joann. She had no motive to commit the crimes. She waived extradition. She didn't set up an airtight alibi—and she easily could have. Even the prosecution agrees that Patty was in North Carolina on December 16. How hard would it have been for her to find a receipt dated December 15? Just drive around the back of any restaurant or store and open the dumpster. I guarantee you, you'll find a receipt from the day before. Patty could have found a receipt dated December 15, tossed it in the back of the van, and then miraculously found it when the police came asking questions. Every one of those things could be considered consciousness of innocence.

You heard a lot about her never mentioning Seth or Cowboys as an alibi too, but you heard the testimony of Agent Ayers. Patty did speak about Cowboys the very first time she was interviewed. You heard her explanation for that, and it makes sense. She also spoke about being with her boyfriend, Jake, and the dance instructor. Did the police realize she was talking about three separate people? Or did they think that Jake was her boyfriend?

There was no "shopping for an alibi" either. Patty was simply trying to find out where she was six months earlier on a Thursday afternoon. Think back six months to a random weekday, and tell me if you can remember where you were. Patty was calling everybody she could think of, as I'm sure each of us would be.

Put yourself in her shoes. What if they wanted to arrest you for these brutal crimes and sentence you to death? Wouldn't you be calling every place you could think of, too? She never asked anyone to provide her with a false alibi, never asked anyone to lie.

The fact of the matter is, the police were negligent in not following up on Patty's alibi, and now they're asking you to punish her for their mistakes. Don't you do it, ladies and gentlemen, don't you do it. It was their mistake, not Patty's.

I think it's significant that the prosecution couldn't come up with one person who was willing to say Patty definitely was not at Cowboys on December 15. Not one. Everyone said they didn't know if she was there. It was just too long ago for them to remember.

Seth Alden and Jake Beamer say Patty was there that night, and initially, Jerry Bogan, the dance instructor, said she was there, too. It wasn't until the police went back to Jerry Bogan over and over and over again that Bogan finally changed his story. Now he says he can't say that Patty was there and he can't say she wasn't. I think that's significant, because even with all the police pressure, they still can't get Jerry Bogan to say Patty definitely was not there.

What about Patty's name not appearing on the sign-in sheets at Cowboys? Wow, now that's proof positive she killed Joann and Alex, isn't it? You all heard the testimony. People didn't always sign in at that club. Even the club's owner told you that. It wasn't a big deal. It wasn't something they watched carefully, especially on Thursday nights. You couldn't sign in when you came for dance class because the sign-in sheets weren't even out yet. Do you really believe that people already in the club were going to go back outside, get in line, and then wait around to sign in? I think we all know no one is going to do that.

Seth Alden said Patty was at Cowboys that night. Do you think Seth would lie for her to let her get away with killing a young mother and her little baby? Seth has a baby. Do you really believe he'd do that? Do you really think he'd want to continue living with a monster capable of doing something like that? Do you think he'd want this sadistic psychopath raising his own child?

I don't believe it, but even if you doubt Seth, can you really doubt Jake Beamer? Why would he lie for Patty? He barely knew her. In fact, he barely knew Seth. They had only met two months earlier. What did

Jake Beamer have to gain by lying to keep a killer out of prison? Absolutely nothing, that's what. He had a lot to lose, though. Perjury is a criminal offense, punishable by jail time. Why would Jake Beamer risk that? The answer is, he wouldn't. Of every witness who took that stand, Jake Beamer would have to be considered the most credible because he had nothing to gain by lying.

What about Audrey Brussels, the lady at the Exxon station? She remembers having problems with the pump and a lady coming in to tell her about it. How did Patty know about the pump problem or that a woman had complained about it if she wasn't that woman?

Michael Gaines remembers someone coming in to inquire about a lost set of keys.

The prosecution wants you to believe that Patty, caught off guard, basically confessed to Detective Suzanne Pearson on the morning she was arrested. That she said to her baby, "If I had known I would get caught, I would never have brought you into this world."

I want you to think about those words. They're overly dramatic. They don't sound like normal speech, and they don't ring true. Patty's not stupid, but she's not educated either, and she doesn't talk like that. You know, it's funny. Patty's house was swarming with police officers that morning. They were in and out of the bedroom, in and out of the house. One was even stationed at the bedroom door the entire time, yet no one heard this incriminating statement other than Detective Pearson.

Detective Coble was there, running in and out of the room, getting the baby a bottle, and he never heard Patty say this. Detective Tony Roberson was there, and he never heard Patty say it. Patty and Coble had a conversation right next to Pearson, and she couldn't hear what they were saying.

Detective Pearson's description makes it sound like Patty was hysterical, like she didn't know what she was saying. Yet the prosecution also wants you to believe that Patty was so sly and cunning, the moment another officer entered the room she got ahold of herself and clammed up. Well, you can't have it both ways. Either she was hysterical and rambling, or she was completely in control of what she was saying and doing.

What kind of police officer doesn't carry a notebook? Apparently, Suzanne Pearson doesn't. Suzanne Pearson doesn't believe getting a confession in a high-profile case like Patty's would help her career. Are we really supposed to believe that? Her work in the case had already earned her a promotion to sergeant, a position that came with more prestige and more money. Believe me, Suzanne Pearson knows that securing a confession from Patty Rorrer would be fantastic for her career. And you know it too.

Do I think Suzanne Pearson is lying? I don't know. Maybe Suzanne Pearson was the one caught up in the moment. Maybe Suzanne Pearson heard what she wanted to hear. What I am sure of, though, is that Patty never said those words. Sure, she told Holly she was sorry. She knew the police were going to take her away, and she knew that Holly was afraid and upset. But I don't believe for a minute that she ever said, "If I had known I would get caught, I'd have never brought you into this world."

Let's talk about the gun. The gun that killed Joann has never been found, and the police can't even tell you if the killer used a rifle or a handgun. There are seven different makes and models of gun that could have fired that shot. Tim Sellers can't tell you the make and model of the gun Patty owned, and neither can the man who sold her the gun. For all we know, the gun Patty once owned wasn't even on that list.

How can they stand here and insist to you that it was Patty's gun that fired that shot? They can't. It's another theory. Another "trust us" situation.

Patty has always maintained that Tim Sellers took her gun, and what evidence is there to negate that? None, other than Tim Sellers himself. Well, we all know how credible Tim Sellers is. He's a fifteen-time convicted felon with a reputation for stealing guns. The prosecution wants you to put Patty to death on the word of Tim Sellers? My God, give me a break.

Imagine for a moment that the roles were reversed. That Tim Sellers was on trial for killing Joann and Alex. Would anyone believe he didn't take that gun? Would anyone ever believe him over Patty? No way. You know it, and I know it. So why would you believe him now?

Tim Sellers is the type of person who would send his own mother to the electric chair if he thought it would benefit him. He's a career criminal. He knows the value of testifying for the prosecution in a high-profile case, and he has an ax to grind with Patty Rorrer. Don't you believe Tim Sellers for a minute, ladies and gentlemen, because Tim Sellers isn't worthy of belief.

There's something else I want to mention about this gun. The police spent weeks digging up places where Patty and Tim used this gun to target practice. They dug at Patty's house, at Telly Fiouris's, at the original gun owner's house, even at the Silver Shadows Stable, and guess what? They found more than seventy-five .22 caliber slugs and fragments, but not one of them matched the murder weapon. Not one.

Did Patty set up a ballistics lab in her house, dig up all the .22 slugs she could find, get rid of those fired from the .22 Jennings and then rebury the rest? Or might the police have actually recovered bullets fired from Patty's gun, and they didn't match the one from Joann because Patty's gun *is not the murder weapon*?

If that's possible, then that's reasonable doubt, and you must acquit Patty of these crimes.

Now, I have spoken to you for a very long time, and I could go on speaking to you for hours more because there are just that many problems with this case. That many doubts, that many mistakes. There is far more in this case that points to Patty's innocence than points to her guilt. I think you know that there's more than enough reasonable doubt to acquit her of these crimes.

I am, however, going to talk to you about one more thing. The most important thing in this case. The thing that will prove Patty's innocence beyond all doubt.

Now, we heard a lot of testimony about that one hair found in Joann's car located fifteen miles from the crime scene. Days and days of testimony about that one hair. But what we haven't heard much about is the physical evidence found right on the body of Joann Katrinak. Physical evidence that did not come from Patricia Rorrer. Physical evidence that came directly from Joann and Alex's real killer.

I'm talking about a hair found in Joann's right hand, a hair that did not come from Patricia Rorrer. It's a human hair, and it's capable of being DNA tested, but the prosecution refuses to test it.

I'm talking about three pieces of fingernail—two found on Joann's bicep and another on her chest. A fingernail that was torn from its owner—not clipped or cut—and that still retains a piece of skin with blood on it. Pieces of fingernail that did not come from Patricia Rorrer. They are perfect samples to DNA test, but the prosecution refuses to test them.

I'm talking about a cigarette butt found with the bodies of Joann and Alex. Again, a perfect specimen for DNA testing, but the prosecution refuses to test it.

Why? Why have the police and the prosecution chosen to disregard the most important evidence in the case? Well, there can only be one reason. The police and prosecution will not test this evidence because they know it won't match Patty Rorrer. And if they admit that to you, there is no way you can convict her of these crimes.

But I'll tell you something. The prosecution's failure to test that evidence *is* an admission that Patty didn't commit these crimes. Because you know as well as I do, if that evidence matched Patty, they'd be presenting it in this courtroom. You know they would.

Their goal is to win, and if they have to disregard evidence to do that, they will. Isn't justice supposed to be a search for the truth, no matter where that truth leads? Whoever left that evidence with Joann and Alex, that's who killed them. And that person is not Patricia Rorrer. The real killer is getting away with murder because the police and the prosecution are letting them. Where's the justice in that? How is that justice for Joann and Alex?

That evidence didn't just float along on a breeze and come to rest on those bodies. Whomever that evidence belongs to was with Joann and Alex at or near the time of death. It came from the last person Joann Katrinak had contact with in life, and that person is *not* Patricia Rorrer.

The police have the real killer's DNA, and they refuse to test it, because they'd rather put an innocent woman to death just to close the books on this case. That's reprehensible. You should be outraged and appalled by that, and you should not let them get away with it.

My God, if that evidence left on Joann is not reasonable doubt, then you tell me what is.

Joann struggled with her assailant, and in doing so, she took from him or her evidence that will prove that person's guilt. We can tell you how the fingernail pieces were left on Joann's body. We know Joann was dragged face down because of the mud on her jeans and boots, but she was found lying on her back. And under her body was her bracelet, broken in half. Now think about that. The bracelet had to be broken at that time, or it wouldn't have been found where it was. We contend that after dragging Joann face down, her killer flipped her body onto its back, and in doing that, he or she snagged a fingernail in that bracelet. And when the killer yanked it free, he or she broke the bracelet, and in the process, ripped off a fingernail, which came to rest on Joann.

That fingernail will tell you who killed Joann and Alex Katrinak, but the prosecution refuses to test it. And if you convict Patricia Rorrer, they will *never* test it. And whoever killed Joann and Alex will simply get away with murder.

Don't let that happen, ladies and gentlemen. As jurors, you have been handed an awesome responsibility. You hold this woman's very life in your hands. I understand that public sentiment isn't for Patricia Rorrer. There's a tremendous amount of pressure from the public, the police, and the victim's family to convict this woman. It won't be easy for you to do the right thing, but remember, you're not doing anyone any good if you convict the wrong person. Not the public and certainly not Joann and Alex or their loved ones. As members of the jury, you were privy to a lot of information the public never heard. Only you know the full story, and you took an oath to do the right thing, no matter what.

If you go into that jury room, and you say, "Maybe she didn't do it," that's reasonable doubt, and you must acquit her.

If you go into that jury room and say, "It's possible somebody else did it," that's reasonable doubt, and you must acquit her.

If you go into that jury room and you say, "I'm not sure she did it," that's reasonable doubt, and you must acquit her.

If the prosecution hasn't proven their case beyond a reasonable doubt—and it's obvious that they haven't—then you must acquit her.

You heard all the evidence. There's nothing tying Patty to these crimes. The prosecution has put up smokescreens here. Smoke and mirrors, ladies and gentlemen, smoke and mirrors. They have not met their burden of proof in proving Patty's guilt beyond a reasonable doubt, and you know it.

Tell them, ladies and gentlemen. Tell them that if they want you to send this woman to her death or condemn her to a life behind bars, then they had better have stronger and more convincing evidence than they have here.

This case should scare the hell out of you because it does me. If the Commonwealth can bring someone to trial on the flimsy evidence they paraded here, then any one of us could be sitting in that defendant's chair.

Tell them, ladies and gentlemen. Tell them with your verdict that it's got to be better than this. Tell them, and do the right thing. Honor your oath as jurors, and find Patricia Rorrer not guilty. Because she's not.

21

All of the evidence I laid out in my summation was either known by the defense or should have been, yet the jury never heard much of it. More startling revelations were to come, but my quest to uncover them was no easy task. It had been twenty years since the murders occurred, and finding information was difficult. Phone numbers were disconnected, people had moved away, died, or seemed to have just vanished off the face of the earth. I sent out countless letters but received few replies. Some of the envelopes came back stamped "Moved, no forwarding address" or "Not deliverable," but others were neither returned nor answered, leaving me to wonder whether the recipient even received them.

In 2013, I sent out Freedom of Information Act Requests to the Catasauqua Police Department, the Pennsylvania State Police, and the FBI, asking for any files or reports pertaining to the case. Almost immediately, I heard back from the PSP, which informed me that it was releasing absolutely nothing. The files, they wrote, contained sensitive information concerning a minor—Alex Katrinak—and therefore, I would not be allowed to see them. Since Alex was dead, this should not have mattered, but I wasn't surprised. It was not the first time I had encountered resistance in the case. A few weeks later I received a call from the chief of the Catasauqua Police Department, who also informed me that he had no reports to divulge. They had remodeled since he had become chief, and he could find no records on the Katrinak case. I thought it odd that the department had nothing on the biggest case it had ever handled, but again, I was not surprised. My last remaining hope was the FBI, which sent me a letter stating that it had received my request and was perusing its files. I suspected I would not get anything from it either, but there was nothing I could do other than wait.

———————

The hair evidence in the case continued to nag at me. How, for more than two entire years, could no scientist have seen a root and then all of a sudden, after Patty's samples are taken a root appears?

I knew there was no proper chain of custody for the hair. I knew the hair was contaminated and the police were hand-delivering it. I knew there was no count taken of Patty's samples, and I knew Dr. Jensen had her samples in the lab at the same time he had the six hairs from Joann's car. Could Dr. Jensen have mislabeled one of Patty's hairs for one of the hairs found in Joann's car? I felt it wasn't only possible but probable.

At least twice during the trial, prosecutor McIntyre discovered evidence of Jensen's mislabeling, and the jury watched as Dr. Jensen relabeled an exhibit that dealt with one of the hairs used to convict Patricia Rorrer. McIntyre also found an envelope that was supposed to contain two hairs but actually contained three, which Dr. Jensen dismissed as "not unusual."

I found it incredible that any reputable scientist would give such an answer in open court. Not unusual to be mixing up evidence and having no idea where that evidence came from? The envelope was marked, "two hairs found with Alex Katrinak." How could Jensen determine which two hairs in that envelope were actually the ones found with Alex? Where did the other hair come from, and where was it found? I'd never heard anything like it.

The reports I had in my possession led me to believe that Patty was probably telling the truth; somehow her hair was switched for that found in Joann's car, but I did not have enough information to show how. I desperately needed to read the trial testimony of Dr. Jensen,

Dr. Deadman, and Dr. Dizinno—each scientist who had worked with the hair—but I didn't have the trial transcript at the time, and obtaining it was much harder than expected.

I phoned the Allentown courthouse and spoke with a woman who seemed very friendly and helpful until she found out what trial transcript I was seeking, then her attitude immediately changed. That was an old case, she said, probably archived somewhere in storage. She'd have to look for it, but she couldn't guarantee she'd be able to find it. That seemed odd, but I asked her to please try.

Days passed, and then a week, but still I heard nothing back from the courthouse. After leaving several messages without a return call, I finally connected with the woman again. She hadn't found the trial transcript, but she did inform me that it consisted of more than 6,500 pages and would cost $3.00 to $5.00 per page—somewhere between $19,000 and $32,000 dollars. There was no offer for me to come into the courthouse and copy only the pages I might need.

Obviously, I didn't have an extra twenty or thirty grand lying around, but my spirits rose when I learned that Margaret had managed to secure a copy of the transcript early in her investigation. The only problem was, Margaret had died years ago, and no one seemed to know what had become of it. I called Patty's Uncle Telly, who told me he thought Margaret's husband had it, which was good, except that Margaret's husband had no telephone. A friend and I spent an entire day driving down to Allentown and knocking on his door, only to find it was a wasted trip; Margaret's husband didn't know what had become of Margaret's files after she passed away.

It was a real letdown. I desperately needed those transcripts and went so far as to have a lawyer draw up a motion for the court to get them. I had no idea how I would pay for them, but I figured I'd find a way. Thankfully, it never came to that. A few months after my trip to Allentown, I received a call from Telly Fiouris, who had just remembered that he gave a copy of the transcript to a private investigator years earlier. Although he had no idea where the PI might be now, he promised to do some checking. It took several months and the aid of an attorney before Telly tracked the PI to Florida. My quest for the transcripts began in 2013, but it wasn't until late November 2014 that a Zip drive with the copied transcripts finally arrived at my house.

I immediately went to work, but it was a mind-boggling task. Whoever had copied the transcript had put each page into its own PDF file—more than 6,500 clicks with my mouse. I worked day and night, eager to find something that would raise Patty's spirits. She had suffered another loss in October when her step-pop, Ray Chambers, passed away after a long battle with cancer. It took nearly two months of daily reading, but I finally hit on something that seemed to bring the puzzle into focus.

When McIntyre had Patty on the stand, he asked her a curious question: "Do you know they took thirty-nine of your hairs? Do you know that?"

Of course, Patty didn't know that, nor did I. I wondered where McIntyre had gotten the figure, since no one I knew had ever seen a documented count on Patty's hair samples. It didn't matter, however; the prosecution had offered a number, and it was now a part of the trial record. Thirty-nine hairs, I thought, quickly beginning to calculate. When Dr. Jensen received Patty's hair samples, the first thing he did was send three of them unmounted to the FBI. He then mounted fourteen more in his lab and tested another two with a methylene blue solution. That made nineteen hairs.

On August 6, 1996, Jensen sent an additional sixteen mounted slides of Patty's hair to the FBI, and there the trail ended. I had no other reports of any activity with Patty's hair samples from Dr. Jensen or the FBI. Combining those last sixteen samples with the previous nineteen accounted for thirty-five of Patty's thirty-nine hair samples. Where were the other four?

I felt a surge of excitement. Four hairs unaccounted for; the exact number needed to frame Patricia Rorrer: one left unmounted to provide the match of one in thirty-seven thousand and the other three *remounted* to ensure the perfect match in 2007.

I had to sit back and take a deep breath. If the theory were correct, that would mean the switched hairs were not an accident. One hair could have been accidentally switched for one of the car hairs, but not all four. Someone would have had to have done it deliberately, a notion I found extremely hard to believe. At the time, I was still under the impression that things like that didn't happen in real life, only in the movies. Besides, why had no one else picked up on this? Who was I to have figured this out? I wasn't a lawyer or a scientist. I had to be missing something. I had to be.

Page by page I went over the reports I had on the hair evidence—not once, but dozens of times—and found absolutely nothing to discredit what I had discovered. Either I was missing some critical reports—which was possible—or it was highly likely that someone had framed Patty Rorrer. But who, and for what reason? The known facts provided some ideas.

- At the time, the Katrinak case was the biggest in Pennsylvania
- The police were under a tremendous amount of pressure to solve it
- Technicians at the PSP crime lab had instructed officers on how to collect evidence—ostensibly so nothing would be mishandled

What, I wondered, was the lab's reaction when they discovered that they had botched the entire investigation by contaminating the most crucial evidence in the case? What had they thought when they realized that they might solely be responsible for letting this "baby killer" walk free? I didn't think it was hard to imagine. At the very least, they were bound to look incompetent, but most likely, their jobs and reputations would have been at risk as well. Perhaps even more important was the fact that they would have known the contamination would follow the case forever. And that somewhere down the road, a judge would probably allow Patty to retest the evidence, which is exactly what happened. It all made sense.

I knew that the PSP had the hairs from Joann's car in their possession at the same time they had Patty's hair samples. Was it possible that someone in the lab, believing that Patty was guilty and desperate to preserve not only the case but his or her job and reputation as well, decided that the end justified the means? Did that person convince him- or herself that there was nothing wrong with switching the hairs because there was a duty to keep this "monster" off the streets?

If someone switched three of Patty's four missing hair samples for the three mounted hairs that were found in Joann's car, it might explain several things:

- Why the hair matched Patty perfectly in 2007 despite Orchid Cellmark using the same method to DNA test it as was used in 1996
- Why Orchid Cellmark didn't find Dr. Jensen's DNA on the hair
- Why Orchid Cellmark didn't find Joann's DNA on the hair
- Why the PSP lab claimed it measured the three mounted car hairs in such a bizarre and complex way *after* mounting them (to explain the lack of Jensen's DNA on the hair)
- Why there was testimony about *three remounted hairs* from Joann's car
- Why the PSP crime lab insisted no pictures of the mounted car hairs were taken before December 1997

Without photos of the mounted hairs from 1995, there was no way to compare them with photos from today and no way to verify if the original hairs had been switched with Patty's samples.

As for the fourth missing Rorrer sample, that one could have been returned to the FBI as one of the unmounted car hairs and then used to secure the initial match to Patty of one in thirty-seven thousand. If one of Patty's samples was substituted for one of the three unmounted hairs, her sample would be the only one that bore a root and thus the only one the FBI would have been able to test. That would explain why no scientist reported seeing a root on the car hairs until after they received Patty's samples and why the PSP lab, again, claimed to have taken only one picture of one of the unmounted hairs, and not the hair that was matched to Patty. The lack of picture taking never made any sense. What police department doesn't take pictures of evidence?

I had to ask myself if I was becoming a conspiracy theorist. Was it really possible that someone had deliberately framed Patty? Most claims of framing would need the agreement and involvement of dozens of people, but I realized that wasn't the case with this theory. Patricia could have been framed by a single person, someone who had access to her hair samples and the hair from Joann's car. No one else need ever have known.

I thought that what I had stumbled upon was important, and Patty fervently agreed. She had worked for a time with the Pennsylvania Innocence Project at Temple University but had been unable to explain to them the switching of the hairs. Now, she asked that I let them know my theory and also that I call her old lawyer, Craig Neely, and let him know too.

I exchanged a few emails with a woman at the Innocence Project who assured me that she would include my findings in Patty's case file. As for Craig, I had spoken to him briefly in the past, but I didn't really know him. When I called him now, however, we ended up talking about the case for well over an hour. I discovered that Craig was one of those rare attorneys—a lawyer with a heart. He was a brilliant man who cared about his clients, the law, and our justice system. He was also cautious in his manner and not one to give undue hope. Although he listened carefully to my story of Patty's four missing hairs, he gave no indication of what he was thinking. The conversation ended on a good note, however, and we kept in more regular contact after that.

After discovering the four missing Rorrer hair samples, things began happening in a domino effect. The first was the *Washington Post*'s breaking news story of faulty hair analysis performed by the FBI in criminal cases before the year 2000. In reviewing more than two hundred cases in which a conviction was secured through FBI hair analysis, 98 percent were determined to contain errors. The story stunned the public and sent shockwaves through the legal community. Unable to refute the story's accuracy, the FBI posted the following information on its website:

> The United States Department of Justice (DOJ), the Federal Bureau of Investigation (FBI), the Innocence Project, and the National Association of Criminal Defense Lawyers (NACDL) reported today that the FBI has concluded that the examiners' testimony in at least 90 percent

of trial transcripts the Bureau analyzed as part of its Microscopic Hair Comparison Analysis Review contained erroneous statements. Twenty-six of 28 FBI agent/analysts provided either testimony with erroneous statements or submitted laboratory reports with erroneous statements. The review focuses on cases worked prior to 2000, when mitochondrial DNA testing on hair became routine at the FBI.

It was an exciting story with the potential to significantly impact Patricia Rorrer. Her case fell precisely within the timeframe and was the first in Pennsylvania to use mitochondrial DNA testing. Even more hopeful was the fact that Dr. Harold Deadman, the FBI analyst who had made the "match" to Patty's hair and helped secure her conviction, had been mentioned in the *Washington Post* article. In an unrelated proceeding, Dr. Deadman had determined a hair to be of Caucasian origin when in fact, the *Post*'s investigation proved, the hair had come from a canine.

I'd barely begun to absorb this revelation when, in July of that same year, I opened my mailbox to find a small envelope with a return address from the FBI, the results of my Freedom of Information Act Request sent out two years earlier. The envelope held a CD containing three hundred FBI reports, and as I eagerly read over them, one stood out in stark clarity. It was a report generated early in the investigation before the police had obtained Patty's hair samples, and it stated unequivocally that the three unmounted hairs from Joann's car "have no roots attached." No roots attached.

I was rendered speechless upon reading it. The magnitude of this find was incredible because not only did it prove that someone had switched Patty's hair samples for those found in Joann's car, but it also wiped out the 2007 hair match. If the hairs tested in 1996 were not the same hairs found in Joann's car, then neither were the ones tested in 2007. Whether that mounted hair matched Patty or not was irrelevant if it was not the same hair that came out of Joann's car. Finally, here was the proof needed to show that someone had deliberately framed an innocent woman and sent her to prison for the rest of her life. I couldn't help but wonder what a jury would have done had they been privy to this FBI report. I thought a jury would have acquitted Patty if they had known all the facts *before* this report surfaced. With the report, I had no doubt of it.

Patty had only sixty days to file an appeal based on this newly discovered evidence, and we were both hoping that Craig Neely would agree to help. I gave him a call and explained to him what I'd found, and he asked that I send him a copy of the CD. I did, and in September 2015, working pro bono, he filed an appeal on Patty's behalf.

Before we even received an answer from the court, a local news channel in Lehigh County decided to interview Craig about his recent PCRA filing. After running a three-minute clip of the interview on the nightly news, Officer Joseph York contacted Craig and relayed his information: that Officer Kicska had told him there was no sign of a break-in at Andy's house on the evening of December 15, 1994, and that he had been threatened by the Lehigh County District Attorney's Office to "keep his mouth shut."

One month later, in December 2015, Judge Reichley sent Craig a "notice of intent to dismiss" on Patty's PCRA. It was incredibly disappointing. We had given the court proof that the prosecution had secured Patty's conviction by using a piece of evidence that had never existed—the alleged hair root on the unmounted hair—but apparently, it didn't matter. Had the judge even read the petition, I wondered? Luckily, Reichley also gave Craig twenty days to respond to his notice and, combined with Officer York's signed affidavit, Craig felt confident that the judge would be compelled to grant him a hearing. Before that could happen, however, another revelation came to light that left all of us reeling.

On February 16, 2016, I opened my email to find a message from Craig that revealed that he might have found additional proof of a hair switch.

According to the police and prosecution, no one had ever tested the three mounted car hairs before Craig had them sent to Orchid Cellmark in 2007. In fact, Dr. Deadman of the FBI sent prosecutor Michael McIntyre a letter in December 1997—less than two months before Patty went on trial—informing him that he had not tested the mounted hairs due to his inability to get into the slides. However, while reading over Dr. Jensen's trial testimony about those three mounted car hairs, Craig had come across something peculiar.

In questioning Dr. Jensen, McIntyre first put up a picture of one of the mounted car hairs and then asked the witness to "Show the ladies and gentlemen of the jury on this particular exhibit what you consider to be apparent dried blood."

After Jensen had pointed out the spot, McIntyre said, "All right, now that particular hair was then mounted by you on a slide?"

"That hair was mounted on a slide by me and at a later date was sent to the FBI, and some tests have been done to some of the red stains on that hair by some people at the FBI."

How could the FBI test the red stains if they never got into the slides?

Still later in his testimony, when McIntyre was again questioning Jensen about the three mounted seat-back hairs, he put up Commonwealth's exhibit 17-D and asked Jensen to tell the jury what it was.

"That's what I call hair number one of the car seat hairs that were mounted. This is hair number one."

"All right," McIntyre said, "let me just take you back for a little background and make something understandable for the jury. When you say you mounted these on slides before sending them to the FBI, can you give us an indication of how permanent your mounting of those hairs were on those slides so that we know that the FBI hadn't done anything with them to alter the way they look before you send them and after you send them?"

Jensen replied that in addition to mounting them in a "permanent mount," he also made Xerox copies of each mount "so that any attempts to change things later would immediately be obvious."

"All right," McIntyre said, "when you got the slides back from the FBI, did you match them with the Xerox copies you made as to how the hairs looked before you sent them?"

"Yes, I did."

"And were the hairs in the same exact position as when you mounted them?"

"Well . . ." Jensen began, hesitating.

"The hairs themselves," McIntyre interrupted.

"Well, the hairs themselves, except sections of one of them were missing."

"So the FBI did get into one of those slides?"

"Oh, yes. Yes." Jensen answered.

Despite the prosecution's denials, it seemed the FBI did manage to get into at least one of the mounted seat-back hairs.

This testimony nagged at Craig, and then it hit him like a bolt of lightning; he had sent the mounted hairs to Orchid Cellmark in 2007, but he didn't recall Cellmark mentioning anything about broken mounts or sections of hair being missing. On a hunch, Craig called the Texas laboratory and asked for their file on the 2007 testing. Upon receiving it, he made an astonishing discovery: Cellmark described the hairs and the mounts as being "intact," with no broken mounts and no sections of hair missing. That wasn't the only unusual thing either; Cellmark also described the mounted hairs as being brown in color—the same color as Patty's given samples—and not blond like those found in Joann's car.

Craig was flabbergasted by the finds, but there was even more to come. The Q4 hair was listed as having no root, while the Q5 hair was listed as having a root, yet in their final results Cellmark had obtained that perfect match to Patty using the Q4 hair! Was this a mistake? A typo? How was it possible to have another DNA match made to Patricia Rorrer from a hair that had no root?

For me, these revelations brought home the truth about the hair evidence: Since it was so unreliable and so screwed up, how could anyone possibly trust it? The only way to either prove or disprove whether Patty's hairs were switched was by reviewing the entire case file, which we did not have, as evidenced by the fact that we had already uncovered several documents that were never handed over to the defense. Craig had asked for the entire case file back in 2007, but the judge denied his request. From the documents in my possession, the theory of the switching of the hair cannot be disproven. If there is any chance that Patricia Rorrer was wrongfully convicted of these two heinous murders, then her case deserves to be completely reviewed. In the interest of justice, I hope one day it is.

CONCLUSION

Eventually, I came to believe that the prosecution of Patricia Rorrer was a classic case of smoke and mirrors. There was scant real evidence against her and more than enough reasonable doubt to acquit her. Had the jury heard all the evidence, there's little doubt they would have acquitted. In hindsight, Patty probably would have fared better by leaving her fate in the hands of a judge rather than a jury. Judges, after all, are supposed to think with the law, not their emotions.

It's too late for that now, but it's not too late to set things right. Patty believes there are still people out there who know what happened, witnesses who never came forward, and people with information they have never divulged. If so, Patty hopes those people have the courage to come forward today.

No one is asking that Muncy just open its doors and allow Patricia Rorrer to walk free, including Patty. "The public needs to understand that I'm not asking to be set free. I just want a fair trial. I want to be allowed to test the evidence and argue my case. That's all I'm asking for. I did not kill Joann and Alex, and I want the chance to prove it. I welcome contact from anyone who has any information."

Joann Katrinak was hardly the only person to go missing from the Lehigh Valley—the county has numerous unsolved cases of missing and murdered women. So many, in fact, that in January 2015, they instituted a cold case squad to work on them. It would seem that in the interest of justice, the Commonwealth should test the evidence left with the bodies of Joann and Alex. Perhaps all these dead and missing women are not unrelated. If a DNA profile could be established and then run through the Combined DNA Index System (CODIS), it's possible the police might get a hit that links it to another crime. For some unknown reason, however, Lehigh County refuses to test the Katrinak evidence. Why? Doesn't it have an obligation and a duty to do so?

The murders of Joann and Alex were a tragedy beyond comparison, and whoever killed them deserves to spend the rest of his or her life in prison. If that person is Patricia Rorrer, then so be it. However, the Commonwealth of Pennsylvania has a duty to make sure it *is* Patricia Rorrer and not some unknown killer still walking the streets today. To date, it has not done that.

The new evidence that's come to light in Patty's case has finally brought her hope. She and her attorney were granted a hearing to "inspect and copy documents" in April 2016. The hearing should have lasted ten minutes, but instead, it turned into a two-hour battle between Craig Neely and Michael McIntyre. Incredibly, McIntyre stood up in open court and made a number of odd admissions, at one point saying, "There's no way that I'll say that I'm one hundred percent sure that Patricia Rorrer is guilty of this crime. We can't be sure of anything."

And, while discussing Craig's decision to send the three mounted hairs to Orchid Cellmark in 2007, McIntyre told the court, "I wasn't a part of this at the time, and so I can't say I'm a hundred percent sure [of what the crime lab did]—like I can say I'm a hundred percent sure that what [Neely] says about me is a lie. I don't know what the crime lab did. I didn't run over to the crime lab and say, 'Oh, let me take a look at the slides before you send them to Attorney Neely's expert.'"

McIntyre also told the judge, "I want to say that we proved her guilt beyond a reasonable doubt and in the eighteen years since her crime, since her conviction, no one has brought any evidence to me to cast any doubt on that conviction. If they do, I hope that I'd be man enough to take a look at it and judge it fairly. But what's hard to do—and for the court too—is when we get blinded by the nonsense that's filed. There might be a kernel of truth in there [Patty's brief], but we might not see it because of all the nonsense."

There might be a kernel of truth in there. Since it seems so obvious that there is a vast amount of doubt in Patty's case, I hope prosecutor McIntyre is sincere in his words. I hope he will be "man enough" to take another look at this case and "judge it fairly."

Despite these astonishing revelations by the man who prosecuted Patricia Rorrer, Judge Reichley denied her appeal.

Hope is not all lost, however. Patty is still in the appeal process with the higher courts, but the wheels of justice turn ever so slowly.

Not long ago, I was thinking about how disappointed I was when I first realized that the only person willing to cooperate with me was Patty Rorrer. Today, I understand how fortunate I was that things turned out that way. What would have happened if Detective Vasquez had not piqued my curiosity with his phone call or if Joann's family and those who investigated the case had agreed to cooperate with me? Would I have taken the time needed to gain Patty's trust? Probably not. Instead, I would have written a book detailing the prosecution's side of the story and omitting all the problems that plague this case.

It was Patty who enabled me to gain access to more than ten thousand documents, both good and bad, pertaining to the case. It's unlikely that the police would have allowed me to access any reports that pointed toward Patty's innocence, and of course, had the police cooperated with me, I would have had no reason to send the FBI a Freedom of Information Act Request. Had I not done that, then all the new evidence that points to a wrongful conviction in Patty's case would never have come to light, and this book would have told a far different tale, an inaccurate story that perpetuated more lies about Patricia Rorrer and helped keep a potentially innocent person in prison.

One day, while visiting Patty at Muncy, the two of us were sitting outside at a picnic table when another visitor walked by and nodded. Patty mentioned that the man was a reporter who had once written to her asking for an interview, but she hadn't replied. It got me thinking about the fact that she had never spoken to anyone about the crimes, and I decided to ask her why she had agreed to speak to me. She looked thoughtful for a moment and then shrugged. "I don't know," she said. "Something just told me to talk to you."

I had to smile. Almost from the beginning, both Patty and I have believed that God was directing our every move, and I saw His hand at work in her answer. My goal in writing this book was to find the truth, and with Patty's help, I feel confident that I have done that. Although people may accuse me of taking her side, I can honestly say that the only side I've ever been on was the side of justice and obtaining it for Joann and Alex.

EPILOGUE

It seems that each time I feel I'm through with this book, something else occurs to bring the case back into focus. In 2016, I was interviewed for a documentary titled *Murder in Lehigh Valley: Keith Morrison Investigates*. The show, hosted by veteran crime reporter and *Dateline NBC* correspondent Keith Morrison, aired on the Investigation Discovery channel in 2017 and chronicled the Katrinak/Rorrer case. Morrison would maintain a neutral stance throughout the program, but he was the first journalist to give both sides of the story, and the only one to ever ask prosecutor Michael McIntyre and PSP captain Robert Werts some very tough questions. Many of their responses are worth repeating.

Werts admitted that he didn't know why the local Catasauqua authorities would fail to take the Katrinak disappearances seriously if they actually saw evidence of foul play at the house on their early visits, and agreed that such inaction was a "mistake." He also, on several occasions, illuminated the double standard I felt the police displayed in their treatment of Andy and Patty as suspects.

When asked about Andy having shown deception on his polygraph tests, Werts sighed, as if to indicate that Andy's results were inconsequential. "He may have shown some deception," the captain said, "but the fact that he said it readily, he didn't try to hold anything back [and] anything we asked for, he did . . ."

What was Werts saying with that response? That it was OK to dismiss anything suspicious in regard to Andy because he was cooperating with the investigation? Patty had initially cooperated with the investigation too, but she certainly never received any benefit of the doubt. Nor should she have—just as Andy shouldn't have either.

When it came to the subject of alibis, Werts claimed that Patty's were untrue, and tried to verify this by saying, "She was not at the bar, because you are required as you come in to sign in, and she never signed in on the fifteenth of December."

"But," Morrison reminded him, "somebody later said, 'You can come into that bar and not sign your name. You're supposed to, but not everybody does.' That doesn't mean she wasn't there."

"Neither does it mean that she was there," Werts shot back.

"But it's ambiguous!" Morrison pointed out.

In regards to Andy's alibi, however, Werts seemed to go out of his way to defend him.

"An alibi from a family member's not as strong as someone you don't know," Morrison noted.

"Yes," Werts said. "But, the work that they said they did that day was in fact done [at the Brenner house]."

How could Werts have verified that? Who told him what work was done that day? Andy? Andy's father? Jim Brenner, Andy's best friend since childhood?

Even more telling was the captain's response to whether it was possible for Andy to have left the job site for a couple of hours and then come back. Werts simply shrugged and said, "If you don't wanna believe them, yes. But we had no reason not to believe them."

If you don't want to believe them? Is that what the police did? Simply believe what Andy and his family and friends told them? Where Patty was concerned, everything she said was a lie, but in regard to Andy, the police seemed to go out of their way to make excuses for him. Apparently they "wanted" to believe Andy; they did not want to believe Patricia.

When it was pointed out to prosecutor McIntyre that it seemed odd that the only evidence linking Patty to Joann's car were those six hairs, he agreed. "You'd definitely think there'd be some blood on her," he said.

"It's kind of curious if there's nothing from her in the car; surely?" Morrison prodded.

McIntyre nodded, then sighed dramatically. "I would expect that maybe we should have found more," he said, before adding, "but what we found was so damning in itself, we don't need to find anything more."

In discussing the FBI's use of mitochondrial DNA testing, McIntyre claimed the hair had a root capable of being nuclear tested, but acknowledged that "[the FBI] didn't go for the root material right away."

"Which seems odd somehow," Morrison said. "I mean, if you can get the absolute answer right off the bat . . ."

"I agree," McIntyre nodded. "I don't know why that happened."

Nor could he explain why he never tested the hair found in Joann's hand.

"Why wasn't it tested? Morrison asked.

"Why wasn't it tested?" McIntyre repeated. "It *was* looked at, and it was already determined that it wasn't Joann's and it wasn't Patricia's."

When his interviewer raised his eyebrows, McIntyre became frustrated. "*Who cares whose [hair] it is!*" he finally shouted.

"Maybe it was the killer's," Morrison fired back.

"You mean the other killer?" McIntyre asked sarcastically. "Because Rorrer's two hairs are out there in the debris too. You know, there were eight hairs, six in the car, two found on the debris. So there was somebody with Patricia Rorrer? OK. Does that make her not guilty?"

It was an incredible comeback to a logical question. Of course if Patty committed the crime with an accomplice that would not make her not guilty. It would, however, make the prosecution and the PSP responsible for allowing a double murderer to walk free, putting the public at risk.

"Why not test the hair?" Morrison asked again.

McIntyre, clearly annoyed and uncomfortable with the subject, first tried to defend himself by saying that in every case there would always be someone who said you should have done more. Realizing, however, that such an argument would never fly, he finally said, "You're right. You got me. We should have tested it."

Indeed they should have.

Captain Werts was also asked about the hair found in Joann's hand. "If it isn't Joann's hair, and it isn't the accused's hair, whose hair is it?" Morrison asked.

"I don't know," Werts answered.

"The killer's hair?"

"I don't know."

"Wouldn't you want to know that?"

"Yeah," Werts said, "I would."

To me, such statements clearly constituted doubt on the part of Werts and McIntyre, so why were they so forcefully objecting to Patty's request for a review of the evidence? Was it their pride? Their reputations? Is there any relevant reason that would excuse not trying to determine if an innocent person was wrongfully convicted of a crime?

Perhaps one of the oddest comments came from prosecutor McIntyre after he described what he believed Patty did immediately following the murders. "Now, she gets back in the victim's vehicle, she drives back, she parks the car in the McCarty's parking lot, walks to her car, and drives home."

"It's an interesting theory," Morrison noted.

"The jury bought it too," McIntyre said with a smile.

"The jury bought it too." What a peculiar thing to say. Not "The jury believed it" but "The jury *bought* it."

Although I have no grand illusion that Michael McIntyre will ever admit it's probable or likely that someone switched Patty's hair samples, it was still encouraging to hear him admit that the notion is not outside the realm of possibility. After adamantly denying that *he* had switched the hairs, he did concede, "But is it possible we had some kind of mole in the state police crime lab? You know, it's—it's so ridiculous, but yet *I can't rule it completely out.*"

Having heard Mike McIntyre, for the second time, publicly admit it's possible Patty's hairs were switched, I'm compelled to once again remind him of his own words at the 2016 hearing: "In the eighteen years since . . . [Patty's] conviction, no one has brought any evidence to me to cast any doubt on that conviction. If they do, I hope that I'd be man enough to take a look at it and judge it fairly."

How much more doubt does one need?

After *Murder in Lehigh Valley* had aired, a woman named JENNIFER STARR contacted me. Jennifer was the sister of Joann's ex-husband, Jhared Starr, and she was extremely upset by the show—not because she thought we were trying to get a killer out of jail, but because, as she said, "For the past twenty years, we've had this woman convicted in our house."

Jennifer knew Joann well and loved her like a sister. Not only were they related through marriage, but they were friends. Over the years, Jennifer had watched all the television shows and read all the newspaper articles that portrayed Patty as guilty. And, like myself initially, she was convinced of Patty Rorrer's guilt. Now, however, having finally learned of the many problems plaguing the case, she wasn't so sure.

Jennifer gave me a vivid picture of Joann and confirmed what I had already suspected: that Joann was a spitfire who would have fought tooth and nail if she honestly believed her life, or that of her child, was in danger.

"Joann would never have gotten into a car with a stranger," Jennifer insisted, "especially not in broad daylight and with people in the vicinity. Joann was a fighter, and she would have fought."

Jennifer was astounded that so much about Joann's murder had been kept from the public. At her request, I have since provided her with the entire case file so that she can reassess the evidence—all of the evidence—with an open mind. "This case is tragic beyond words," Jennifer said, "and if there's any chance that the police convicted the wrong person, we need to know. Joann and Alex deserve justice, and if Patricia Rorrer isn't guilty, then justice has not been served."

It's a sentiment I agree with completely.

PATTY'S WORDS

I was asked if I wanted to say anything in this book. After thinking it over, this is what I want to say to you:

I've been approached before, by mail and phone, so what made me answer this [author]? I can't truly tell you, other than a spiritual leading. I had it with Margaret [Sneary]; two rows of reporters at [my] trial, and she is the only one I agreed to meet and put on my visiting list.

By Tammy's first letters, I knew she thought I was guilty. By the two books she had sent, I knew she believed murderers belonged in prison until they died. But, when I tested her back, and, believe me, she tested me too, she was honest. If she had lied when I asked her if the man in *Little Girl Lost** should not have been released, this book would [have] never been written.

For every question [Tammy] asked me, I probably had one for her. God led me. She'll have to tell you what led her. Letters turned into phone calls. Questions into answers, usually followed by lab or police reports. And then the visits. At first just her. So much in her voice and tenacity reminded me of Margaret. The first call and hearing her dogs in the background: Margaret. Did I just miss the woman who spent nearly seven years trying to help me, until her unexpected death? Or

---

* AUTHOR'S NOTE: A book about a murderer whom I felt should not have been released from prison.

did [Margaret] help arrange this whole thing? Because upon meeting her, Tammy is her own person.

I hope anyone who reads this book can grow like we both had to in creating it. Me to trust a stranger. She, to see how our system really works—or doesn't. I used to be like her; I imagine like you. "Those in jail must belong there. It's not my problem. It doesn't affect me." The time and effort Tammy has taken to [write] this book had to [have] changed her. Visits and stories of actual prison life, reading transcripts, dealing with my lawyer, it would challenge and change anyone. The nineteen years [I've spent] falsely imprisoned have [changed] me. And touching on my lawyer, Craig Neely, I know it has changed him too. He'd hate that I am writing anything on him. [He's] modest, not a showboat, or as he says, "an actor," but a lawyer, one raised in a family with a legal background, one that I know has taken heat for representing me, a lawyer with a heart: "Free nine guilty to stop one innocent from being jailed." He may have put his career on the line for that one. It's just who he is.

Tammy, thank you. Thank you for not just believing me but for making me prove it to you. Thank you for spending more time, effort, and money than we both know [was] needed to produce a book. I've repeatedly said this case is about more than me. I've had to lose everything and everyone to accept that thought. May it allow people to truly see the heart you have in not just writing but in digging deep before you put your name on something. And may it allow those reading it to realize it may not be you, but it could be. Or your child or grandchild.